MASS VIOLENCE IN AMERICA

MASS VIOLENCE IN AMERICA

LOYALISM IN NEW YORK
DURING THE AMERICAN REVOLUTION

Alexander Clarence Flick

ARNO PRESS & THE NEW YORK TIMES

New York • 1969

Editorial Note

NATIONS, LIKE MEN, ARE SOMETIMES INTERESTED IN BURYING THE PAST. In early 1968, after more than five years marked by political assassinations, racial uprisings, campus disorders, mass demonstrations and the violent suppression of protest, *The New York Times Magazine* asked a group of distinguished scholars to reply to the question, "Is America by nature a violent society?" In answer, University of Chicago anthropologist Clifford Geertz wrote:

> "We do not know very well what kind of society we live in, what kind of history we have had, what kind of people we are. We are just now beginning to find out, the hard way . . ."

The proposition was astonishing but correct: what was least understood about domestic political violence was its role in American history. It was common knowledge that the United States had had a Revolution, a Civil War, some trouble with the Indians and a period of labor-management conflict. But one could search the shelves of the nation's great libraries without discovering more than a handful of works on the subject of violence in American history, and these hopelessly out of date.

Historians had generally ignored or soft-pedaled the history of farmer uprisings, native vigilantism, labor-management struggles, ethnic conflicts and race riots; comparative work in the history of social conflict was particularly weak. Sociologists and political scientists in the grip of "consensus" theory tended to treat episodes of mass violence in America as insignificant or aberrational—temporary exceptions to the norm of peaceful progress. Psychologists and behavioral scientists discussed "mob violence" in terms which suggested that riots, revolts, insurrections and official violence were the products of individual or group pathology. All such interpretations had the effect not only of minimizing group violence in America, but of depriving it of political content—hence, of relevance to the present.

As a result, as late as 1968, the rich, multifarious and often terrifying history of domestic political violence was still largely *terra incognita.* So long as most Americans wished to keep certain skeletons locked away in their closets, few scholars would attempt to open doors. Conversely, once the American people, frightened yet emboldened by the sudden reappearance of intense social conflict, began to ask new questions about the past, so did the scholars.

Our purpose in helping Arno Press and *The New York Times* select and publish significant documents in the history of political violence has not been to compound past errors by overemphasizing the role of conflict in American history. On the contrary, our aim has been to provide materials which will aid in the search for an accurate perspective on the present. MASS VIOLENCE IN AMERICA includes eyewitness reports, government documents and other descriptive and analytic material relating to mass political violence in the United States. These documents not only provide information—they give the "feel" or "flavor" of past eras of civil disorder by evoking the emotional and political context in which revolts took place. Most of them have long been out of print and are obtainable, if at all, only in the nation's largest libraries.

The scope of this series is wide, ranging from accounts of Indian warfare to descriptions of labor-management violence, from narratives of colonial insurrections to reports on modern racial uprisings. It is not, however, limitless, nor were the constituent volumes carelessly selected. The principle of coherence which guided the selections is implicit in the phrase "mass political violence." "Mass" denotes activity engaged in by large groups rather than individuals acting alone; "political" suggests a relationship between such activity and competition among domestic groups for power, property and prestige; and "violence" is narrowly construed as resulting in physical damage to persons or property. In short, the materials reproduced herein are intended to illuminate the resort to violence by American groups seeking to change or to preserve the status quo. Although historical, they are of interest to any who wishes to understand the causes, nature and direction of domestic political violence, whether they be social scientists, historians or just interested Americans.

Of course, we are particularly hopeful that these volumes will prove useful to those now engaged in curriculum-revision and the teaching of high school and college courses in the area of American studies. What Christopher Jencks and David Reisman term "the Academic Revolution" has made difficult demands on all educators, not the least of which is the demand for courses which are both relevant to the condition of modern America and of the highest academic quality. These volumes are meant to provide raw material for such courses—primary source matter which will help both instructors and students to deepen and enrich their views of the American experience.

Most important, the editors and publisher recognize that these volumes appear during a national crisis which is also a crisis of the spirit, a time in which the public response to various manifestations of civil disorder is increasingly governed by anger, fear and hysteria. In such an atmosphere it is important to recognize that one is not alone in time—that such events have taken place before in America and, unless fundamental changes in our social and political life take place, will probably recur in the future. Our fondest hope is that this work, and others like it, will help to keep alive, in a time of growing unreason, the spirit of reasoned inquiry.

RICHARD E. RUBENSTEIN
The Adlai Stevenson Institute
Chicago, Illinois

ROBERT M. FOGELSON
Harvard-MIT Joint Center
for Urban Studies
Cambridge, Massachusetts

LOYALISM IN NEW YORK
DURING THE AMERICAN REVOLUTION

CONTENTS

CHAPTER I

RISE OF THE LOYALIST PARTY

CHAPTER II

FINAL ORGANIZATION OF THE LOYALIST PARTY

CHAPTER III

WAR AGAINST THE LOYALISTS

CHAPTER IV

County Inquisitorial Organizations

CHAPTER V

Activity of Loyalists Subsequent to the Issue of the Declaration of Independence

CHAPTER VI

Commissioners on Loyalists, 1776-1781

CHAPTER VII

Confiscation and Sale of the Property of the Loyalists

CHAPTER VIII

The Emigration of Loyalists

CHAPTER IX

Treatment of the Loyalists by Great Britain

CONTENTS

APPENDIX

CHAPTER I

RISE OF THE LOYALIST PARTY

LOYALISM, as believed and practiced during the American revolution, had both a religious and a political side. It was based upon the fundamental teachings of Anglicanism, which made loyalty to the ruler and obedience to law religious duties.[1] This did not mean abject submission to acts looked upon as blunders, or as being unjust. It was not " non-resistance and passive obedience," for none upheld and used with more telling effect than the loyalists the sacred right of petition and remonstrance.[2] Only when the issue came to be one between submission to the will of the king and parliament, as expressed in law, and resistance by rebellion or revolution, did religious duty enforce obedience. The political science of Anglicanism was, therefore, a fundamental principle in loyalism.

[1] Dr. Myles Cooper, the President of King's College and the recognized clerical leader of the loyalists in 1774, set forth this phase of loyalism best. God, he said, established the laws of government, ordained the British power and commanded all to obey authority. *American Querist*, etc., queries 90–100. " The laws of heaven and earth " forbade rebellion. To threaten open disrespect to government was " an unpardonable crime." *A Friendly Address*, etc., 5. " The principles of submission and obedience to lawful authority are inseparable from a sound, genuine member of the Church of England as any religious principles." That church had three homilies on obedience and six on rebellion. Its members prayed to be made loyal. The church was ashamed of those who disregarded these sacred principles. *Ibid.*, 45–49.

[2] Dr. Myles Cooper asserted that subjects might remonstrate against unjust laws forced upon them. *A Friendly Address*, etc., 5, 43. Other loyalists took the same position. Chandler, *What Think Ye of Congress Now ?*, 44–48.

Anglicanism did not appear as a factor in colonial politics in New York until the latter part of the seventeenth century, though introduced with the English occupation of New Netherland.[1]   From that time until the revolution, however, it was one of the most potent influences in shaping colonial parties.   It valiantly upheld royal prerogatives.[2]   Its clergy were "nurtured in sentiments of loyalty."   Its prayers ascended constantly for the king and his officers.   It furnished the best arguments for loyalism and taught them to its communicants.   It spread rapidly over the colony.   The conservative Dutch and not a few of the aristocratic Huguenot families joined the English church.[3]   By 1775 the Episcopalians constituted the most influential element of the population.

With scarcely an exception the Anglican ministers were ardent loyalists and the leaders in their communities.   The writers and pamphleteers, who furnished the keen, brainy defense of loyalism, were teachers and priests of that faith.[4] The leading loyalists, who were active in a military or civil capacity during the war, were members of that church. The rank and file of loyalists were to a large extent believers in that creed.   Thus loyalism and Anglicanism were largely united in practice as they were in theory and in logic.[5]

---

[1] *Docs. rel. to N. Y. Col. Hist.*, iii, 59.

[2] *Ibid.*, viii, 208; *N. Y. Hist. Soc. Colls.* (1877), 211.

[3] *Cf. John Adams' Diary* for August 21, 1774, while visiting in New York city.

[4] *Docs. rel. to N. Y. Col. Hist.*, viii, 208.

[5] In the time of the tea riots a loyalist wrote from New York: " You would perhaps think it proper to ask whether no Church of England people were among them [the rioters].   Yes, there were, to their eternal shame be it spoken !   But in general they were interested in the motion, either as smugglers of goods, or as being over-burdened with dry-goods they know not how to pay for. . . . But, sir, they are few in number.   Believe me, the Presbyterians have been the chief and principal instruments in all these flaming measures. . . .   Government at home,

On its political side loyalism stood for the recognition of law as against rebellion in any form,[1] for the unity of the empire as against a separate, independent existence of the colonies, and for monarchy instead of republicanism.[2]   It clung to the established order of things; in its conservatism it avoided dangerous "revolutionary principles" and shunned association with those "that are given to change."[3]   This did not mean that the loyalists upheld England's colonial system in all its features, or that they sanctioned her unwise policy in dealing with the colonists.[4]   If anything, in the days before the revolution, they were more active than the whigs in seeking to modify that system and to correct the known abuses.[5]   Their method was to operate through legally organized bodies in ways provided by the constitu-

if they mean to look for genuine loyalty and cordial affection to the state, will nowhere find it except in the hearts of the professors of the Church of England. . . . The Church of England people . . . did, from principle . . . everything they could . . . to stop the rapid progress of sedition." *Am. Archs.*, 4th ser., i, 301.

[1] Whether the British parliament is right or wrong, our actions have been "intolerant," asserted Dr. Cooper. *A Friendly Address*, etc., 4.   He despised the radical whigs of Suffolk co., Mass., whom he called "these rebellious republicans, these hair-brained fanatics, mad and distracted as the Anabaptists of Munster." *Ibid.*, 29.   "Count the cost of rebellion and you will stop it." *Ibid.*, 33; *ibid.*, 43, 45.   "If one can violate law, all can—then anarchy results." Seabury, *The Congress Canvassed*, etc., 39–43; Chandler, *What Think Ye of Congress Now?* 41–43, 44–48.

[2] Cooper, *American Querist*, etc., queries 80–89; Cooper, *A Friendly Address*, etc., 24: Seabury, *The Congress Canvassed*, etc., 52–59.

[3] Cooper, *American Querist*, queries 99–100.

[4] Dr. Cooper was inclined to think the tea duty "dangerous to constitutional liberty." *A Friendly Address*, etc., 13, 31; Seabury, *A View of the Controversy*, etc., 23; Chandler, *What Think Ye of Congress Now?* 7.

[5] Dr. Cooper declared the Stamp Act to be contrary to American rights, and approved of the opposition to the duties on paper, glass, et cetera. *A Friendly Address*, etc., 43.

tion. They had positive remedies to suggest which, they constantly insisted, would have secured in time every demand of the whigs except independence.[1]

The loyalists were Americans, not Englishmen. They felt, however, that the best interests of the colonies would be served by remaining a part of the great empire,[2] even though laboring under heavy and grievous burdens, because they believed that England's sense of justice would soon lead to the removal of the hardships. Hence, before independence through revolution became the paramount issue, many loyalists favored mild measures such as non-importation and non-exportation, while only the royal officials and Anglican clergy and teachers—the ultra-loyalists—de-

[1] The plan submitted by Dr. Cooper was " a formal allowance of the rightful supremacy in general of Great Britain over the American colonies—a declaration of our opposition to a state of independence with a corresponding behaviour—a respectful remonstrance on the subject of taxation—an assurance of our willingness to contribute, in some equitable proportion,towards defraying the public expense—and the proposal of a reasonable plan for a general American constitution." *A Friendly Address*, etc., 43; Seabury, *Free Thoughts*, etc., 46–48; Seabury, *The Congress Canvassed*, etc., 44–47, 48, 52–59. Seabury advocated the "settlement of an American constitution," granting self-government under the sovereign imperial parliament. Prudence would secure that. Then "the dependence of the colonies . . . will be fixed on a firm foundation; the sovereign authority of parliament over all dominions of the empire will be established; and the mother country and her colonies will be knit together in one grand, firm and compact body." *A View of the Controversy*, etc., 21–23; Chandler, *What Think Ye of Congress Now ?* 42–48.

[2] " My ancestors were among the first Englishmen who settled in America. I have no interest but in America. I have not a relation out of it that I know of. Yet, let me die ! but I had rather be reduced to the last shilling, than that the imperial dignity of Great Britain should sink, or be controlled, by any people or power on earth." Seabury, *A View of the Controversy*,etc., 23. Another prominent loyalist said, " My most earnest wish is for the happiness of America. I consider Great Britain and her colonies . . . as but one body, which must be affected throughout by the sufferings of any one member. I consider them as constituting one great and illustrious family to which I have the honor to belong; and I pray that its tranquility may be speedily restored, and that peace and harmony may forever reign through every part of it." Chandler, *What Think Ye of Congress Now ?* 44–48.

nounced them.[1] After July 4, 1776, the loyalists, seeing
that the day of argument and moderation was past, believed
that the integrity of the empire and the happiness of America could be secured only by crushing the revolutionary
spirit and by subduing their rebellious brethren by force.
This conviction, supplemented by the bitterness caused by
the hardships and persecutions suffered at the hands of
their whig countrymen, led them to sanction England's
military program.[2] As they viewed the situation, their personal hopes and the future of their country now depended
entirely upon the success of British arms.

The imperial government had the encouragement, advice,
material aid and services of the loyalists. For seven years
their cause was common with that of England in the means
used and the immediate object, but not in the purpose or
ultimate end. The loyalists had no more idea of surrender-
ing the principles involved in the contest before 1775 than
the whigs. But revolution had first to be crushed. The
unexpected success of the revolution, however, blasted all
their hopes and threw them upon either the tender mercies
of their victorious fellow citizens, or the charity of Great
Britain.

The colonial parties of New York, or more strictly the
groups representing certain political tendencies, were primarily religious and social. Out of these elements and the
local and imperial civic conditions and relations grew the
political differences.[3] With the planting of officialism, the

---

[1] For the attitude of extreme loyalists, *cf.* Cooper, *A Friendly Address*, etc.,
35–42; Seabury, *Free Thoughts*, etc., 3–36; Chandler, *What Think Ye of Congress Now?* 27–37.

[2] They maintained that the ground of contest had been completely changed
Before, it was a struggle against English despotism, but now it was a fight against
American independence and tyranny. *The Letters of Papinian*, Preface, iii,
probably written by Rev. Charles Inglis.

[3] Colden wrote in 1770: " From the different political and religious principles of

introduction of Anglicanism, the development of a type of feudalism and the growth of large fortunes in trade, came that community in interests, unity in beliefs and aristocratic rank which formed the environment for the doctrine of loyalism.

Whatever force or influence tended to emphasize or magnify centralized imperial or colonial power, to sanctify kingly prerogative, to subordinate colonial to imperial affairs, to enforce obedience to law, to develop social interests which depended for their triumph on the maintenance of a connection with England, to extend the Anglican church, to suppress the hazy democratic ideas that were in the air, to curtail the growing power of the general assembly, or to accumulate property in the hands of the few, was laying the foundation for the loyalist party.

The colonial period was marked by a contest between a strong and exclusive executive power, such as was upheld by the directors of the West India Company, the English government, and the Anglican church, on the one hand, and local rights and privileges, such as were demanded by the Dutch, French and English subjects and set forth in the Calvinistic creeds and the acts and resolves of the assemblies, on the other hand. This struggle had most to do with the formation of those religious-political groups which were to develop into the whig and loyalist parties of the revolution. The dominant political force in the conflict was officialism, that system by which the king's powers were extended to the province through a distinct class of dependent agents. The governor, as the representative of the doctrine,[1] gathered about him all those elements that upheld

the inhabitants, opposite parties have existed at all times, and will exist in this Province, which at different times have taken their denominations from some distinguished person or family who have appeared at their head." *N. Y. Hist. Soc. Colls.* (1877), 223.

[1] "We derive our authority from God and the Company, not from a few ignorant subjects," boasted Stuyvesant. *Cf.* the statement of Lord Cornbury, *Docs. rel. to N. Y. Col. Hist.*, iv, 1122.

the royal prerogatives and sought to maintain them un-
changed. Hence every concession demanded and every
privilege assumed by the popular branch of the government were contested by the crown officers.

The numerous petitions sent to England by the colonial
executives [1] begging for help did not go unheeded. British
authorities appreciated the necessity of upholding the hands
of the colonial royal officials in order to keep the colonies
in a state of subordination. Again and again decisions were
rendered to strengthen the governor's powers or to support
his recommendations. [2] The trade laws, the billeting act, the
stamp act, the tea-tax, the declaratory act, and finally, war
itself, were simply parts of the policy of the English government to support its powers as exercised through the
king's agents. Nevertheless, by 1774 many of the powers
which the governors possessed in 1689 had been lost. [3]
The strength of the official class had been much diminished,
though its pretensions were still large and its influence war
sufficient to make it the nucleus about which rallied the
loyalist party. [4]

Not until 1689 did social-political groups appear with
clearness in the province. Then it became apparent that
the shop-keepers, small farmers, sailors, shipwrights, poor
traders and artisans were not in sympathy with the patroons,
rich fur-traders, merchants, lawyers and crown officers. At
that time the two groups were called "Leislerians" and

---

[1] *Docs. rel. to N. Y. Col. Hist.*, v, 900, 902, 937, 941, 975; vi, 76, 285, 287, 379, 404, 408, 529, 536; vii, 548, 832, 994.

[2] *Ibid.*, viii, 815; *N. Y. Assemb. Jour.* (1767–1776), 34; *N. Y. Hist. Soc. Colls.* (1876), 421.

[3] *Cf.* Explanation of the loss of the New York governor's prerogatives, by Gov-
ernor Shirley. *Docs. rel. to N. Y. Col. Hist.*, v, 432–437; *Cf.* Smith, *Hist. of N. Y.* (Albany, 1814), 441.

[4] *Cf. Am. Archs.*, 4th ser., vi, 45.

"Aristocrats."[1]   The leaders of the latter faction were Peter Schuyler,[2] Nicholas Bayard,[3] Frederick Phillipse,[4] Stephen Van Cortlandt[5] and Robert Livingston.[6]   They wished to continue government under authority from James II, until definite instructions should be received from king William.[7] Both factions professed loyalty to the new sovereign, but the aristocrats insisted upon showing it in a strictly legal way and denounced the hasty, unwarranted course of the Leislerians.   The issue at this time, therefore, was one of law and precedent rather than of loyalism.   It must be remembered, however, that legality was one of the prime factors in the loyalist's creed.

From 1690 until the events of the revolution brought about a final readjustment of party lines and the appearance of whigs and loyalists, these two factions can be traced more or less distinctly.   In the modern sense they were not parties, but they did bear a resemblance to the parties in England at that period.   Membership was not determined by race or speech, Dutch, French and English being found on both sides; nor was it determined even by a decided difference in political principles, but rather by creed, wealth and social position.   A divergence, however, in political ideas is early noticeable, which became more defined with the passing of time, until at the outbreak of the revolution it had become fundamental.

---

[1] *Cf. Docs. rel. to N. Y. Col. Hist.*, iv, 508.   The " Aristocrats" were also called " Jacobites" by the " Leislerians."

[2] In the contest over the courts he joined the popular party.

[3] He was a deacon in the Dutch Reformed Church.

[4] His family were loyalists.

[5] He was also a Dutch Reformed Church deacon.

[6] He joined the liberal party in 1698.   Dunlap, *Hist. of the Province of N. Y.*, i, 230.   For a further list of " Aristocrats," *cf. Docs. rel. to N. Y. Col. Hist.*, iv, 849.

[7] *Ibid.*, iii, 636.

Important events like Leisler's rebellion, the contest over courts and the tenure of judges, Zenger's trial, the founding of King's College, the stamp act, the laying of the tea duty, the first Continental Congress, and the Declaration of Independence called forth an intense partisan spirit and produced readjustments of party adherents and a further differentiation of principles. / After allowing for these changes in the membership and motives of the two groups, it can be said that they were representative of those elements which, after nearly a century, were to produce the whig and loyalist parties of the revolution. Neither side held a fixed set of political tenets from 1690 to 1776, but only revealed connected tendencies.[1] At times the aristocratic party was in accord with the liberty party in its contest for some of the elements of self-government, but as a rule it upheld parliamentary supremacy and the royal prerogatives.

Party feeling was moulded by circumstances. After the death of governor Bellomont, it was so intense that civil war was scarcely averted,[2] while in 1719 governor Hunter wrote that "the very name of party or faction seems to be forgotten."[3] Under Cosby it was embittered by rival newspapers and personal and family feuds.[4] Zenger's trial, which was made a party issue, shows the construction of the two factions.[5] In the days of Leisler the groups were formed on lines of wealth and social rank. Persons of all faiths and tongues were found on both sides. Fifty years later, the

---

[1] Crown officials with liberal views were sometimes found on the popular side· *Docs. rel. to N. Y. Col. Hist.*, iv, 303, 322, 323, 379, 380, 400, 401, 508, 515 620, 848, etc.

[2] *Ibid.*, 848, 881, 916, 925, 946–948.

[3] *Ibid.*, v, 493, 522, 529; Smith, *Hist. of N. Y.* (Albany, 1814), 227.

[4] *Docs. rel. to N. Y. Col. Hist.*, vi, 636. Report of Privy Council on New York.

[5] *Ibid.*, v, 982; vi, 5, 6, 7, 72, 74, 75, 76, 77, 80; vii, 528, 909.

"court party" no longer held all the aristocracy in its ranks. The Livingstons, Philip Schuyler, Adolph Phillipse and others, all Calvinists or Lutherans, had then shifted to the popular party. Religion had become a political factor of considerable force. Nearly all the Anglicans of property and wealth, but only a few rich Hollanders and Huguenots of other creeds, were then in the "court party." The two parties had also become more clearly divided on political issues, though they still held common ground on some of the great questions at issue between the mother country and the colony.

The sectarian controversy over King's College helped to define the parties still further.[1] It threw into the foreground individual animosities and denominational bigotry. The "Episcopalian party" and the "DeLancey party" now came to be synonyms for the "court party," while their opponents were called the "Presbyterian party" or the "Livingston party."[2] Creed had become an important basis of political organization. William Livingston voiced the sentiments of his party when he· declared that the proposition of Archbishop Secker to establish an Anglican college at public expense, and the tory strivings of the DeLancey clique, were all parts of one plan to strengthen the royal prerogatives at the expense of popular rights, and to enlarge the power and organization of the episcopacy against non-conformists.[3] Whatever may have been the motives involved, the Angli-

---

[1] *Docs. rel. to N. Y. Col. Hist.*, vi, 625, 685, 777, 910, 913, vii, 217, 371; Jones, *Hist. of N. Y.*, i, 3, 10–16; *cf. Am. Hist. Rev.*, i, 240; *cf. Mem. Hist. of N. Y. City*, ii, 303; *cf.* Beardsley, *Life of Samuel Johnson.*

[2] Smith, *Hist. of N. Y.* (*N. Y. Hist. Soc. Colls.*, iv), 273. These names were still used for the parties in 1774. *Cf. John Adams' Diary* for Aug. 20, 1774. For leading members of each party, *cf.* Dunlap, *Hist. of Province of N. Y.*, i, 395–396.

[3] *Independent Reflector* in *Gaine's N. Y. Mercury*, no. 43, June 4, 1753; *cf.* Jones, *Hist. of N. Y.*, i, 12–17; *cf.* Smith, *Hist. of N. Y.* (*N. Y. Hist. Soc. Colls.*, iv), 191; *cf. Docs. rel. to N. Y. Col. Hist.*, vi, 913.

cans won an immediate victory in the contest, though it cost them defeat at the polls in the next election.[1]

Both parties united against the stamp act. " It occasioned," said Colden, " a universal tumult." [2] He complained for months of standing almost alone in upholding the acts of parliament and the royal rights. Only a few " disinterested friends," like General Gage, Major James, Sir William Johnson and the Church of England ministers, supported him.[3] He believed, however, that " great numbers in the city " were intimidated, and that the people outside of the metropolis were "absolutely free from the seditious spirit." [4] The anarchy of the fickle mob soon alienated the conservatives.[5] The great body of the business men, professional men and land-owners began to urge moderation and the adoption of legal methods of redress. At first they had encouraged the mob and used it, but they soon began to fear it. Many of the DeLancey party took the first opportunity to desert the " opposition." [6] A few extremists, the Episcopalian clergy and royal officers, horrified at the thought of rebellion, took the British side and defended the stamp act.[7] They sneered at the Stamp Act Congress and denounced it as " unconstitutional and unlawful." [8] With the repeal of the stamp act,

[1] *N. Y. Hist. Soc. Colls.* (1876), 34.

[2] *Ibid.* (1877), 27; Jones, *Hist. of N. Y.*, i, 18; *cf.* Dawson, *Westchester Co.*, 4, n. 2.

[3] *N. Y. Hist. Soc. Colls.* (1876), 462, (1877), 27, 44, 49; *Docs. rel. to N. Y. Col. Hist.*, vii, 790.

[4] *N. Y. Hist. Soc. Colls.* (1877), 61, 62, 77. But this was one of Colden's hasty judgments. *Cf. Ibid.*, 115, and *Docs. rel. to N. Y. Col. Hist.*, vii, 812, 838, 845, 849, 910.

[5] *N. Y. City during the Revolution*, 41–49; *cf. Mag. of Am. Hist.*, i, 361–362.

[6] *N. Y. Hist. Soc. Colls.* (1877), 61.

[7] *N. Y. Mercury*, May 20, 1765, no. 708; June 17, 1765, no. 712. *Cf. N. Y. Assemb. Jour.*, ii, 787.

[8] *N. Y. Gazette*, Feb. 3, 1776; *N. Y. Hist. Soc. Colls.* (1877), 35.

the party lines, obscured by the excitement over that
measure, reappeared.   In the election of 1768 "the whole
force of both sides" was exerted, and the "whig interest"
was overwhelmingly defeated.[1]   All the DeLancey men who
were elected, save one, became loyalists.[2]   Peter Van Schaack
predicted that the "party spirit which had been aroused
would never be extinguished."[3]

By 1770 the two parties had become fairly well distinguished and defined.   Each was now more nearly than ever
before a distinct political organization, with its own caucus,
leaders, candidates, platform and method of work.   Each
side was subdivided into liberals and conservatives.   The
extreme wing of the tory party was still led by Colden and
his coterie.   They stood for a rigid execution of imperial
law.   The moderates, who constituted a large majority of
the party, did not wholly sympathize with the conservative
element.   They were guided by the aristocratic landholders,
merchants and traders, mostly of the Anglican persuasion.
But some Lutherans, members of the Dutch Reformed congregations and even "several Presbyterians" were found
among the "friends of government."[4]   That party was no
longer co-extensive with the established church, a proof that
political issues were fast becoming paramount.

The party was bound together by a social network of the
influential families like the De Puysters, the Waltons, the
Crugers, and the De Lanceys, who were united by blood or
marriage to more than half of the aristocracy of the Hudson
Valley.[5]   Its members venerated forms and traditions.   Loy-

---

[1] *N. Y. Hist. Soc. Colls.* (1877), 182, 211.   [2] Jones, *Hist. of N. Y.*, i, 18.

[3] Van Schaack, *Life of Peter Van Schaack.*

[4] *N. Y. Hist. Soc. Colls.* (1877), 211.

[5] A few of the other prominent families were the Verplancks, Rensselaers, Wattses,
Van Cortlandts, Joneses, Coldens, Morrises, Lispenards, Johnsons, Bayards and
Cuylers.   *Cf.* Dunlap, *Hist. of the Province of N. Y.*, i, 396; *cf.* Smith, *Hist. of
N. Y. (N. Y. Hist. Soc. Colls.*, iv), 273.

alty was a part of their religious teaching. The republican spirit in the colony was by them condemned and the empire praised. They loved the king and respected parliament, but many of them stood up as valiantly as the whigs for the American interpretation of the British constitution. Their rights once secured, their fondest hope was peace, a united empire, and friendly commercial relations. Owing to these political beliefs many of the loyalists were not averse to a mild show of force in order to bring Great Britain to terms.

After 1770, every important event became a party question. The McDougal trial was made a distinct political issue,[1] but in this neither party won a decisive victory.[2] The parties divided over non-importation, when all duties but that on tea were removed. "We have two parties violently opposed to each other," wrote Colden.[3] The popular party still favored boycotting all English goods.[4] The tories wished to confine this policy to tea alone, canvassed the city, found that 3,000 out of 4,154 favored the course they recommended, and won the day.[5] The attempt made to collect the tea-tax aroused party discussions.[6] The three "public gazettes teemed with articles upon it."[7] The Sons of Liberty favored a general non-consumption agreement,[8] but the tories

---

[1] *N. Y. Hist. Soc. Colls.* (1877), 212; *Docs. rel. to N. Y. Col. Hist.*, viii, 208, 213.

[2] Jones, *Hist. of N. Y.*, i, 29–33.

[3] *N. Y. Hist. Soc. Colls.* (1877), 220.

[4] Leake, *Life of John Lamb*, 63–64.

[5] *N. Y. Hist. Soc. Colls.* (1877), 220, 223, 224, 227, 228, 230, 251. *Docs. rel. to N. Y. Col. Hist.*, viii, 218.

[6] *Ibid.*, 400–401.

[7] *Ibid.*, 408. Governor Tryon said they were written "alternately by good citizens and fair traders, by men of cool sense and just discernment, on the one hand, by fraudulent dealers, artful smugglers, inflamatory politicians and patriots on the other." But this is a prejudiced loyalist's statement.

[8] *Docs. rel. to N. Y. Col. Hist.*, viii, 403, 408.

were not with them in 1773 as in 1765. Having a majority
in the three branches of the government,[1] the latter took
things rather, moderately though in the assembly they
named a committee of correspondence.[2] Although the Boston Port Bill became " the subject of all conversation," many
ardent tories believed that Boston ought to pay for the
" drowned tea."[3] Fearing that the whig leaders would " run
the city into dangerous measures," they attended the mass
meeting called to discuss the situation and elected a safe
majority of the committee of fifty-one.[4]

It must be remembered that at this time the contest was
not one between those who favored and those who opposed
the acts of the English government—for both parties opposed
them—but was over the form which that opposition should
take. The ultra-tories who upheld the acts of parliament
took no part whatever in these proceedings.[5] The liberal
tories acted with " a resolution to prevent any violent or rash
measures being entered into, and to preserve the peace of
the colony."[6] A general non-importation agreement was
not revived, since all the counties but Suffolk opposed the
idea.[7] The committee of fifty-one was controlled by moderate loyalists, yet it was one of the strongest factors in under-
mining the power of the crown and parliament. It helped
to call the Continental Congress, which usurped authority

---

[1] *Docs. rel. to N. Y. Col. Hist.*, viii, 248, 249; *N. Y. Hist. Soc. Colls.*(1877), 218.

[2] *N. Y. Assemb. Jour.* (1767–1776, 8th part), 7, 13, 14, 16, 102, 105; *Docs. rel. to N. Y. Col. Hist.*, viii, 417.

[3] *N. Y. Hist. Soc. Colls.* (1877), 339; *Am. Archs.*, 4 ser., i, 289.

[4] *Ibid.*, 302, 293; Jones, *Hist. of N. Y.*, i, 439, 467; *N. Y. Hist. Soc. Colls.* (1877), 342. No less than twenty-one members of the committee later became avowed loyalists.

[5] Jones, *Hist. of N. Y.*, i, 34; Dawson, *Westchester Co.*, 11.

[6] *N. Y. Hist. Soc. Colls.* (1877), 342.

[7] *Am. Archs.*, 4th ser., i, 297, 702, 703; Leake, *Life of John Lamb*, 87.

not delegated to it, raised the standard of armed revolution and closed the door of reconciliation, which it was instructed to open as widely as possible, overthrew monarchy and created a republic.[1]

The election of delegates to the Continental Congress was made a political issue.[2] Each party had its ticket. In the committee of fifty-one the moderate loyalists won,[3] as they also did at the polls.[4] Livingston and Low were moderate whigs, while Duane, Jay and Alsop were looked upon as loyalists.[5] All except Livingston were Anglicans.[6] " A great deal of pains has been taken," wrote Colden, " to persuade the counties to choose delegates for the Congress, or to adopt those sent by the city." [7] Westchester, Dutchess and Albany authorized the " city delegates " to act for them.[8] Kings, Suffolk and Orange sent representatives of their own.[9] Cumberland, Gloucester, Charlotte, Tryon, Richmond, Ulster and Queens paid no attention to the demand.[10] Not even half a dozen in Queens county could be induced to meet to consider the matter, while in Orange and other counties twenty out of over a thousand freeholders elected the delegates.[11] In Westchester county representatives were chosen by only four towns.[12] " It is notorious," asserted Seabury, "that in some districts only three or four met and chose

[1] *Cf.* Dawson, *Westchester Co.*, 12, 13.

[2] *Am. Archs.*, 4th ser., i, 302, 307, 308.

[3] *Ibid.*, 308; *Rivington's Gazette*, July 14, 1774; *N. Y. Hist. Soc. Colls.* (1877), 346, 348.

[4] *Ibid.*, 352; *Am. Archs.*, 4th ser., i, 320, 321; Leake, *Life of John Lamb*, 94; Jones, *Hist. of N. Y.*, i, 464.

[5] *Ibid.*, 34; Dawson, *Westchester Co.*, 11, n. 1, 34, n. 3.

[6] *John Adams' Diary*, August 22, 1774.

[7] *Docs. rel. to N. Y. Col. Hist.*, viii, 493.

[8] *Jour. of Cont. Cong.*, Sept. 5, 1774.   Credentials of delegates.   [9] *Ibid.*

[10] *Docs. rel. to N. Y. Col. Hist.*, viii, 493.   [11] *Ibid.*

[12] Dawson, *Westchester Co.*, 29.

themselves to be a committee on this most important occasion. So that, taking the whole province together, I am confident your delegates had not the voice of an hundredth part of the people in their favor." [1]   Statements like this represent the feelings of the ultra-loyalists.   Though they are exaggerations, still they show the significant fact that the rural districts of New York were indifferent or hostile to the Continental Congress. [2]

The moderate loyalists looked not unfavorably upon the Continental Congress. [3]   While the extremists did not wholly sanction it, yet they hoped for some beneficial result.   Dr. Cooper rejoiced that it took the dispute out of the hands of the rabble. [4]   " A redress of grievances, and a firm union between Great Britain and America upon constitutional principles, was their only aim," wrote the severe loyalist historian, Judge Thomas Jones. [5]   Even Colden hoped that Congress would " produce some good." [6]   Others thought the " wisdom and prudence of Congress " might avert rebellion. [7]   All hoped or expected that peace would be the result. [8]   The first public declaration of the thorough-

---

[1] Seabury, *The Congress Canvassed*, etc., 13, 14; Chandler, *What Think Ye of Congress Now ?*, 18.   He asserted that in every place outside of New York city the non-voters far outnumbered the voters.

[2] *Docs. rel. to N. Y. Col. Hist.*, viii, 488, 492, 493; Onderdonk, *Queens Co.*, 16; Dawson, *Westchester Co.*, 35; Chandler, *What Think Ye of Congress Now ?*, 18.

[3] Jones, *Hist. of N. Y.*, i, 34, 35, 449–468.   All moderates, and they were not a few, looked to a general American Congress for obtaining a restoration of tranquility and a reconciliation with Great Britain.   Cooper, *A Friendly Address*, etc., 30; Seabury, *Free Thoughts*, etc., 2; Seabury, *The Congress Canvassed*, etc., 20–24; Chandler, *What Think Ye of Congress Now ?*, 6.

[4] Cooper, *American Querist*, etc., Queries 90–100.

[5] Jones, *Hist. of N. Y.*, i, 35.   [6] *N. Y. Hist. Soc. Colls.* (1877), 350.

[7] Seabury, *Free Thoughts*, etc., 2.

[8] Seabury, *The Congress Canvassed*, etc., 12, 22, 24; Cooper, *A Friendly Address*, etc., 30; Cooper, *American Querist*, etc., query 90; *N. Y. Hist. Soc. Colls.* (1877), 341.

going loyalists came from the town of Rye, Westchester
county, September 24, 1774.   It was a manifesto of loyalism.
Content with English rule, as organized in the imperial
parliament and in the province, and happy as subjects of
George III., they discountenanced all attempts to disrupt
the existing relations.[1]

Nothing is clearer than that the Continental Congress did
not meet, intentionally, as a revolutionary body.   There was
no design to declare for armed resistance and few, if any,
dreamed of a Declaration of Independence.   The sole object was to uphold the American interpretation of the political relations of the various local governments to the imperial
government, and to accomplish that by united but moderate
measures.   Yet this body, to the horror of the loyalists,
was soon diverted from its original purpose and became an
instrument for the promotion of revolution and independence.

No sooner had Congress convened than the loyalists became very active.   They expressed their political beliefs
with a greater liberty than had been known in years.[2]   More
loyalist tracts, pamphlets, sermons and letters were printed
" in favor of administration, and against measures which may
be offensive to parliament, than in all the colonies put together."[3]   Foremost among the loyalist writers were Dr.
Myles Cooper,[4] Dr. Samuel Seabury, Rev. T. B. Chandler,
Isaac Wilkins, Rev. Charles Inglis and Rev. John Vardill,
all staunch Episcopalians, whose philippics were hurled
against Congress.[5]   "The turbulent, factious few" were sup-

---

[1] *Rivington's N. Y. Gazetteer*, no. 78, Oct. 23, 1774;   Dawson, *Westchester Co.*,
32;   Cooper, *A Friendly Address*, etc., 34.

[2] *N. Y. Hist. Soc. Colls.* (1877), 359, 360, 367;   *Am. Archs.*, 4th ser., i, 373.

[3] *N. Y. Hist. Soc. Colls.* (1877), 368.

[4] Colden said he was the supposed author of almost every loyalist pamphlet.
Docs. rel. to N. Y. Col. Hist., viii, 297, 898.

[5] *Cf.* Tyler, *Literary Hist. of Am. Rev.; cf.* Perry, *Hist. of Am. Episc. Church.*

pressed.[1] It was generally believed, however, that the "moderate, prudent men" would prevent radical measures.[2] Galloway's "Plan of Accommodation" was regarded by some as
a solution of the problem. Duane and Jay favored it[3] and
Colden pronounced it a "rational mode of proceeding, evidently tending to a reconciliation."[4]

The loyalists watched Congress with the keenest interest,
but they hoped for bread and got a stone. Peace and not war
was what they wanted. The counties were almost wholly
for moderate measures.[5] "A large majority of the merchants and people" of the city opposed a non-intercourse
act. After Congress adjourned Colden wrote to Lord Dartmouth that "a great majority in this province are very far
from approving of the dangerous and extravagant measures"
and longed for a reconciliation.[6] Loyalists felt that Congress
had betrayed them. They had hoped, wrote Seabury, that
"the wisdom and prudence of Congress" would deliver the
colonies from rampant rebellion and bring peace, but that
body broke up "without ever attempting it," and "basely
betrayed the interests of all the colonies."[7]

It was asserted that the New York delegates must have
been forced to sign the acts to make the colonies rebels, to
shut the courts, to replace the regular government by committees and to call a second congress.[8] The delegates had

---

[1] *N. Y. Hist. Soc. Colls.* (1877), 367, 368; *Am. Archs.*, 4 ser., i, 327.

[2] *N. Y. Hist. Soc. Colls.* (1877), 360.

[3] Dawson, *Westchester Co.*, 33, 34.

[4] *N. Y. Hist. Soc. Colls.* (1877), 374.

[5] *Ibid.*, 368; Seabury, *The Congress Canvassed*, etc., 1–6; *Cf. Memoirs of Henry Van Schaack*, 33.

[6] *N. Y. Hist. Soc. Colls.* (1877), 369, 375.

[7] Seabury, *Free Thoughts*, etc., 1, 2; *cf.* Cooper, *A Friendly Address*, etc., 30; *Cj. Memoirs of Henry Van Schaack*, 28, note.

[8] Seabury, *The Congress Canvassed*, etc., 7–11.

been unfairly elected. The committee of New York city had no right to dictate to the counties, or to regard silent counties as favoring a congress. Should they be bound by its acts then?[1] The people were quiet only because they expected peace.[2] But congress assumed the power of legislation and foisted the association upon the people and ordered committees to enforce it.[3] The laws of a congress were made to supersede the provincial laws, and liberty to depend upon the will of a committee.[4] "You have blustered and bellowed," mockingly wrote a loyalist pamphleteer, "and swaggered and bragged that no British parliament should dispose of a penny of your money without your leave, and now you suffer yourselves to be bullied by a congress and cowed by a committee." Now you find that legislation and taxation go together. Your liberty and property are at the mercy of a committee. This is indeed a new " passive obedience and non-resistance."[5]

The non-intercourse and non-consumption agreements, it was said, will shut the colonies off from the whole world. " Can we think to threaten and bully and frighten the supreme government of the nation into a compliance with our demands?" The injury to America in one year will be greater than the three-penny tea-duty will amount to in twenty years. The farmers will suffer most, since scheming merchants and wily traders are at the bottom of all this confusion.[6] But "our sovereign lords and masters, the high and mighty delegates in grand Continental Congress assembled have ordered and directed it." Tyrannical committees have been appointed to execute it. Obedience to such a command is slavery. The New York city committee will then

---

[1] Seabury, *The Congress Canvassed*, etc., 13, 14.   [2] *Ibid.*, 20–24.
[3] *Ibid.*, 25–29.   [4] *Ibid.*, 30, 31.   [5] *Ibid.*, 33–38.
[6] Seabury, *Free Thoughts*, etc., 10, 11, 19–31, 33, 34.

order the county committees to enforce the edicts. Will you submit to such tyranny and abject slavery? Will you choose committees or let them be chosen? "Let us ignore the half-dozen fools who meet and choose themselves a committee. Let us assert our freedom and, if necessary, assemble ourselves."[1] These seditious committeemen are not defending our rights and liberties, but are "making us the most abject slaves that ever existed." "Renounce all dependence on congresses and committees. They have neglected or betrayed your interests. Turn your eyes to your constitutional representatives." They will soon meet. Trust them to secure peace.[2]

You are honor-bound to the English government. You ought, therefore, to oppose the laws of congress. They cannot be executed without violating known laws. The laws of God, nature and New York all forbid your hindering a man in his regular business. Can the laws of congress do it, then? Is any one bound to obey the acts of that body?[3] Why, all your imagined evils endured for a century are not so bad as these for a year. You can never justify violent means of redress until all peaceable, constitutional ones have been tried.[4]

The disappointment of the loyalists at the course followed by Congress is not difficult of explanation. That body was a voluntary association, with no legal authority to bind the colonists in any degree. It was not empowered to exercise legislative functions, nor to exact obedience under legal pen-

---

[1] Seabury, *Free Thoughts*, etc., 37. *Cf.* Chandler, *What Think Ye of Congress Now?* 6. Let the "friends to order and government," suggested Dr. Cooper, "assume the courage openly to declare their sentiments." *A Friendly Address*, etc., 34.

[2] Seabury, *Free Thonghts*, etc., 39–48.

[3] Seabury, *The Congress Canvassed*, etc., 39–43; *Free Thoughts*, etc., 46–48; Chandler, *What Think Ye of Congress Now?* 6–17.

[4] Seabury, *The Congress Canvassed*, etc., 44–47.

alties. At most it could only recommend certain lines of action. The loyalists declared that it exceeded the authority delegated to it, and therefore its acts were unwarrantable and revolutionary. Hence it was to be expected that discontent and alarm should arise in the hearts of those who hoped for, and were promised, something quite different. They merely refused to be forced into rebellion, and decided to repudiate the decrees which were bringing war and ruin to them instead of peace and quiet. Consequently, the discontent and opposition which sprang up all over the province were not so surprising.

The agriculturists, who had refused to take action in seven counties regarding the calling of a Continental Congress, were not injured by a tea-tax nearly so much as by political disturbances, non-intercourse and war. Hence they turned a deaf ear to the complaints of the city merchants and of the Sons of Liberty, and ignored the methods of redress ordered by Congress. New York city and Albany, the mercantile centers, were most active in calling Congress and in obeying its decrees.[1] This great body of moderate business-men, whose political principles were naturally tinged with commercialism, were opposed by the handful of explosive revolutionists, the Sons of Liberty, because they did not go far enough, and by the king's agents and the Anglican clergymen for having gone too far.

When that Congress, supported in New York by classes which on the whole were aristocratic, anti-revolutionary and commercial, was diverted from its original purposes, the Sons of Liberty continued to give it hearty support,[2] the farmers

[1] Not a voice in the city was raised against the recent acts of Congress. Seabury, *Free Thoughts*, etc., 21, 22.

[2] They applauded as if " *There* a regular American Constitution was to be established and our liberties and privileges fixed on a foundation so stable that neither Lord North nor Old Time himself should ever make any impression on them." Seabury, *The Congress Canvassed*, etc., 12.

remained indifferent or became hostile, while the extreme "friends of government" became open and pronounced in their opposition.[1]   The liberal loyalists who had joined the whigs in convening Congress were divided.[2]   One part joined Colden, the De Lanceys and the Anglican pamphleteers in order to oppose the revolutionary program; the other acquiesced in the measures of Congress and served in extra-legal bodies to enforce them until moderate resistance developed into confessed revolution with independence as its object, when most of them were driven into the ranks of the loyalist party.

The loyalist now had a positive part to play.   While on the one hand he was opposed to revolution, on the other, he was not satisfied with the pretensions of parliament.   His duty, therefore, was plainly to propose terms of an "accommodation" with the parent country,[3] which would secure "the settlement of an American constitution" with colonial self-government under a sovereign, imperial parliament.[4] But this, the loyalists insisted, could not be done through despotic committees,[5] which enforced laws made at Philadelphia, and collected money without consent, but only through the provincial assembly.[6]   Hence New York loyalists felt under obligations to repudiate congress, to refuse to sign the association and to carry out their program through their local representatives. [7]

It was not until after the first Continental Congress that

[1] Shown in all the loyalist pamphlets.

[2] Many who worked hard to elect delegates were the foremost now in denouncing the results.   Chandler, *What Think Ye of Congress Now ?* 18.

[3] Seabury, *The Congress Canvassed*, etc., 52–59.

[4] Seabury, *A View of the Controversy*, etc., 21–23.

[5] Seabury, *An Alarm*, etc., 4, 5.

[6] *Ibid.*, 7, 8;   *Am. Archs.*, 4 ser., i, 1211–1213.   "To the Americans."

[7] Chandler, *What Think Ye of Congress Now ?* etc., 41–43.

an unmistakable meaning was attached to the party names, whig and loyalist.[1] Political organization was complete by that time, though not final. The loyalist party had been formed out of those social, religious, political and commercial tendencies which appeared here and there during more than a century of colonial history and had come to be marked characteristics. Antecedent groups and factions made the transition easier, since they contained the essential elements of loyalism and paved the way for the party as it came into existence in 1774. The Continental Congress gave a definite form to the organization and furnished a general platform for action, but complete unification did not come until the act of separation.

In character the loyalists have been judged too harshly on the one hand, and too leniently on the other. Most American historians have characterized them as unprincipled royal office-holders, scheming political trimmers, a few aristocratic landlords and merchants, who were fearful of losing their wealth and indifferent to the rights of man, together with their dependents, and the preachers and teachers of the Anglican church. Not a few English historians take this same view. These writers look upon them as a negative force in the revolutionary movement without any positive program and as unqualified supporters of England's conduct. The loyalists themselves and their apologists, on the contrary, have asserted that their ranks included all the best, the wealthiest, the most educated and those of highest social rank in the colony. Both of these views are partly right, but mostly wrong. Among the loyalists were all grades of worth and unworthiness, as among the whigs.

The loyalists may be divided into the following general classes:

---

[1] *Cf. Am. Archs.*, 4 ser., v, 845; *cf. N. Y. Hist. Soc. Colls.*, Lee Papers, iii, 417.

1. Royal officials—governors,[1] lieutenant-governors,[2] councillors,[3] many assemblymen,[4] judges,[5] military and naval officers,[6] and other royal agents[7] on down to the petty district squires.[8] These persons were led by a variety of motives—self-interest, official bias, fidelity to oaths, and conviction of duty. They formed a powerful network of loyalists over the

[1] William Tryon.

[2] Cadwallader Colden and Andrew Elliot.

[3] William Axtell, John Harris Cruger, Oliver De Lancey, James Jauncey. Jr., Roger Morris, William Smith, Hugh Wallace, John Watts and Henry White.

[4] James De Lancey, John De Lancey, John Cruger, James Jauncey, John Rapalje, Jacob Walton, Frederick Phillipse, Daniel Kissam, Simon Boerum, Peter Van Cortlandt, John Coe, Zebulum Williams, Benjamin Seaman, Samuel Gale, Christopher Billopp, Samuel Wells, etc.

[5] Thomas Jones, G. Banyar, Richard Floyd, Jonathan Fowler, Joseph Lord, Noah Sabin, H. P. Valentine and Samuel Wells.

[6] Sir Samuel Auchmuty, Capt. Ball, Col. George Brewerton, Ensign Elisha Budd, Capt. Bull, Col. John Butler, Col. Thomas Chandler, Col. Isaac Corsa, Capt. Oliver De Lancey, Jr., Capt. Richard Hewlett, Major D. Kissam, Capt. Lewis McDonald, Capt. Charles Cornell, etc.

[7] George Clark, Sec. of N. Y.; Alex. Colden, Surv. Gen.; Richard C. Colden, Surveyor and Searcher of Customs of N. Y. city; Abraham C. Cuyler, Mayor of Albany; James De Lancey, Sheriff of Westchester county; Andrew Elliott, Collector of Customs; Samuel Gale, Court Clerk of Cumberland county; John Tabor Kempe, Attorney General; Abraham Lott, Treasurer; Maurice Lott, Sheriff of Queens county; Cary Ludlow, Surrogate and Master of Chancery; David Mathews, Mayor of N. Y. city; James McEvers, Stamp Master; John Moore, Deputy Collector of Customs; William Patterson, Sheriff of Cumberland county; Philip Skeene, Lieutenant-Governor of Crown Point and Ticonderoga; John Thompson, Chamberlain of New York city; Alex. White, Sheriff of Tryon county; William Knox, Sec. of N. Y., etc.

[8] Bartholomew Crannell, Public Notary in N. Y. city; James Harper, Justice of the Peace in Queens county; Daniel Kissam, a magistrate; Peter Meetin, Magistrate of N. Y. city; Lambert Moore, Notary Public; John Collin, Magistrate of Tryon county; Stephen Tuttle, Justice of the Peace for Albany county. MS., *Transcript of . . . Books and Papers . . . of American Loyalists*, vol. i, pp. 195–196, gives a list of 32 civil officers for New York, Oct. 7, 1783. *Cf. John Adams' Diary* for August 22, 1774, which gives a general view of the factions of loyalists in New York.

province, were so many centers of influence advocating loyalism and gave political organization to the loyalist party. They were the most powerful and at the same time the most active class.

2. Large landed proprietors with their tenants—like the Johnsons, the De Lanceys, Roger Morris, the Skeenes, the Jessups, Frederick Phillipse and others.[1] At heart and by habit they were true aristocrats and denunciators of the democratic movement. They were loyal to the crown because of received and anticipated favors, their material interests were connected with the established order of things, and their convictions tended to loyalism. A few of this class were inactive during the war, but most of them unhesitatingly joined arms with Great Britain against the revolution. An undoubted majority of this group were loyalists.

3. Professional classes—lawyers,[2] physicians,[3] teachers[4] and ministers.[5] A very large proportion of these persons were loyalists—some from a sense of duty, others because

[1] The Crugers, Joneses, De Puysters, Waltons, Robinsons, Baches, Wattses, Rapaljes, Floyds, Purdys, Cuylers, Van Cortlandts, Bayards, etc.

[2] Among them were Crean Brush, Cumberland co.; Walter N. Butler and Benjamin Hilton, Albany Co.; Benjamin Kissam, David Matthews, John C. Knapp, D. G. Ludlow, Lindley Murray, Isaac Ogden and Beverly Robinson, Jr., of New York city; John L. Roome and Peter Van Schaack.

[3] Among the physicians were Dr. Azor Betts, Dr. Adams, Dr. Richard Bonsall, Dr. Magra, Dr. Alexander Kellock, Dr. Peter Huggeford, Dr. Peter Middleton, Dr. William Moore, Dr. R. H. Auchmuty, Dr. S. Bard, Dr. R. Bayley, Dr. Barrant Roorback, Dr. George Smith and Dr. Henry Van Buren.

[4] Education was controlled largely by the Episcopal Church. Among the educators were Dr. Myles Cooper, Prof. Alexander Girard and Dr. Samuel Classey, of King's College; James Harper, of Queens co.; Mr. Ritzema, of Tarrytown; Dr. Samuel Seabury, of Westchester.

[5] Those of the Anglican church were all loyalists. Benjamin Abbott and Thomas Rankin were Methodist clergymen, Mathias Burnett was a Presbyterian parson of Queens co., John Mackenna was a Roman Catholic priest, Domine Rubell was of the Dutch Reformed church, and Bernard Houseal and John M. Kern were Lutherans.

of a distrust of the success of the revolution, a few through a hope of reward, and many on account of an alliance with royal officials and the aristocracy.

4. The wealthy commercial classes, mostly in New York City and Albany, whose interests were affected first and most by civil war. They were anxious for the victory of the American interpretation of the British constitution and therefore championed the revolutionary movement in its early stages, but opposed war and independence on principle and on business grounds.[1]

5. Conservative farmers in all parts of the colony, but especially in Queens, Kings, Richmond, Westchester, Albany and Tryon counties. They were happy and prosperous under the old regime. They did not feel the burdens complained of by the revolutionists, and consequently, had no sympathy with whig principles. But when their incomes were injured by the edicts of congress and committees and by war, their eyes turned toward the king's army to restore their former peace and security.

6. Colonial politicians, who neither cared for nor even saw any principle involved in the contest. They changed sides with the greatest ease as victory, and with it the hope of reward, passed from the English to the American side, or the reverse. With nothing to lose and everything to gain, policy made them loyalists.[2]

---

[1] Leading loyalists of this type were James Duane, Isaac Low, A. Van Dorn, William McAdam, William Walton, Isaac Corsa, Robert Murray, John Moore, William Laight, Theophylact Bache, Thomas Buchanan, William Seton, Thomas Miller, Edward Laight, Hugh Wallace, Gabriel H. Ludlow, William Steeple, Henry White, Benjamin Booth, Alexander Wallace, Robert R. Waddel, Richard Yates, Gerard Walton, August Von Horne, Lawrence Kartright and John Alsop. Cf. *N. Y. Hist. Soc. Colls.*, 2 ser., vol. ii, pt. 2, p. 381, etc.

[2] *Am. Archs.*, 5 ser., i, 40, ii, 967–970; cf. *Rivington's Royal Gazette*, July 7, 1779; cf. Allen, *The Am. Rev.*, i, 417, 483, 554, 571. Capt. David Fenton was a fair example of this class of loyalists.

7. Conservative masses, of no trades and all trades, of all grades of wealth, education and social position, in all parts of the province, who through loyalty, religion, interest or influence disapproved of independence. Loyalists of this character were found in every village, district, city and county in New York. They formed the great majority of the loyalist party. They were not conspicuous for wealth, social influence, office, professional prominence, or active hostility; hence in thousands of cases they were not known outside of their respective localities. They formed a large part of the loyalist soldiers and sailors, carried out the will of their leaders and made loyalism an-efficient force in coping with the revolution.[1]

Thus it appears that the loyalists of New York had within their ranks persons of all social positions from that of the poor emigrant but recently come to America, to the oldest and wealthiest family in the colony; of all grades of intelligence from the ignorant agriculturist to the president of the only college in the province; of all lines of work from the humble cobbler and blacksmith to the most celebrated lawyer and physician in the metropolis;[2] of all creeds; and actuated by all motives from the basest material greed to the loftiest sense of religious duty and highest type of

---

[1] Jones, *Hist. of N. Y.*, ii, 437, gives a list of thousands of "signers," who were loyalists, with their race and trade. The diversity of occupation is quite striking. Other lists of the rank and file of loyalists show the same variety in vocations.

[2] Out of a list of 17 Orange co. loyalists, there was a tanner, a tavern-keeper, several servants, a saddler, a silversmith, a gunsmith, a constable, a soldier, and a shoemaker. *Cal. of N. Y. Hist., MSS.*, i, 351. On April 15, 1776, a return of prisoners in the New York city jail gave 3 soldiers, 8 sailors, 2 pilots, 2 naval officers, a hatter, a farmer, an oysterman and an armorer. Out of 117 petitioners to the British government asking for compensation for losses through loyalty, 35 were farmers, 20 were laborers, 22 were widows mostly of loyalist soldiers, 17 were crown officers, 12 were merchants, 4 were doctors, 4 were clergymen, 2 were sailors and 1 was a lawyer. MS., *Transcript of . . . Books and Papers . . . of Am. Loyalists,*" vols. 17–22.

patriotism. The party included most of the leaders in culture, religion and society, many of the solid business men and also much of the brawn and muscle of the common people.

The loyalists were not a party wholly of negation and obstruction. They differed from the whigs in the method, process and scope of reform only in degree. They loved their country, they fought for it when both sides appealed to the sword, and they died for it. When the Declaration of Independence became the thoroughly understood issue between the whigs and loyalists, it soon became manifest that political principles were more potent than religious creeds, race,[1] family ties,[2] or social rank. Although the party was predominantly Anglican in its faith,[3] still Methodists, Catholics,[4] Presbyterians,[5] Lutherans[6] and Quakers[7] were found among the loyalists.[8] The vast majority were Englishmen, but there were also many Irish, Scotch, Germans, Dutch, French, Indians and Negroes true to the British flag.

[1] Out of 363 petitioners to the king for compensation for losses, 200 were native Americans, 60 were Scotch, 40 were Irish, 30 were English, 28 were Germans, 2 were Welch, 2 were French and 1 was a Hollander. MS., *Transcript of . . . Books and Papers . . . of Am. Loyalists*, vols. 17–22.

[2] These families were divided—the De Lanceys, the Livingstons, the Van Schaacks, the Crugers, the Morrises, the Youngs, the Boyntons, the Van Cortlandts, the Floyds, the Lows, the Herkimers, the Jays and the Subers.

[3] The whole congregation of Trinity church went to Nova Scotia with their venerable pastor. *The United Empire Loyalist Centennial* (1884), 110. Address by William Kirby, Esq. *Ibid.*, 111. *Can. Archs.* (1894), 407, Carleton to North, Aug. 26, 1783.

[4] Many of the Irish loyalists were Catholics.

[5] MS., *Transcript of . . . Books and Papers . . of Am. Loyalists*, vol. 18, p. 81.

[6] Rev. John M. Kern was a German Lutheran minister. *Ibid.*, vol. 19, p. 389.

[7] Gordon, *War in America*, i, 223; Allen, *Am. Rev.*, i, 571; MS., *Associations and Miscl. Papers*, 63, 469; *Am. Archs.*, 4 ser., iii, 707, 883, iv, 780–787, v, 826, 872, vi, 1055; *Min. of Prov. Cong.*, iii, 27, 67.

[8] *Can. Archs.* (1896), 76; *The United Empire Loyalists Centennial* (1884), 111. Sir John Johnson's Royal Regiment of New York, consisting of 800, were mostly Lutherans and Presbyterians. Croil, *A Sketch of Canad. Hist.* (1861), p. 128.

CHAPTER II

FINAL ORGANIZATION OF THE LOYALIST PARTY

THE loyalist opposition to Congress and its " recommend-ations " was soon felt in every section of New York. In some localities it was manifested only in sentiment, while in others it took the form of united action. This hostility did not mean, necessarily, that England's course was approved, but, for the most part, simply indicated that the loyalists did not sanction whig methods of seeking the redress of griev-ances. In Queens county the authority assumed by the New York city committee was wholly ignored.[1] To offset some whig resolves of December 6, 1774,[2] and the appointment by the whigs of a committee, the Jamaica loyalists issued a pro-test signed by 91 of the 160 freeholders in the township and " 45 other very respectable inhabitants," January 27, 1775.[3] At Newtown 56 loyalists signed a similar protest.[4] The Oyster Bay loyalists outnumbered the whigs and prevented action.[5] The same thing happened at Flushing.[6]

Suffolk county was almost unanimously whig. There were not more than a dozen loyalists in the whole county.[7] Kings county, full of easy-going Dutch, who were passive loyalists, repudiated the acts of Congress by silently ignoring

---

[1] Onderdonk, *Queens County*, 16.   [2] *Ibid.*, 14.   [3] *Ibid.*, 17.

[4] *Rivington's Gazetteer*, no. 92, Jan. 12, 1775; Ricker, *Annals of Newtown*, 175–178; Onderdonk, *Queens County*, 17–20.

[5] *Ibid.*, 20.   [6] *Ibid.*, 21; *cf. Memoirs of the L. I. Hist. Soc.*, 268.

[7] Flint, *Early Long Island*, 340; *cf. Am. Archs.*, 4th ser., ii, 117; *cf.* Stiles, *Hist. of Kings Co.*, i, 32.

them.[1]   Most of Staten Island was loyalist, but no decisive action was taken.[2]

Westchester county disapproved of the acts of Congress and disregarded the New York city committee entirely.   At White Plains 45 freeholders suppressed the whig movement.[3] The loyalists of Rye were outspoken and pugnacious.[4]   Both parties were very busy in Ulster county.   The whigs carried the day, but the loyalists at Showangunk were especially active.[5]   From the first the loyalists of Dutchess county repudiated committees and congresses.[6]   After Congress laid down a program they refused to follow it.[7]   In Albany county the loyalists of Kings district resolved to obey the law and to resist all efforts to violate it.[8]   In Tryon county the loyalists, led by Sir William Johnson, practically controlled the situation and held the German whigs at bay.[9]

With insufficient data, it is impossible to say just how many in the province advocated peaceable means of redress and what number favored force and violence as a means of securing their rights and privileges.   Certainly New York was far from unanimously favoring the harsher course, and it is even a question whether a majority held this idea.   Early in 1775 Colden asserted that a " good majority" of the most respect-

---

[1] Onderdonk, *Revolutionary Incidents*, etc., Preface; Stiles, *Hist. of Brooklyn*, i, 243; Flint, *Early Long Island*, 340; Ostrander, *Hist. of Brooklyn and Kings Co.*, i, 208–211.

[2] Brooks, *Hist. Records of Staten Island*; Clute, *Centennial of Northfield*, 13; Tyson, *Lecture on the Hist. of Staten Island*, 9; *Holt's N. Y. Journal*, no. 1676; *Am. Arch.*, 4th ser., i, 1249.

[3] *Cf.* Dawson, *Westchester County*, 36–40.

[4] Baird, *History of Rye*, 222.

[5] *Am. Archs.*, 4th ser., i, 1230.

[6] *Ibid.*, 702–703.   [7] *Ibid.*, 1164.   [8] *Ibid.*, 1063.

[9] Campbell, *Annals of Tryon County*, 31–35; Benton, *Hist. of Herkimer County*, 66–67.

able people urged peace and discountenanced violence.[1]   But
radicals north and south of New York were trying her
moderation, for it was hard to resist the contagious enthus-
iasm "when propagated by every artifice."[2]   Still the governor believed that the people were not inclined to copy
the "extravagant schemes" of other colonies.[3]   He certainly
had many reasons for his belief.

The loyalists refused to recognize Congress as either entitled to obedience, or possessed of the power to exact it.
As it could only recommend, they felt free to reject its recommendations.   The leaders urged that course and advised
all to place their hope in the general assembly, their lawful
representatives.[4]   The loyalist pamphleteer, Seabury, best
stated the attitude of his party in "An Alarm to the Legislature."   "A foreign power is brought to govern this province," he wrote.   "Laws made at Philadelphia . . . are
imposed upon us by the most imperious menaces.   Money
is levied upon us without the consent of our representatives
. . .   Mobs and riots are encouraged, in order to force submission to the tyranny of Congress. . . .   To you, gentlemen, the good people of this province look for relief; on
you they have fixed their hopes; from you they expect de-
liverance from this intolerable state of slavery. . . .   If you
assert your dignity, if you maintain your own rights and
privileges, we shall again be a free and happy, and, I trust,
not an ungrateful people. . . .   If laws made and decrees
passed at Philadelphia, by the enthusiastic republicans of
New England and Virginia, are to bind the people of this

---

[1] *N. Y. Hist. Soc. Colls.* (1877), 378.

[2] *Ibid.*, 378, 387.   [3] *Ibid.*, 390.

[4] Seabury, *The Congress Canvassed*, etc., 48–49; Seabury, *Free Thoughts*, etc.,
46–48; Chandler, *What Think Ye of Congress Now?* 42–43; Onderdonk, *Queens
County,* 17; *Am. Archs.*, 4th ser., i, 702–703; *N. Y. Hist. Soc. Colls.* (1877)
374–375.

province, and extort money from them, why, gentlemen, do you meet?   Is it barely to register their edicts, and rivet the fetters of their tyranny on your constituents? . . . Your duty requires you to interpose your authority, and to break up this horrid combination of seditious men, which has already enslaved this province, and which was intended to draw the faithful subjects of our most gracious sovereign into rebellion and civil war." [1]

The last session of the general assembly began January 13, 1775.[2]   The loyalists watched it with anxious hearts and largely dictated its course of procedure.   Colden's opening message was an earnest prayer that its members would follow a wise, moderate course, which would secure a "permanent reconciliation." [3]   This they solemnly promised [4] in a "loyal and affectionate address." [5]   The governor, council and assembly were in accord in their desire to secure peace and avert civil war, and gave expression to the sentiment of the entire loyalist party.

In the assembly the moderate loyalists had a solid majority, and consequently all the radical measures of the whigs were voted down.[6]   The lower house refused to consider the recommendations of Congress,[7] to thank the merchants for obeying the non-intercourse acts,[8] and to select delegates to

---

[1] *An Alarm*, etc., 4–8.

[2] *N. Y. Hist. Soc. Colls.* (1877), 382.

[3] *N. Y. Assemb. Journ.* (1766–1776, 8th part), 4.

[4] *Ibid.*, 14.

[5] *Ibid.*, 12; *N. Y. Hist. Soc. Colls.* (1877), 384.

[6] *N. Y. Assemb. Journ.* (1766–1776, 8th part), 18, 28, 37, 38, 40, 44–45; Seabury, *Free Thoughts*, etc., 46–48; *Am. Archs.*, 4th ser., i, 1188, 1203; Jones, *Hist. of New York*, i, 36–37; *Docs. rel. to N. Y. Col. Hist.*, viii, 532; *N. Y. Hist. Soc. Colls.* (1877), 381, 383, 386, 389.

[7] Jones, *Hist. of N. Y.*, i, 36–37.

[8] *N. Y. Assemb. Journ.* (1766–1776, 8th part), 40.

the second Continental Congress.[1]   The loyalist majority
declared that their "allegiance to George III., was the same
as if they were in England."   They admitted that they owed
"obedience to all acts of parliament . . . for the general
weal," but insisted upon the right of personal representation
before taxation.[2]   This, it was believed, would lead to reconciliation.[3]

The "loyal petition" to the king, the memorial to the
House of Lords and the remonstrance to the Commons em-
bodied the true political views of the great mass of moderate
loyalists.   The pamphlets of Seabury, Wilkins, Inglis,
Cooper and Chandler expressed the feelings of the churchmen and crown officials.   The assembly could not recede
from the encroachments made on the royal prerogatives.
The American interpretation of the British constitution was
stated in a clear, dignified manner.

Parliament was acknowledged " as the grand legislature of
the empire,"[4] and the colonies to be parts of that empire.
They recognized the "supreme, regulating power" of parliament, but denied its right to bind "in all cases whatso-
ever," for that would make them slaves.[5]   Hence "the line
of parliamentary authority and American freedom" must be
found and then firmly established "on just, equitable and
constitutional grounds."[6]

Since 1691 New York had had a measure of home-rule,
with a local tax-granting assembly.   Therefore, it was held
that contributions to the imperial government could be secured only through the assembly of the province.[7]   The

---

[1] *N. Y. Assemb. Journ.* (1766–1776, part 8), 44–45; *Docs. rel. to N. Y. Col.
Hist.*, viii, 543.

[2] *N. Y. Assemb. Journ.* (1766–1776, 8th part), 59–64.

[3] *N. Y. Hist. Soc. Colls.* (1877), 387.

[4] *N. Y. Assemb. Journ.* (1766–1776, 8th part), 109.   [5] *Ibid.*, 112.

[6] *Ibid.*, 114–117.   [7] *Ibid.*, 110.

scheme to tax America without the assent of the assemblies was branded as an " innovation."[1] To restore peace, acquired rights must be recognized.[2] At the same time they were quite willing to admit that parliament could act for the " general weal of the empire, and the due regulation of the trade and commerce thereof."

" The honest, though disorderly, struggles for liberty " on the part of the revolutionists were condemned.[3] They had no desire for independence, and emphatically denied charges to the contrary.[4] They yearned for reconciliation, with the constitutional rights and privileges, which they felt they had enjoyed for almost a century, guaranteed to them.

This was the last attempt in New York to secure by legal means the rights to which the colonists considered themselves entitled under the British constitution. It failed and gave way to a revolutionary procedure which the king and parliament could not recognize. The loyalists, after this, centered their hopes first in the leniency and justice of the sovereign power,[5] and finally, in the strong arm of force. The whigs based their expectations upon ultra-legal congresses, conventions and committees, later on civil war, and ultimately on independence.

The committee of inspection and observation, appointed to enforce the decrees of congress,[6] proposed the election of delegates to the next Continental Congress.[7] The loyalists had had a surfeit of revolutionary congresses and decided, if possible, to thwart the election.[8] In a mass meeting of both factions

---

[1] *N. Y. Assemb. Journ.* (1766–1776, 8th part), 114–115.   [2] *Ibid.*, 111.

[3] *Ibid.*, 109, 114.   [4] *Ibid.*, 115–117.

[5] *Am. Archs.*, 4th ser., ii, 513.

[6] *N. Y. Hist. Soc. Colls.* (1877), 372, 373.

[7] Jones, *Hist. of N. Y.*, i. 480; *Am. Archs.*, 4th ser., ii, 4.

[8] *Am. Arch*, 4th ser., ii, 44–46, 48, 49–50; *N. Y. Hist. Soc. Colls.* (1877), 395.

in New York City the loyalists were defeated.[1]   The next step
was to send deputies to a convention for the purpose of
electing delegates to congress.[2]   This was strenuously opposed by the loyalists.   In Ulster county they protested
that the election of deputies was not sanctioned by a hundredth part of the inhabitants.[3]   In Westchester county
hundreds objected to sending representatives.[4]   The Queens
county loyalists outvoted the whigs on all occasions, but did
not prevent the minority from sending deputies.[5]   Three-
fourths of Dutchess county disapproved of the convention.[6]
Staten Island almost unanimously refused to send deputies.[7]
The Kings county loyalists were indifferent.[8]

The Provincial Convention was the first revolutionary
body in New York which acted as a legislature.   It was
called because the loyalist assembly had refused to approve
of the acts of congress.[9]   The proposition to call it came
from the whigs alone.   The loyalists opposed its call both
on constitutional and party grounds, but were defeated,
partly through the fear or indifference of many of their own
members.

The skirmish at Lexington, following on the heels of the

---

[1] Jones, *Hist. of N. Y.*, i, 481–483; *Am. Archs.*, 4th ser., ii, 49, 138.

[2] Jones, *Hist. of N. Y.*, i, 484–486; *Am. Archs.*, 4th ser., ii, 138.

[3] *Cal. of N. Y. Hist. MSS.*, i, 22–23.

[4] *Am. Archs.*, 4th ser., ii, 282, 314–322, 323–324; *Cal. of N. Y. Hist. MSS.*, i, 20–21.

[5] *Ibid.*, 38–39, 40, 41; *Am. Archs.*, 4th ser., ii, 273–275; *Min. of Prov. Conv.*, i, 2, 7.

[6] *Cal. of N. Y. Hist. MSS.*, i, 41.   The whigs denied this statement and placed the number at one-half or one-third. — *Am. Archs.*, 4th ser., ii, 176, 304–305.

[7] *Ibid.*, 313.

[8] *Cal. of N. Y. Hist. MSS.*, i, 41–42.

[9] *N. Y. Hist. Soc. Colls.* (1877), 389–390; *N. Y. Assemb. Journ.* (1766–1776, 8th part), 44–45.

Provincial Convention, was another sad blow to the loyalists. It put the mob in power. The "friends of government" now came to be despised and maltreated, Rivington, the loyalist printer, was forced to recant. President Cooper had to flee before a mob. Others followed his example, so that the city of New York was soon rid of the loyalist leaders, while the rest of the party became quiet through fear.[1] "It was with much difficulty that the people were prevented from taking the lives of those whom they have considered as traitors to their country."[2] Colden was powerless,[3] and had to admit that the province was in a "state of anarchy and confusion."[4] "A committee has assumed the whole power of government," he complained,[5] and retired to his farm on Long Island.[6] The loyalists were broken-hearted. Until Lexington they had hoped to win through the assembly. They could not believe that civil war was upon them. Several left for England "with hopes . . . to stop the effusion of blood, and the horrors and calamities of a civil war, which has already had such terrifying effects."[7]

The committee of one hundred which had been elected May 1, 1775, conservative though it was, led New York into armed resistance. The genuine loyalists denounced it, but the moderates had countenanced it. Its president was a loyalist.[8] Some members never attended and over a third remained away most of the time.[9] From the first it exercised judicial powers

[1] *Am. Archs.*, 4th ser., ii, 448.   [2] *Ibid.*, 448–449.

[3] Jones, *Hist. of N. Y.*, i, 40–41.

[4] *N. Y. Hist. Soc. Colls.* (1877), 404.   [5] *Ibid.*, 406.   [6] *Ibid.*, 413.

[7] *N. Y. Hist. Soc. Colls.* (1877), 404. Among them were Col. Maunsell, Isaac Wilkins, Col. Morris and Mr. Watts.

[8] Isaac Low. For list of members *cf. Docs. rel. to N. Y. Col. Hist.*, viii, 600; Jones, *Hist of N. Y.*, i, 488.

[9] *Am. Archs.*, 4th ser., ii, 898, 933, 940, 409, 410.

and acted as a board of censors on obnoxious loyalists,[1] while congress and itself were the only bodies which could declare a person a public enemy.[2] It made arrests, imprisoned and denounced violators of the association,[3] and after continuing this work for a time finally surrendered its powers to the provincial congress.

The general association, signed by congress October 20, 1774, and sent to the colonies for enforcement,[4] had served as a political thermometer to test party spirit in New York. From the first the extreme loyalists denounced this measure. They objected to both the act itself and the methods of enforcing it. They ridiculed the idea of boycotting the whole world in order to get rid of a three-pence duty on tea, and said that the remedy was "ten thousand times worse than the disease." "It was like cutting off your arm to remove a sore on your little finger." It would throw thousands out of work, and riots and acts of violence would result. It would hurt England, but would be doubly injurious to the colonies and would force them to be the first to yield. Farmers would be the worst sufferers. Prices would go up in spite of agreements to the contrary. Parliament would close the port of New York as it did that of Boston. The rich would swallow up the poor. Americans would have to live like dogs and savages until the English government relented.[5] If non-importation were confined to tea and respectful petitions sent to the home authorities, no doubt the duty would be removed, but never under the association.[6]

[1] *Am. Archs.*, 4th ser., ii, 1574.

[2] *Ibid.*, 532.   [3] *Ibid.* 1576, iii, 15, 21.

[4] *Ibid.*, i, 914–927, v, 874–878; *Jour. of Cont. Cong.*, 57, 68–77; *Docs. rel. to N. Y. Col. Hist.*, viii, 69, 80, 176.

[5] Cooper, *A Friendly Address*, etc., 36–42; Seabury, *Free Thoughts*, etc., 3–36; Seabury, *The Congress Canvassed*, etc., 25–29: *Am. Archs.*, 4th ser., i, 1211–1213; Chandler, *What Think Ye of Congress Now?* 27–32.

[6] Cooper, *A Friendly Address*, etc., 43; Seabury, *The Congress Canvassed*, etc., 44–48.

The loudest cry was raised against the provincial and local committees which were appointed or chosen to execute the association. The loyalists asserted that obedience to such tyrannical bodies was slavery. These illegal committees were to enforce the association like "the Popish Inquisition." No proofs were admitted, no evidence, no defense, no jury, no appeal; judgment was rendered on appearance only; the accused were condemned unseen and unheard, and finally outlawed or otherwise punished by the committee acting as the highest court on earth.[1] "Will you choose such committees?" asked Seabury. "Will you submit to them should they be chosen by the weak, foolish, turbulent part of the country people? Do as you please; but by Him that made me, I will not. No, if I must be enslaved, let it be by a king at least and not by a parcel of upstart, lawless committeemen."[2] The loyalist assembly also refused to approve of the association or to suggest means for its execution.[3]

The committee of sixty had been chosen expressly to enforce this coercive measure.[4] The committee of one hundred and the Provincial Congress, both whig bodies, were expected to complete the work.[5] But not until April 29, 1775—subsequent to the encounter at Lexington—was an effort made to enforce the association in New York.[6] County and district committees were then appointed to oversee the work.[7] The names of signers and of those who refused to

---

[1] Seabury, *Free Thoughts*, etc., 35–45; Seabury, *The Congress Canvassed*, etc., 30–39; Seabury, *An Alarm*, etc., 4–5; *Am. Archs.*, 4th ser., 1211–1213; Chandler, *What Think Ye of Congress Now?* 30–37.

[2] Seabury, *Free Thoughts*, etc., 37.

[3] *N. Y. Hist. Soc. Colls.* (1877), 401.

[4] *Am. Archs.*, 4th ser., i, 328–329.   [5] *Ibid.*, ii, 400, 470.

[6] *Ibid.*, 471; *Min. of Prov. Conv.*, i, 34–35, gives a copy of the association used in New York.

[7] *Rivington's N. Y. Gazetteer*, no, 107, May 4, 1775; *Holt's N. Y. Journal*, no. 1687, May 4, 1775; *Min. of Prov. Conv.*, i, 82.

sign were to be returned to the Provincial Congress.[1] No " coercive steps " were to be used,[2] but still the committees might pass judgment on violators of the association.[3]

So far as the incomplete records show, about 12,000 persons signed the association and nearly 6000 refused to sign.[4] It must be remembered, however, that these reports came from whig committees. Besides, the returns from the loyalist strongholds were very meagre or not given at all. In Albany and Westchester counties only the county committees signed the association, while no returns of those who refused to sign in Queens, Kings, Richmond and Gloucester counties are known to be in existence. It is true, also, that, owing to the threats of the whigs and the force of public pressure, many, who at heart were loyalists, had not the courage to refuse to sign the association.[5] Others, who became loyalists after July 4, 1776, entered, in 1775, heartily into this method of obtaining a redress of colonial grievances.[6] It seems reasonable to conclude, therefore, notwithstanding the disparity in the figures preserved, that the association indicates the existence of almost as many loyalists as revolutionists in the province at this time.[7]

The " non-associators " were pointed out as objects of contempt and suspicion. Later the refusal to sign the association was taken as the basis for summary punishment. The names of those who refused were published and they were

[1] *Min. of Prov. Conv.*, i, 97.   [2] *Ibid.*, 98.

[3] *Am. Archs.*, 4th ser., ii, 1838.   Case of the Murrays.

[4] These figures were obtained from lists given in local histories, *Minutes of the Provincial Congress, American Archives, Cal. of N. Y. Hist. MSS.*, and other sources.

[5] *Docs. rel. to N. Y. Col. Hist.*, viii, 582.

[6] *Memorial of Henry Van Schaack*, 27; Van Schaack, *Life of Peter Van Schaack*, 59; *Docs. rel. to N. Y. Col. Hist.*, viii, 582.

[7] O'Callaghan, *Doc. Hist. of N. Y.*, iv, shows that there were 41,616 males above 16 in New York in 1774.

boycotted as "enemies to their country."[1] Violators of the
agreement were treated in a similar way.[2] The county committee acted finally in most cases, but doubtful and obstinate
ones were sent to the Provincial and even to the Continental
Congress. March 14, 1776, the latter body ordered all who
refused to join the association to be disarmed.[3] Later a
milder form of association was submitted to them and pressure was brought to bear upon them to force them to sign it.[4]

The association thus became the first decisive test of the
politics of individuals to which resort was had during the
revolution. It stamped the individual as a whig or a tory in
the eyes of his neighbors, and treatment was meted out to
him accordingly. It proved his political rectitude or de-
pravity. Hesitation involved suspicion; refusal, guilt. The
loyalist who was true to his convictions, creed and king was
detested, reviled, and, if prominent, ruined in business, tarred
and feathered, mobbed, ostracised, or imprisoned; and all
this at the will of a committee, self-constituted and respon-
sible to no one.[5] The weak and timid were silenced and
made secret enemies of the deadliest type until the arrival of
British troops gave them a chance to throw off their decep-
tive cloaks. That so many disapproved of the mild form of
opposition in 1775, is very significant, because it meant that
when independence was thrust into the conflict in 1776 and
became a second and final test of men's political views, the
number of loyalists would be greatly increased.

The loyalists made little open opposition to the calling of
the first Provincial Congress.[6] Opposition to the second

---

[1] *Am. Archs.*, 4th ser., ii, 606–607.

[2] *Ibid.*, 12, 13, 35, 298, 448, 887–889, iii, 21, 22, 439, 451, 880, 1626, 1627, iv,
690–691, vi, 1433–1434.

[3] *Ibid.*, vi, 1419.   [4] *Ibid.*, 1420, 1421.

[5] *Cf.* "A Loyalist's Soliloquy." Moore, *Diary of the Am. Rev.*, i, 169.

[6] *Cf. Min. of Prov. Cong.*, i, 31, 32, 197; *cf. Cal. of N. Y. Hist. MSS.*, i, 23,

Provincial Congress was far more pronounced, especially in
Queens, Richmond, Kings and Gloucester counties   In the
first three counties a majority voted against sending deputies.[1]
Richmond was threatened with an interdict, and then sent two
representatives.[2]   Queens county[3] was outlawed by the Continental Congress, all trade with the traitors was cut off, they
were confined to the county, were ordered to be disarmed,
their names were ordered to be published in all local newspapers for a month, and twenty-six leaders, together with
other notorious loyalists, were ordered to be arrested and
imprisoned.[4]   Even in New York city the twenty-one deputies who were chosen were so objectionable that the Provincial Congress ordered the committee of one hundred to
choose new ones.[5]

The Provincial Congress assumed all governmental powers
and brought loyal government practically to an end in the
colony.[6]   Fearing arrest,[7] Governor Tryon went on board a
British war-ship, where all business pertaining to his office
was transacted.[8]   There he remained from October, 1775,
until the occupation of New York by the British in September, 1776, when civil government was finally superseded by

---

42–44, 64–68, 97–98; *cf. Am. Archs.*, 4th ser., ii, 959; *cf.* Seabury, *The Congress
Canvassed*, etc., 48–51.

[1] *Cf. Min. of Prov. Cong.*, v, 931, iii, 368; *cf. Cal. of N. Y. Hist. MSS.*, i,
200–201; *cf. Am. Archs.*, 4th ser., iii, 1388–1391, 1754, 1756, 1762, iv, 428.

[2] *Ibid.*, iii, 1762, iv, 428, 1069–1070, Jan. 19, 1776.

[3] Only 221 in the county voted for representatives, while 788 opposed them.
Ibid., iii, 1389–1391.

[4] *Am. Archs.*, 4th ser., iv, 1630–1632.   [5] *Ibid.*, v, 255.

[6] *Docs. rel. to N. Y. Col. Hist.*, viii, 579–580, 650; *Am. Archs.*, 4th ser., ii, 966;
Min. of Prov. Cong., i, 180.

[7] *Am, Archs.*, 4th ser., iii, 1052–1053; *cf.* Jones, *Hist. of N. Y.*, i, 61–63,
559–560.

[8] *Ibid.*, i, 62; *Am. Archs.*, 4th ser., iii, 1053–1054, 1311–1315; *Docs. rel. to N.
Y. Col. Hist.*, viii, 638–644.

military rule.¹ He assured the " friends of order and good
government " that they would be protected, but that all
others would be dealt with as rebels.²

The course taken by the Provincial Congress was satisfac-
tory to neither loyalists nor ardent whigs. Complaints were
heard on all sides,³ and these forced that body to name a
committee to investigate the rumors so " inimical to this colony and its inhabitants." ⁴ Sincere efforts for reconciliation
had been made ⁵—a plan had been approved by the moderates in both parties—but to no purpose. The day for
reconciliation was fast passing away.⁶

All of the loyalists, save a few extremists, desired peace
on the broad ground of the American interpretation of British constitutional rights. They dreaded and feared civil war
as the greatest obstacle to reconciliation, for they knew that
with rebellion rampant Great Britain would not and could
not compromise. Therefore they denounced the military
program of the whigs, and insisted that the contest be carried on constitutionally. Many of them labored as indefa-
tigably to stay the iron hand of Great Britain as to check
the seditious and revolutionary actions of the whigs. They
wrote to England that sending an army and navy to America had " disconcerted and unhinged a concilatory proposition respecting a revenue." ⁷ They recommended a suspen-
sion of the restraining acts, the withdrawal of armed forces,
the recognition of the right of self-taxation, and an annual

¹ Jones, *Hist. of N. Y.*, i, 560.

² *Am. Archs.*, 4th ser., iv, 307, 308–309.

³ *Ibid.*, iii, 18–19, 50, 135, 262–263, 974, iv, 193, 694, 830.

⁴ *Ibid.*, v, 328.

⁵ *Min. of Prov. Cong.*, i, 112–113, 140–141, 307–313, 325, 340–341, 424, 347–348,
ii, 10–11.

⁶ *Am. Archs.*, 4th ser., iv, 470–473, v, 854, 931, 942, 945, 947, 1055, 1078, 1169.

⁷ *Ibid.*, 4th ser., ii, 1526–1528.

colonial congress, on all whose acts a veto right of the crown should be reserved.[1]   The prospect of independence seemed intolerable to them.   " The tories dread a declaration of independence, and a course of conduct on that plan, more than death," wrote a prominent whig.[2]   That would be an anarchistic blow at church and state.   The loyalist presses were busy waging this new battle.[3]   They asserted their right to discuss the momentous question " without being charged with sentiments inimical to America."   They insisted, with truth, that this was a new issue, wholly inconsistent with the declarations and professions of individuals, committees, conventions and congresses in 1774 and 1775, and hence ought not to be forced upon them against their protest.[4]

The loyalists were encouraged by Governor Tryon's letter " To the Inhabitants of the Colony of New York," March 16, 1776.[5]   He extended his thanks to the loyalists " for their zealous attachment to our happy constitution and their obedience to the sovereignty of the British empire."   By the king's orders he promised " every assistance and protection the state of Great Britain will enable his majesty to afford them " for withstanding the revolutionary acts.   He urged all good loyal citizens to be firm for a few months, when rebellion would be suppressed.   But that was a vain promise.

All parties on both sides of the Atlantic professed a desire for peace, but neither the revolutionists nor British authorities seemed willing to sacrifice or compromise the prin-

---

[1] *Am. Archs.*, 4th ser., ii, 1527, v, 1011,   [2] *Ibid.*, v, 1168.

[3] *Ibid.*, v, 514, 542, 802, 839, 1036, 1049, vi, 1348, 1363.

[4] *Ibid.*, v, 1011–1016. They denied " that those who hesitate to embrace an immediate independency, * * * * * would sacrifice their country for the sake of a re-union with Great Britain."

[5] *Ibid.*, 248–249; *Min. of Prov. Cong.*, v, 161–163; *Constitutional Gazette*, March 20, 1776.

ciple on which the contest rested.   Meanwhile the colonies
declared themselves independent, and all prospects of peace
were at an end.   A fierce war of extermination had begun,
and loyalists were forced to act on the defensive.

In the colonial history of New York nothing is more patent than the fact that at no time, prior to the close of 1775,
was total independence desired.   The charge that independence was desired was resented publicly and privately, individually and collectively, on all occasions, by all classes and
all parties.   Complete separation did not become the issue
of the contest until early in 1776, and was certainly not the
the original object of the war.   The whigs and loyalists
stood together in demanding their constitutional rights, but
differed more and more widely as to the means of securing
them.   When, at last, the whigs proclaimed the new issue
of independence, the loyalists branded it as revolution, anarchy and political suicide.   They declared that it was not
only a violation of all earlier professions, but that it was
the course least likely to secure the end desired.   Therefore they fought it bitterly with the pen, the sword and the
Bible.[1]

The loyalist literature, both before and after July 4, 1776,
reflects the attitude of that party toward the Declaration of
Independence.   These loyalist writers asserted over and over
again that independence would be the direst calamity;[2] that
the attempt to secure it was heretical, sinful and impractic-
able;[3] and that, if obtained, it would lead to internecine war
and ruin, and would force the colonies to seek the protection

---

[1] Seabury, *The Congress Canvassed*, etc., 52–59; Cooper, *A Friendly Address,*
etc., 24, 44; *cf. Am. Archs.*, 4th ser., v, 1067.

[2] Seabury, *The Congress Canvassed*, etc., 52–59.

[3] Inglis, *The True Interest of America*, etc.; *Plain Truth*, etc., and *Additions to
Plain Truth*, etc., both very likely by Inglis; *cf.* Tyler, *Lit. Hist. of Am. Rev.*, i,
479.

of some foreign sea-power, for which they would have to pay
in one year more than for all British duties.[1] One loyalist pamphleteer no doubt expressed the biased thought of his party
when he declared that, of the seventy men who constituted
the Continental Congress, which issued the Declaration of
Independence, all but eight or nine were deeply in debt or
very poor, and hoped for great benefit from the change.[2]
" Republicans, smugglers, debtors and men of desperate fortunes were the principal promoters of this unnatural rebellion." [3]   Adding the politicians, he said, you have the " sum
total of those who were active and zealous for independence." [4]
Others were inveigled into joining the movement.   But the
loyalists on every hand were convinced that independence
was unattainable, and that the idea "must vanish like the
baseless fabric of a vision." [5]

"The Declaration of Independence," said Thomas Jones,
the loyalist historian, " was the first act that put an end to
the courts of law, to the laws of the land, and to the administration of justice under the British crown. . . . The
revolt was now complete. . . . A usurped kind of government took place; a medley of military law, convention
ordinances, congress recommendations and committee resolutions." [6]   Every American now had to choose between remaining a subject of Great Britain—which had always been
his pride—and thus becoming a traitor to the United States
of America, and declaring himself a citizen of the latter newly-
born nation, and, consequently, a traitor to the crown.
There was no compromise and no middle ground.   Those

---

[1] Cooper, *American Querist*, etc.,queries 80–89; Seabury, *The Congress Canvassed*, etc., 52–59.

[2] *Letters of Papinian*, etc., preface, iv.

[3] *Ibid.*, 107.   [4] *Ibid.*, 108.   [5] *Ibid.*, 125–130.

[6] Jones, *Hist. of N. Y.*, ii, 115.

who tried the neutral course were treated by the revolutionists as enemies and harried out of the land.[1]

The act of July 4, 1776, led to a final readjustment of
party lines. It gave finality to loyalism. The great " party
of opposition," composed of whigs and liberal loyalists,
broke up. Loyalists now gave up all hopes of carrying out
their moderate program, and relied upon British military
power to suppress revolution and to destroy treason. Many
took up arms against the insurgents, others fled to Canada
or England, while the rest either tried to brave the storm in
their own localities or else sought protection within the British
lines. The loyalist party now reached its high-water mark
as a political organization with a positive part to play. It
was composed of three classes. The first and most influential group was the conservative loyalists, who had denounced
all show of armed resistance, and had either upheld Great
Britain in her course, or, at furthest, had favored petitions
and remonstrances through legally constituted bodies. The
second class consisted of those moderate loyalists who
meant to be true to the king and parliament, but who looked
at these from the standpoint of an American. They championed the claims of the colonists as just, approved of the
extra-legal bodies and in many instances were members of
them, and even sanctioned a show of resistance in order to
compel a recognition of their rights. One of the most conspicuous examples of this class was John Alsop, one of New
York's delegates to Congress. He wrote to the New York
Provincial Convention July 16, 1776, that he was surprised at
their resolution in favor of the Declaration of Independence.
Such action was against his " judgment and inclination."
As long as a door was open for reconciliation with Great

---

[1] The case of Peter Van Schaack, a loyalist lawyer, was a typical example. Van
Schaack, *Life of Peter Van Schaack*, 60.

Britain, he was ready to serve his country with all his power, but now that his hope of that event was destroyed, he resigned his office.[1]   The Convention promptly resolved that it cheerfully accepted Mr. Alsop's resignation of his seat in the Continental Congress.[2]   The third faction of loyalists in 1776 was composed of conservative whigs who had been willing to fight to defeat a bad ministerial policy and to secure their rights as British subjects, but who now halted when treason and national disruption were decreed, and refused to be coerced into an approval of total separation from the crown.   Isaac Low and James Duane represent this class.[3]

Men must now take sides either for or against independence.   The issues were clear and well understood.   There could be no recognized middle ground.[4]   All had to choose whom they would serve.   Those who desired to remain neutral, and they were very numerous, were treated as more dangerous traitors than those who openly espoused the British side, and were forced in self-defense to seek royal pro-

---

[1] *Am. Archs.*, 5th ser., i, 368, 1428–1429.

[2] *Ibid.* 1429, 1431.   Peter Van Schaack, a moderate loyalist, who desired to remain neutral in the conflict, summed up the attitude of a majority of the party, when he said that they were " disposed to go along with Congress to a certain limited extent, hoping in that way to fix what they conceived to be the rights of their country upon the firmest foundation; but as soon as they found that the views and designs of the American leaders rested in nothing short of a dissolution of the union between Great Britain and her colonies, they refused any longer to participate in public measures."   Van Schaack, *Life of Peter Van Schaack*, 60.

[3] *Cf.* Jones, *Hist. of N. Y.*, i, 712–713, note lxvii; *cf. Am. Archs.*, 5th ser., i, 468.

[4] " I could hardly own the king and fight against him at the same time; but now these matters are cleared up.   Heart and hand shall move together.   I don't think there will be five tories in our part of the country in ten days after matters are known.   We have had great numbers, who would do nothing until we were declared a free state, who are now ready to spend their lives and fortunes in defence of our country."   Joseph Barton, of N. J., to Henry Wisner, of N. Y., July 9, 1776.   *Am. Archs.*, 5th ser., i, 139.

tection.[1]   Though not a few loyalists now openly advocated the extreme claims of the mother country, still the majority, while far from approving the spirit of the British colonies or sanctioning the demands of parliament, were determined to maintain union with Great Britain.[2]   The party was a unit on this question if not on others.   Its members soon saw that the day of argument, of political agitation and of effective action through legal bodies was past.[3]   Through force alone could they win victory for their principles.[4]

Therefore, in the early months of 1776, the loyalist party reached its summit as a political organization and began to decline.   Of course it continued as a factor in the struggle till 1783, when its members were scattered over the various divisions of the British empire and as a party it ceased to exist.   But from and after 1776 the loyalists were compelled to appear as unqualified supporters of the impolitic treatment by Great Britain of its colonies, and therefore were forced to play a part which was to an extent inconsistent with their assertions and convictions.   It is a gross error, however, to believe that the loyalists as a whole were willing to submit without a protest to the invasion of American rights and liberties.   They were Americans and proud of it. They felt the grievances as keenly as did the whigs, but they desired to secure relief in ways provided in the British constitution.   But the folly of the English king, and, as they regarded it, the dogmatic fanaticism of many of the colonists, destroyed all hope of an amicable settlement, caused civil war and led to a result unexpected by either party at the

[1] *Am. Archs.*, 5th ser., iii, 1292.

[2] *Ibid.*, 4th ser., vi, 1431, 1720.

[3] This was very noticeable in the amount and character of their literature after July 4, 1776. *Cf.* Tyler, *Lit. Hist. of the Am. Rev.*

[4] " It then evidently appeared that nothing but the sword could decide the contest." Cooper, *A Sermon*, etc., 17.

outset.   When independence became the great issue, the loyalists took the same view the North did in the late rebellion :
they held that " loyalty " was one of the highest virtues ; that
the supporters of the majesty of law and the established
government were acting an honorable part ; that the national
state, the constitution and the flag must be preserved, and
that rebellion must be suppressed at all hazards and even, if
necessary, by the sword.

CHAPTER III

WAR AGAINST THE LOYALISTS

PRIOR to August 3, 1775, the attitude of the revolutionary government toward obnoxious loyalists was not clearly defined. Cases were determined according to circumstances and exigencies; there were no fixed rules of action either continental or provincial. The Provincial Congress felt it necessary, therefore, to take decisive action against these internal foes. By dealing with special cases precedents were established which gradually developed into principles of action.

The first case brought before the Provincial Congress was that of Guy Johnson, who was warned not to interfere with their plans.[1] No doubt he expressed the sentiment of his faction when he replied that, since reconciliation could come through the assembly alone, he had refused to participate in seditious public meetings called by "leather dressers." He denounced the efforts to injure him in his office, and closed his letter with the words: "I should be much obliged for your promises" of safety, "did they not appear to be made on condition of compliance with continental or provincial congresses, or even committees . . . many of whose resolves may neither consist with my conscience, duty or loyalty."[2]

The next case was that of Angus McDonald, arrested for enlisting loyalist troops. He confessed his guilt and was sent as a prisoner to Connecticut.[3] A letter found on his

[1] *Min. of Prov. Cong.*, i, 153–154.   [2] *Ibid.*, ii, 110–112.
[3] *Min. of Prov. Cong.*, i, 234–240, 243–244; *Am. Archs.*, 4th ser., iii, 89, 913.

person showed that Alexander McDonald was similarly engaged in Richmond county. His arrest was ordered, but he
fled to Boston.[1] These three cases mark the beginning of
armed resistance to the revolutionary government of New
York by congresses, conventions and committees. They
also mark the beginning of the policy of arresting, imprisoning, exiling and otherwise punishing loyalists who dared oppose the revolutionary authority and favor the established
power which the whigs themselves still professed to respect.

In June, 1775, Congress, suspicious of the loyalty of
Queens county, requested the delinquent deputies from that
section to attend and explain their negligence. The Queens
county members who were present were asked to report the
sentiments of their constituents. " It appearing that a great
number of inhabitants of the said county are not disposed
to a representation at this Board and have dissented there-
from," the Congress resolved, as a guardian of the people,
that Queens county "must necessarily be bound by the de-
termination of this Congress." [2] Richmond county was also
forced to send representatives. By this action the Provincial Congress asserted the right of the majority of the counties to coerce the minority. It is not strange that the loyalists declared this to be a violation of the very rights for
which Americans were contending with England.

The committee of safety, acting for the Provincial Congress,
in July, 1775, had before it a case of still another type. Peter
Herring, of New York, aided a loyalist prisoner to escape to a
British man of-war. He was arrested and ordered to be im-
prisoned in Connecticut until released by the Continental
Congress.[3] Cases tried before county committees were sent

---

[1] *Am. Archs.*, 4th ser., iii, 240–242; *cf. Public Papers of George Clinton*, i, 203.

[2] *Min. of Prov. Cong.*, i, 293, 344; *Am. Archs.*, 4th ser., ii, 1328.

[3] *Min. of Prov. Cong.*, ii, 1–2, 3, 19; *Am. Archs.*, 4th ser., ii, 1645.

to the Provincial Congress for final action.[1] Whenever reports of serious disaffection reached the Provincial Congress
a committee was sent to investigate.[2]

Here was a variety of cases, from the individual who was
" inimical to the grand cause " to the " inimical " county. So
numerous and so dangerous were the loyalists that regulations
must be adopted to control them, or the whole cause might
be lost. Law and not the tyranny of a mob must be the
basis of action. Consequently a series of resolves was
passed August 3, 1775. They stated that, since efforts were
made to aid the British army and navy in enforcing the
" cruel and oppressive acts of parliament against the liberties of America," " and as the immutable laws of self-defense
and preservation justify every reasonable measure entered
into to counteract or frustrate such attempts," therefore it was
resolved that any person found guilty before any city or
county committee of supplying " the ministerial army or
navy," or of revealing secrets or giving advice to the same,
should be punished by the committee or Provincial Congress. Those guilty of furnishing supplies were to be disarmed and forfeit to the province double the value of the
articles they supplied. They were to be imprisoned for
three months after the forfeiture was paid. A second offense
would be followed by banishment from the colony for seven
years. Those who denied or opposed the authority of the
Continental or Provincial Congress, or the committe of safety,
or the committee of any county, city, town, manor or precinct,
or dissuaded others from obeying the same, were to be tried
by the county committee. If found guilty, they were to be
disarmed, and, for a second offense, they were to be confined
at their own expense. In case a committee could not execute these resolves it was authorized to call upon the com-

[1] *Min. of Prov. Cong.*, ii, 54–57, 103–104.
[2] *Ibid.*, 167; *Am. Archs.*, 4th ser., ii, 16, 527, 573–574.

mittee of the next county, or the militia, or congress for aid.
If no committee existed in any county, cases were to be tried
before committees of neighboring counties.   Every person
" discovered to be in arms against the liberties of America "
was to be seized by the local committee or militia, and held
in custody for punishment by the Provincial Congress.   His
property was to be put into the hands of " some discreet person," appointed by the committee, who was to pay all profits
to the provincial treasury.   All persons arrested were to
have immediate trial before committeemen sworn to render
judgment "without partiality, favor or affection, or hope of
reward, according to evidence." [1]

Here was an edict passed by the representatives of the
people, and, therefore, having, in the opinion of the whigs,
the force of law.   They argued that in the future the treatment
of loyalists obnoxious to the community could not be called
arbitrary, because it was founded on law.   But loyalists could
not understand how a revolutionary congress, called in the
sacred name of liberty, could refuse to their fellow-subjects
the privilege of securing those same rights in a different way.
Trial and punishment for refusing to be revolutionists sav-
ored more of despotism than the injuries they suffered from
the hands of an overbearing parliament.   These resolves
mark the beginning of that harsh policy of the revolutionists
toward the loyalists, founded on resolution and precedent,
which, in turn, were based on natural rights and the necessity for self-preservation.   Nothing is more striking in the
revolutionary history of New York than the constant attempt to make the treatment of loyalists, whether by the
pettiest committee or by the Provincial Congress, appear to
be legal.   In taking this action the Provincial Congress anticipated the Continental Congress by two months, for it was

---

[1] *Min. of Prov. Cong.*, ii, 314-319.

not until October 6, 1775, that the body at Philadelphia recommended the arrest of dangerous characters.[1]

To take from the loyalists their means of defense and to secure a supply of arms for the troops, the committee of safety decided, September 16, 1775, to seize all arms found in the possession of "non-associators." A list of such confiscations was to be kept, with the appraised values, so that the weapons might be returned or paid for after the war. County committees were to receive the arms subject to the will of Congress. Suffolk county troops, aided by Colonel Lasher, were sent to Queens county to execute the resolution. The chairman of the county committee and Captain Dutcher, aided by the militia and by General Wooster's troops, were to do the same in Westchester county. In other counties the head of the local committee, assisted by the militia, was to enforce the measure. If loyalists resisted, they were to be seized and taken before the Provincial Congress.[2] This was the beginning of that system of confiscation which ended in the sale of all real and personal property of the loyalists. On October 24, the Provincial Congress disapproved of the resolutions of the committee of safety,[3] but they had been in operation long enough to result in the disarmament of many of the loyalists on Long Island, Staten Island, in New York city, Westchester county and elsewhere, and to arouse the most bitter hatred against the revolutionary government and the whigs. In Queens county especially the loyalists resisted, denounced Congress, concealed their valuable arms, and threatened to kill any who tried to seize them.[4]

The disarming of loyalists, which was recommended by

[1] *Am. Archs.*, 4th ser., iii, 1891; *Min. of Prov. Cong.*, iii, 188, 190–191.

[2] *Ibid.*, 73–76.

[3] *Ibid.*, 267–268; *Am. Archs.*, 4th ser., iii, 1303.

[4] *Min. of Prov. Cong.*, iii, 113–117, 124.

the committee of safety in September and the next month repudiated by the Provincial Congress, was recommended by the Continental Congress on March 14, 1776. Now all persons "notoriously disaffected to the cause of America," as well as non-associators, were ordered to be disarmed. The object was to make the foes at home harmless and to arm the continental troops and militia.[1] Hence again the committee of safety instructed all local committees to disarm every one who was " disaffected to the cause of America," or who refused to take an oath of loyalty to the revolutionary powers.[2] Local bodies were cautioned to act moderately, but to use the militia if necessary. The arms were to be appraised by "indifferent persons," marked, recorded, and then turned over to the chairman of the county committee, who, in turn, was to send them with the records to the Provincial Congress.[3] Whole neighborhoods, whose loyalty was too pronounced, were thus disarmed.[4] The loyalists who were deprived of their weapons had to swear that all arms had been surrendered; but many refused so to do,[5] and, as a punishment, were fined or taxed five shillings a day while the district militia was in service.[6] If the fine was not paid, it was collected from the property of the loyalists. This money was used to help arm the "associators." [7] To guard against the influx of loyalists from other colonies every stranger was forced to show from his home committee a certificate " of his

[1] *Am. Archs.*, 4th ser., iii, 989, v, 244, 1409, 1638, 1646.

[2] *Ibid.*, 1409–1410; *Min. of Prov. Cong.*, v, 25, 410.

[3] *Am. Archs.*, 4th ser., v, 274, 1409–1410.

[4] *Ibid.*, 1469, 1487; *Min. of Prov. Cong.*, v, 410, 485, 612.

[5] *Ibid.*, 494, 512.

[6] *Ibid.*, 529; *cf.* Act in Pa. *Am. Archs.*, 4th ser., v, 703; *Ibid.*, 1504. In Albany County the loyalists had to pay an equal share of the military service. *Proceedings of the Alb. Co. Com.*, i, 451.

[7] *Am. Archs.*, 4th ser.. v, 1504. Amendment to the Militia Act, May 11, 1776.

friendliness to the liberties of America," or be subject to trial "as a person inimical thereto."[1]   The silence and, in many cases, the known co-operation of the loyalists with the British led the blustering whigs to conclude that the few tories who dared to open their mouths, together with the placemen in church and state, composed the loyalist party.[2]

The acts of the Provincial Congress were confirmed and supplemented by a series of resolves of the Continental Congress, passed January 2, 1776.   They defined, though rather indefinitely, the status of the loyalists, and outlined the general policy to be enforced regarding them.   They assumed that the loyalists were "honest, well-meaning, but uninformed people," led astray by the "art and address of ministerial agents."   The various committees were instructed, therefore, to explain to them the real situation by conversation and printed matter.   Should "unworthy Americans" still side with the oppressors of America, the various governmental bodies of the colonies were recommended, "by the most speedy and effectual measures, to frustrate the mischievous machinations, and restrain the wicked practices of these men" by disarming them and by exacting a heavy bond for good behavior from the worst among them, or else by imprisoning them.   This, it was thought, would meet the need.   To this end the colonies were authorized to call upon continental troops if necessary.[3]

The resolutions of the sovereign body of the United Colonies, and of the provincial government, formed the groundwork for a complete system of regulations concerning the loyalists.   To loyalists, however, these regulations and edicts, originating in revolution, seemed despotic and tyrannical.   They denied and resisted the right of the revolutionists to dictate what they should believe and how they should

[1] *Am. Archs.*, 4th ser., iv, 438.   [2] *Ibid.*, iii, 940, 1563.
[3] *Ibid.*, vi, 1628–1629.

act, as contrary to all natural, divine and constitutional rights. In the opinion of the whigs, the loyalists were traitors to a just cause, hence these laws were looked upon as moderate, right and needful. Every effort, too, was made to establish their legality.[1] Indeed, so lenient was the Provincial Congress that General Washington complained to the Continental Congress, and that body ordered New York to provide better "for detecting, restraining and punishing disaffected and dangerous persons in that colony," and for preventing loyalists from corresponding with the British. Washington was instructed to help enforce the order.[2]

By the early months of 1776 the status of the loyalists was well defined. The inquisition for dealing with them was thoroughly organized and in active operation. From the sovereign Continental Congress to the pettiest district committee there was a comparatively uniform procedure, based on continental and provincial regulations and supplemented by precedents. Authorization came from the supreme representative bodies, but the enforcement of the scheme was left to minor boards. The Continental Congress laid down the program on general lines, but let each colony devise its own ways and means.[3] A few special cases were sent to the supreme body for action. In New York itself the Provincial Congress took cognizance of very dangerous or difficult cases.[4] Loyalists themselves again and again appealed to it.[5] County and district committees received their instruc

---

[1] *Am. Archs.*, 4th ser., vi, 1716. Act of Prov. Cong., June 18, 1776.

[2] *Ibid.*, 4th ser., vi, 1706, June 14, 1776.

[3] *Ibid.*, 4th ser., vi, 1084; *Gaines' N. Y. Gazette*, no. 1291.

[4] *Am. Archs.*, 4th ser., vi, 725, 1327.

[5] *Ibid.*, iii, 451, 630, 907, 908, 910, 916, 1016, 1267, 1300, 1303; iv, 923, 1017, 1111, 1120; v, 192, 193, 341, 342, 348, 390, 991; vi, 446, 1055, 1315, 1348, 1354, 1355, 1360, 1362, 1365, 1391: *Min. of Prov. Cong.*, iii, 153, 161; iv, 165, 168, 170.

tions from it.   The acts of military officers were counter-
manded by it.[1]   It advised local committees when in doubt,
interpreted law, acted as a final court of appeal, raised and
disbursed money—in short, was the powerful head of the
provincial inquisition.[2]

In May, 1776, a committee, appointed by the Provincial
Congress, on ways and means for dealing with "intestine
enemies" recommended that Queens county loyalists should
be disarmed by force and compelled to take an oath to support the American cause; that all British officers, both military and civil, should be arrested; that all who promised to
favor the American cause should be released; that dangerous loyalists should be sent to Connecticut, New Jersey or
Pennsylvania on parole; and that all who refused paroles
should be imprisoned until the Provincial Congress passed
on them.   The report was adopted.[3]   But finding that the
trial of loyalists took too much time, a "standing committee" of five was appointed, May 27, 1776, to try all tories
arrested by Congress or by the committee of safety.   It was
empowered to call and examine witnesses, to send for papers,
and to discharge all the innocent.   A record was to be kept,
and all proceedings were to be reported to the superior
body.   Three were a quorum.[4]

This committee was deluged with business.   June 5th,
1776, forty-four loyalists, fifty-five royal officers and many
suspects were brought up for trial.[5]   So arduous were the
duties that a new committee of nine was soon appointed

[1] *Min. of Prov. Cong.*, v, 707; *Am. Archs.*, 4th ser., vi, 676, 1358; Dawson, *Westchester Co.*, 172.

[2] *Ibid.*, 174; *Am. Archs.*, 4th ser., iii, 439, 446, 451, 880; iv, 187–188.

[3] *Ibid.*, vi, 1324, 1327, 1328, 1331, 1342, 1365–1370; *Cal. of N. Y. Hist. MSS.*, i, 338; *cf.* Dawson, *Westchester Co.*, p. 165.

[4] *Min. of Prov. Cong.*, v, 632–636, 649; *Am. Archs.*, 4th ser., vi, 1337.

[5] *Min. of Prov Cong.*, v, 737–747.

with increased powers. It could issue warrants for arrest, try loyalists and declare them guilty or innocent.[1] A sub-committee was named to try loyalists at a distance.[2] The proceedings of these committees reveal the hopes, fears, numbers, character and treatment of the loyalists in New York before July 4, 1776.[3] The purpose of the Congress in creating the general committee of nine and its duties may be seen in the resolves of June 5, 1776. That body was convinced that the loyalists of New York and the neighboring colonies were in communication with one another, and were thus strengthening the cause of the English ministry. Certain persons in the counties of Queens, Kings, Westchester, Richmond and New York and elsewhere were represented " as disaffected to the American cause." Since the colony could not tolerate annoyance by " domestic enemies," when a hostile army was daily expected, it was resolved to appoint a special committee, distinct from the committee of safety, to summon or arrest and bring before it obnoxious loyalists for trial. All persons found guilty of aiding the enemy, persuading persons from uniting against parliament, preventing the circulation of paper money, or hindering united action against the British ministry were to be imprisoned, put under bond for good behavior, or removed from their localities on parole. The innocent were to be given certificates and discharged. The continental troops stationed in the province, and not the local militia, were to be used by the committee. County committees were urged to discover and to seize loyalists and to report to Congress. Town and district committees were authorized also to arrest the " dangerous and disaffected," to give them a preliminary hearing and to send them to the county committees. If the accused should decline to give security for such appearance, they should be kept in

---

[1] *Min. of Prov. Cong.,* v, 737–747, 835; *Am. Archs.,* 4th ser., vi, 1400.
[2] *Ibid.,* vi, 1152–1183.   [3] *Ibid.*

safe custody till the next meeting of the general committee. Fifty-five crown officers, specified by name, and all others of like character were to be called before the committee. If they ignored the summons, they were to be arrested by a warrant executed by any militia officer in the colony. The " friends to the American cause " were to be discharged and certificated. The loyalists of influence were to be removed to a neighboring colony and put on a parole of honor. Those refusing to give a parole were to be imprisoned. The less dangerous were to be bound over to keep the peace, or confined, as seemed necessary. This provincial committee and the county committees were instructed to keep a complete record of all their proceedings and report the same to the Provincial Congress. The committee had power to send for witnesses and papers, while its members and those of the county committees were put under oath to perform their duties impartially.[1]

On June 15 the committee of nine met in New York city, and elected a president, secretary and assistant secretary, messenger and doorkeeper.[2] A form of " summons " to be issued to loyalists was adopted.[3] This was served on twenty royal officers of " equivocal character." [4] A special warrant was adopted for arresting those of " equivocal character" who had disobeyed the summons, and also those "supposed to be inimical and dangerous." [5] With these weapons the committee began its work. Washington was ordered to turn loyalists over to it.[6] Suspects were occa-

---

[1] *Am. Archs.*, 4th ser., vi, 1365–1370.

[2] *Proceedings*, etc., June 15, 1776; *Am. Archs.*, 4th ser., vi, 1152, 1400, 1403; *Cal. of N. Y. Hist. MSS.*, i, 340.

[3] *Proceedings*, etc., June 15, 1776; *Am. Archs.*, 4th ser., vi, 1153.

[4] *Proceedings*, etc., June 19, 1776.

[5] *Ibid.*, etc., June 19, 1776, and June 21, 1776; *Am. Archs.*, 4th ser., vi, 1153.

[6] *Ibid.*, 4th ser., vi, 1158.

sionally examined by a sub-committee,[1] but notorious loyalists were tried by the committee in full session.

The first prominent person examined was Whitehead
Hicks. He said he held crown offices and had sworn allegiance to the king, and hence would not take up arms
against him. He was not willing to be taxed by parliament,
yet he had refused to sign the association. He believed arms
should be used only as a last resort, and he was not prepared
to say that all other measures had been exhausted. The
committee decided that he was not a friend to the American
cause and put him on parole.[2] Samuel Martin denied the
right of internal taxation by Great Britain and was released
on parole. Samuel Whitten signed the association and was
set free.[3] William Axtell did not believe parliament had a
right "to bind the colonies in all cases," nor did he approve
of the program of opposition. He wished to remain neutral for the sake of his property, objected to the parole and
was then turned over to the Provincial Congress.[4] Captain
Archibald Hamilton boasted "that he loved America, that
he had fought, bled and been in irons for her, that he wished
her free and happy," and that he would not "draw his sword
against her." Neither would he unsheath it against his
brothers on the king's side. He was dismissed on his parole
of honor. John Willett denied the right of parliament to
levy internal taxes in America, but would not take up arms
against the king. His other answers were so equivocal that
he was released under a bond of £2,000.[5]

These are fair examples of the ideas and convictions of
the rather extreme type of loyalists, and of the examinations
held by this first provincial inquisitorial committee. Other
"equivocal characters" and "inimical persons" were exam-

[1] *Am. Archs.*, 4th series, vi, 1154–1157, 1161 *et seq.*

[2] *Ibid.*, 4th ser., vi, 1159.   [3] *Ibid.*, 1160.   [4] *Ibid.*, 1180–1181.

[5] *Proceedings*, etc., June 24, 1776.

ined prior to July 7, 1776. The number of these and the results of their examination cannot be definitely ascertained from the meagre records.[1]   The Ulster county jail was made a provincial prison where loyalists were confined at their own expense.[2]   Goshen township, Orange county, was chosen as the place of detention for loyalists on parole.[3]   On June 28, a committee of three was named to take charge of prisoners, continental and provincial, and instructed to treat them " with justice and humanity."[4]

The Constitutional Convention of the state of New York held at White Plains reorganized the " standing committee" July 9, and reduced its membership to six.   With it was com bined a committee of three, which had been appointed, June 17, to confer with Washington about dangerous conspirators, and with power to arrest loyalists and to call on the militia or continental troops for aid, if needed.[5]   The powers of the joint committee were enlarged,[6] and it was now to dispose of all loyalist prisoners, to remove them to places of safety and to appoint a commissary to care for them.   It relieved Washington of the jurisdiction over them, given to him on June 30 by Congress.   In general it was instructed to do what was most " advancive " for the public good.   But the committee was revived only to disappear, for soon all trace of it is lost in the turmoil following July 4, 1776.[7]

[1] *Proceedings*, etc., June 27, 1776;   *Am. Archs.*, 4th ser., vi, 1181.

[2] *Ibid.*. iv, 437.   At one time there were 57 loyalists in jail there from New York, 4 from Kings, 38 from Queens, 13 from Westchester, and 6 from Richmond county.   *Cal. of N. Y. Hist. MSS.*, i, 340–341.

[3] *Am. Archs.*, 4th ser., v, 1496–1497.   [4] *Ibid.*, vi, 1437, 1442.

[5] *Ibid.*, 1412, 1419, 1435;   5th ser. I, 1391.   [6] *Ibid.*, 1391–1392.

[7] *Proceedings*, etc., July 12, 1776.   This seems to be the last session of the committee.   The records end here.   *Am. Archs.*, 5th ser., i, 1415, 1417, show that 17 loyalists were reported to the Convention July 18, 1776, for treason, counterfeitng, s upplying the British, being " notoriously disaffected," and being " too good a pilot to be trusted at large."   Of them 13 were sent to Connecticut, 2 to Albany, and 2 were released.   *Ibid.*, 1419, 1441, 1445.

The firm but comparatively moderate treatment of loyalists by the revolutionary government of New York was very
exasperating to patriots, civil and military, within and without the province.   John Hancock urged New York to attaint
all traitors, as well as counterfeiters.[1]   Washington complained to the Continental Congress of her inactivity, and
readily accepted General Charles Lee's scheme of dealing
with the " dangerous banditti of tories."[2]   John Adams told
Washington that loyalists were identical with British troops,
and hence that he had jurisdiction over them in New York.[3]
But the Provincial Congress peremptorily forbade the execution of the military program, and was supported by the
Continental Congress.[4]   It regarded the army and all general and local committees as instruments to carry out its wil .

The revolutionary authorities sought to bring their deal-
ings with the loyalists into harmony with the law and regulations which were laid down by the Provincial and Continental Congress.   When the Albany county committee sent
six loyalists out of the colony, the Provincial Congress demanded an explanation.[5]   When General Charles Lee imprisoned Samuel Gale in Connecticut, the same body denounced the act as arbitrary.[6]   When a mob arrested Charles
Oliver Bruff on suspicion of being a loyalist, the New York
city jailer refused to receive him, and applied to General
Washington for instructions.[7]   Although the Provincial
Congress discountenanced mobs and declared that riots
were a violation of the laws of the land, and urged that all
disputes be sent to it for adjudication,[8] still the mob broke
out again and again against particularly obnoxious loyalists.

[1] *Min. of Prov. Cong.*, v, 899, June 25, 1776.
[2] *Am. Archs.*, 4th ser., iv, 582–583, 595, 604, 605, 623, 624; v, 57, 74–75, vi, 790.
[3] *Ibid.*, iv, 604; v, 342–343, 347–348.   [4] *Ibid.*, v, 1391–1393.
[5] *Ibid.*, vi, 1432; *cf. ibid.*, 1716.   [6] *Ibid.*, v, 341.   [7] *Ibid.*, vi, 430.
[8] *Holt's N. Y. Journal*, no. 1692, June 8, 1775.

In New York city, however, there was a social element, ignorant, excitable and combustible, which furnished excellent material for mobs. The leaders of both parties had used this weapon, but by 1775 it was wholly devoted to revolution. The revolutionists, now holding the upper hand, had no difficulty in using it, for it could be easily aroused by talks about natural rights, taxation, slavery and the cruel acts of parliament. Before the appearance of the British army, in the summer of 1776, the mob was likely to take vengeance on every objectionable tory of prominence, and many a one felt its heavy hand. The sentiment for liberty was strong, but it was crude and not self-consistent. In practice it was exclusive, because it denied to others what it claimed for itself. Those who cried loudest for it denied it to their neighbors. A loyalist, viewing the violence of a revolutionary mob in the metropolis, exclaimed: "These are the people who are contending for liberty; they engross the whole of it to themselves and allow not a tittle to their opponents." Unlimited freedom was made an equivalent of political liberty. A whig asked his loyalist neighbor whether he might cut down a valuable tree on his land, and received this reply: "Why do you ask? You are for liberty; why do you not go and take it?" The wife of a soldier was ordered by her landlord to leave her house for not paying her rent, hence she wrote to her husband to go to his commanding officers to "see wether D. has any right to turn me out of door, since you have listed to go and fight for liberty. Why should not I have liberty whilst you strive for liberty?"[1] The ladies of Ulster and Dutchess counties surrounded the committee chamber and declared that they would have the liberty to drink tea, or else their husbands and sons should fight no more for liberty.[2]

The "excess of the spirit of liberty" was made a painful

[1] *Jour. of Prov. Cong.*, ii, 342.   [2] *Ibid.*, i, 590.

object lesson to the loyalists in the destruction of tory print-
ing presses, types, manuscripts and books;[1] the burning of
individuals in effigy,[2] tarring and feathering,[3] rail-riding
through the streets and other personal outrages;[4] breaking
windows, stealing live stock and personal effects[5] and de-
stroying property.[6] "Disaffection" simply meant a refusal
to accept as true the opinions of the party in power and to
support its policy, and the slightest suspicion of this was
quite sufficient to cause arrest, and imprisonment or banishment at the victim's expense. In case it was necessary, his
property was confiscated and sold to pay expenses.[7]

The action of the "republican mob," led by Colonel
Lasher, John Smith, Joshua Hett Smith, Peter Van Zandt and
Abraham Lott, toward loyalists in New York city will illustrate the customary procedure of that unruly force. The
whole city was searched for "tories," and several were
dragged "from their lurking holes, where they had taken
refuge to avoid the undeserved vengeance of an ungovern-
able rabble." These "unhappy victims" were put "upon
sharp rails with one leg on each side; each rail was carried
upon the shoulders of two tall men, with a man on each side

---

[1] James Rivington and Samuel Loudon.

[2] This was a very common practice. *Constitutional Gazette*, March 23, 1776.

[3] Cases of Judge James Smith and Coen Smith, given in Upcott, iv, 327. Quoted in Moore, *Diary of Am. Rev.*, i, 138. *Am. Arch.*, 4th ser., iii, 823; iv, 203.

[4] Numerous instances are recorded. *Memoirs of L. I. Hist. Soc.*, iii, 92.

[5] All over the colony, especially on Long Island, Staten Island, Westchester and Tryon counties, such cases were reported.

[6] *Rivington's Gazette*, Jan. 12, 1775; *Ibid.*, March 6, 1775; *Ibid.*, March 9, 1775; *Holt's N. Y.*, *Journal*, March 23, 1775; *Pennsylvania Evening Post*, Jan. 25 and Feb. 3, 1776.

[7] This was almost the "soupçonné d' être suspect" of the French Revolution. *Cf. Holt's N. Y. Journal*, Feb. 16, 1775, for an account of the enforcement of the association in New York. Yet the king was prayed for publicly down to July 4, 1776.

to keep the poor wretch straight and fixed in his seat."
"Numbers" were thus paraded through the streets, and at
every corner loudly denounced as notorious "tories." The
procession passed the buildings occupied by the Provincial
Convention and the committee of public safety, then in session,
and before the very door of General Washington, who so far
approved of "this inhuman, barbarous proceeding that he
gave a very severe reprimand to General Putnam, who acci-
dentally meeting one of these processions on the street, and
shocked by its barbarity, attempted to put a stop to it,
Washington declaring that to discourage such proceedings
was to injure the cause of liberty in which they were engaged, and that nobody would attempt it but an enemy to
his country." [1]   Generals Mifflin and Putnam appealed to
the Provincial Congress to stop the cruelty.[2]   But that body
did not dare to condemn outright the course of the "warm
friends of liberty," and hence disapproved of the transaction
in a mild resolution, to the effect "that this Congress by no
means approve of the riots that have happened this day;
they flatter themselves, however, that they have proceeded
from a real regard to liberty and a detestation of those persons, who, by their language and conduct, have discovered
themselves to be inimical to the cause of America.   To urge
the warm friends of liberty to decency and good order, this
Congress assures the public, that effectual measures shall be
taken to secure the enemies of American liberty in this colony; and do require the good people of this city and colony
to desist from all riots and leave the offenders against so

---

[1] Jones, *Hist. of N. Y.*, i, 101–103.   His description is supported by Pastor
Schaukirk's Diary, quoted in *Mem. Hist. of N. Y. City*, ii, 495; by a MS. letter in
the N. Y. Mercantile Lib., quoted in Lamb, *Hist. of N. Y. City*, ii, 77–78; by a
letter from Surgeon Solomon Drowne, published in the *Revolutionary Documents*
of the N. Y. Mercantile Lib. Ass'n; and by a letter from Staten Island in *N. Y.
Hist. Soc. Colls.*, iv, 288.

[2] *Am. Archs.*, 4th ser., vi, 1397–1398.

good a cause to be dealt with by the constitutional representatives of the colony." [1]   But loyalists were able to see
little difference, in essence, between the disorderly mob and
the orderly Congress or committee.   Both were revolutionary bodies which deprived them of their rights and liberties.

The mob afforded concrete proof of what loyalists justly
feared in the revolutionary program.   The 76th query of
" The American Querist" was: " Whether the Colonies, in
a great measure, have not, for the past ten years, been under
an iniquitous and tyrannical government, namely, the government of unprincipled mobs." [2]   In December, 1776, the
Provincial Congress ordered the committee of public safety
to secure all the pitch and tar " necessary for the public use
and public safety." [3]   To this act the loyalists pointed as
evidence of the alliance between pretended legal bodies and
the lawless mobs.

The heated times produced the most violent abuse and vi-
tuperation.   Neither party could see honesty or honor in the
other.   The whigs charged the loyalists with looking upon
the "rights of mankind" as altogether visionary, patriotism
as hypocrisy and liberty as a shadow, because too corrupt,
mentally, to reach the sublime in morals and devoid of soul-
expansion. [4]   Their behavior was the " severest satire upon
the species "—a compound of inconsistency, falsehood, cow-
ardice and selfishness.   In 1765 they were patriots, clamor-
ers for liberty and property, the life and soul of mobs.   In

[1] *Jour. of Prov. Cong.*, i, 491.

[2] Cooper, *American Querist*, etc., 24-25.   *Cf.* " Speech of I—c W—s, Esq.,"
in N. Y. Assembly.   *Rivington's Gazette*, no. 103, April 6, 1776.   *Cf. Short Advice to the Counties of New York*, 11.   *Cf.* James Stewart, *Total Refutation of
Dr. Price*, 3-4.   *Cf.* Hamilton, *Works*, i, 149.

[3] *Jour. of Prov. Cong.*, i, 232.

[4] *Am. Archs.*, 4th ser., iii, 1414-1417; *cf. ibid.*, ii, 508-509.

1774 they called the Continental Congress and denied the right of parliament to tax them. But in 1775 and 1776 they joined the enemy, condemned the very principles they once advocated, treated congresses with contempt and even denounced the assembly for acting too radically. This "set of wretches," "shameless apostates," "a puny tribe of voluntary slaves," "most obnoxious animals," should be hunted out and destroyed for self-preservation.[1]

The loyalists returned these compliments so far as they dared. They still remained divided into two classes—the extremists, or "non-associators," who believed rebellion was wicked and hopeless;[2] and the moderates, who wished to be neutral. The radicals thought the colonies ought to have a greater share in local and imperial affairs, but advocated obedience to existing authorities until the constitution could be changed legally and peaceably. The other faction was willing, under public pressure, to sign the association, but yet were at heart loyal to the king. By sympathy or silence they helped on the revolution in its first stages. "We at present are all whigs," wrote a loyalist, in June, 1775, "until the arrival of the king's troops."[3] The ultra-loyalists hated the usurped government and looked with contempt upon the weakness and timidity of the legal powers, whose temporizing inactivity had given the revolutionists the advantage, and therefore turned their eyes to the British army and navy for relief and protection. Orderly despotism was preferred to the tyranny of a fickle and bloodthirsty mob. They de-

---

[1] *Am. Archs.*, 4th ser., ii, 508–509: iii, 1552–1554, 1735–1738; vi, 787–788; 5th ser., iii, 1292. *Cf. Gaine's N. Y. Gazette*, nos. 1678, 1682, 1698, " Whigs and Tories;" *ibid.*, no., 1680, "The Tory Creed;" *Holt's N. Y. Journal*, no. 1721, "Conduct of Loyalists;" *Rivington's N. Y. Gazetteer*," no. 99, " Whig and Tory."

[2] *Am. Archs.*, 4th ser., ii, 149–150. Loyalist sermon with doctrines of passive obedience and non-resistance.

[3] *Am. Archs.*, 4th ser., ii, 238–242, 1087; iii, 884, 1552–1554. *Min. of Prov. Cong.*, iii, 30–31.

nounced the policy of the whigs in supporting a scheme of
independence as the "basest hypocrisy." They wished
themselves in free England instead of tyrannous America.[1]
"Are the friends of Great Britain and their property," cried
one, "to be left exposed . . . to the dictates of an inhuman rabble?"[2]

Before loyalist pamphleteers like Cooper, Wilkins, Seabury
and Inglis fled or were exiled, tory articles and tracts were
numerous. After that there was comparative silence until
the Englisn took southern New York. An answer to "Common Sense" appeared, but a whig mob destroyed both the
manuscript and impression.[3] All printers were warned not
to publish loyalist tracts on pain of "death and destruction,
ruin and perdition." "From this time," says Judge Jones,
"no publication, in pamphlet or book form, ever appeared
in New York, unless from England, in favor of the cause of
Britain or in opposition to the tyranny of Congress."[4] But
this is not wholly true, for although the loyalist literature
from now on was of an inferior character, still more or less
continued to issue from the tory presses in New York city
until the war closed.

[1] *Am. Archs.*, 4th ser., ii, 479; *N. Y. Hist. Soc. Colls.* (1883), 62; *cf. ibid.*,
(1882), 205.

[2] *Am. Archs.*, 4th ser., iii, 3, 1745–1752.

[3] Jones, *Hist. of N. Y.*, i, 63, 64; *Jour. of Prov. Cong.*, i, 377, 405, 406, 750;
Am. Archs., 4th ser., v, 187, 440, 514, 1389.

[4] Jones, *Hist. of N. Y.*, i, 65.

CHAPTER IV

COUNTY INQUISITORIAL ORGANIZATIONS

COUNTY committees and district committees had been called into existence to enforce the non-importation agreements and to carry out the general association, and were soon principal organs of local government. By 1776 every county, except possibly Kings, had its committee.[1] Tryon county led by organizing its committee in August, 1774,[2] and others followed. There was little uniformity in method of election, number and activity. In Albany county eighteen districts elected 154 members of the county committee,[3] while Cumberland county had only five members.[4] Westchester county had ninety members, elected at a mass meeting.[5] New York's committee of one hundred was elected by the voters.[6] In the other counties the committees were smaller, but varied greatly in numbers.

The sub-committees also varied in numbers and in the

---

[1] It seems that Queens county was the last to organize. *Cal. of N. Y. Hist. MSS.*, i, 334; MS. *Revolutionary Papers*, iv, 121, 195; *Gaine's N. Y. Gazette*, nos. 1264, 1284. There is no record of the formation of a committee in Kings county. *Cf. Memoirs of L. I. Hist. Soc.*, ii, 12, for an account of the revolutionary records of Kings county. They were carried away by the loyalists. Johnson, *Campaign of 1776 around New York and Brooklyn*, published as vol. iii of *Memoirs of L. I. Hist. Soc.*, speaks on page 60 of the "committee of Kings county;" *cf. Am. Archs.*, 4th ser., v, 219.

[2] Campbell, *Annals of Tryon Co.*, 31–33.

[3] *Proceedings of Alb. Co. Com.*, i, 426.

[4] *Am. Archs.*, 4th ser., ii, 1064–1066.

[5] *Rivington's N. Y. Gazetteer*, no. 108, May 11, 1775.

[6] *Am. Archs.*, 4th ser., ii, 427, 459; Jones, *Hist. of N. Y.*, i, 489.

manner of appointment. In Albany county they were appointed by the county committee[1] and numbered at least nineteen.[2] New York had no sub-committees. In Queens county they were organized by minorities.[3] Town committees were formed very early in Suffolk county.[4] The same was true of Tryon county.[5] In Ulster county every precinct had its local board, as was true also in Westchester county.[6]

These committees in southern New York disappeared with the British occupation, but continued in northern New York and along the Hudson until superseded by the state system of local government. In matters of organization there was considerable uniformity. Each body formed its own rules[7] and had a chairman, secretary, and other necessary officers; but there was great divergence in tenure of office. As was natural, the most ardent whigs were members of the boards, but during the period from 1774 to 1776 not a few of the members were pronounced loyalists.[8]

There was a definite relationship among all the bodies growing out of the revolution. The Continental Congress stood at the head; then came the Provincial Congress or Convention, then the general committee on tories, then the county committees, and at the base, the district committees.

---

[1] *Proceedings of Alb. Co. Com.*, 21–22, 24.

[2] *Ibid.*, 32–33.

[3] Onderdonk, *Queens County Incidents*, 29–30: *Cal. of N. Y. Hist. MSS.*, i, 304; *Am. Archs.*, 4, iii, 887, 889; *Min. of Prov. Cong.*, iii, 39, 41; iv, 50.

[4] *Am. Archs.*, 4th ser., ii, 117.

[5] Campbell, *Annals of Tryon Co.*, 31–33.

[6] Dawson, *Westchester Co.*, 113.

[7] In Oct., 1775, 22 absent members were fined 20 shillings each by the Tryon county committee. MS. *Sir William Johnson Papers*, xxvi, no. 110.

[8] *Am. Archs.*, 4th ser., vi, 1073, for Albany county; *ibid.*, ii, 644, iii, 457–459, 696, 825, for Dutchess county; MS. *Revolutionery Papers*, iv, 189; *Proceedings of Alb. Co. Com.*, i, 145, 146, 173, 183–187, 198, 364, 365; Van Schaack, *Life of Peter Van Schaack*, 57–63; *cf. Public Papers of George Clinton*, i, 246.

The district committees watched the loyalists, made reports to the county committees, arrested dangerous tories and carried out instructions from the superior boards.[1] Trial and punishment were usually left to the higher powers, although in some instances the local authorities tried and sentenced loyalists.[2] Each body in the inquisitorial organization had a wide field for independent action, but there was always a marked respect for instructions from above.[3]

Before August 3, 1775, when a case demanding action was presented, the county committees followed their own judgment and initiative, in accordance with the exigencies of the case. It was easy for these revolutionary bodies, varying in number and activity in each county, to become inquisitorial boards for the seizure, trial and punishment of loyalists. In fact, their work in connection with the association was of this character in a mild form—a fact which made the transition naturally easier. With no laws and few precedents to guide them, these committees at first acted rather hesitatingly. Most cases of importance were referred to the Provincial Congress or Convention.[4] At first there was a general conviction that all obnoxious loyalists should be tried, or at least sentenced, by the supreme body as a final court.[5] As time passed, the county committees became more accustomed to their duties, cases multiplied, precedents grew up and regulations were adopted until these boards acted finally on all cases.[6]

Though elected by the people, all the county committees,

[1] *Am. Archs.*, 4th ser., iv, 210, 211–212.

[2] *Ibid.*, iii, 134–135; v, 518, 548, 821, 1428; vi, 446; *Proceedings of Alb. Co. Com.*, i, 384; *Min. Prov. Cong.*, ii, 54–57, 103–104; iii, 50; Dawson, *Westchester Co.*, 113.

[3] *Proceedings of Alb. Co. Com.*, i, 272, 416.

[4] *Am. Archs.*, 4th ser., ii, 12, 13, 35, 298, 448, 548, 1730–1731; *Proceedings of Alb. Co. Com.*, i, 361, 364, 372, 444, 449.

[5] *Am. Archs.*, 4th ser., vi, 1421–1422.   [6] *Ibid.*, v, 250.

after the system became established, were dependent upon the provincial bodies.[1]   From them instructions were received, and to them appeals were constantly made for advice and help.[2]   The decisions of county boards were often reversed by them.[3]   Frequent reports were made by the lower to the higher authorities.   Greater harmony and uniformity gradually prevailed in the inquisitorial machine, since one common object was sought by all.   All expenses were paid from the state treasury.[4]   County committees could call out the militia, and if the need was urgent, even use the regulars, or ask a neighboring colony for aid.[5]   The Provincial Congress took great care to guard its own powers, as well as those of the local committees, against rival civil and military authorities.[6]   When the Westchester committee sent a "dangerous man" to the committee of safety for final action, that body returned him saying that the "county committees are altogether competent" for such cases.[7]

In making arrests[8] there was no regular procedure by warrants.   Any body chosen by the people, from the Provincial Congress to a precinct committee, was authorized to seize

---

[1] *Am. Archs.,* 4th ser., 1473–1474; vi, 1442–1443.

[2] *Ibid.,* iii, 1248, iv, 186, vi, 1349, 1385–1386, 1415, 1416; *Cal. of N. Y. Hist. MSS.,* i, 88–89; Dawson, *Westchester Co.,* 174, 175, 176, 177.

[3] *Am. Archs.,* 4th ser., v, 1484–1485; 5th ser., i, 1441, 1447, 1472, 1473.

[4] *Ibid.,* 4th ser., v, 1458–1459.

[5] *Min. of Prov. Cong.,* iv, 46; *Am. Archs.,* 4th ser., iv, 402–403, vi, 1442–1443.

[6] *Ibid.,* iv, 185–186, 401, 1033–1034, 1398, for Sears' raid; *ibid.,* 1498; v, 283, 955, for Richmond county; *ibid.,* v, 192–193, 341, 342, 348, 390, 991, for case of Samuel Gale.

[7] *Ibid.,* iii, 916; *cf. Min. of Prov. Cong.,* ii, 54–57, 103–104.

[8] *Am. Archs.,* 4th ser., ii, 917, iii, 134–135, Ulster co.; *ibid.,* iii, 50, 87, 96, Tryon co.; *ibid.,* iii, 331, 333, 457–459, 466, 569, 879, 900, 1761, iv, 187, Dutchess co.; *ibid.,* iii, 1263, iv, 393, New York co.; *ibid.,* iii, 827; *Min. of Prov. Cong.,* iii, 37, Queens co.; *Am. Archs.,* 4th ser., iii, 826, 838, 902, 916, 1707; *Min. of Prov. Cong.,* iii, 319, Westchester co., etc., etc.

obnoxious loyalists and punish them "at the discretion of the committee," according to the penalties prescribed in the act of August 3, 1775. Under the intense hatred and bigotry of the times, loyalists were not infrequently punished on insufficient and questionable testimony,[1] but on the whole, strenuous efforts were made by all bodies to give the accused fair trials.[2] In fact few loyalists objected to the actual trial; it was the assertion of the right to try them which they denounced.

In Albany county loyalists were permitted to demand that their accusers should face them, and they were allowed to produce witnesses to prove their innocence;[3] but counsel was denied them.[4] While imprisoned, their families might visit them.[5] Prior to July 4, 1776, the same moderation characterized the treatment of loyalists in all the counties. In some cases, as has been shown, loyalists were treated in an extremely arbitrary and even inhuman manner, but as a rule, and taking the state as a whole, mobs, riots and the violation of law were denounced by whigs nearly as much as by loyalists.[6] In practice, however, neither whigs nor loyalists lived up to their professions. Loyalists arrested outside the counties where they resided, were returned for trial,[7] or sent

---

[1] *Cf. Am. Archs.*, 4th ser., iv, 693; *Min. of Com. of One Hundred*, Jan. 16, 1776.

[2] *Am. Archs.*, 4th ser., iii, 894, v, 192–193, 293, 342, 348, 390, 991; *cf. ibid.*, iv, 115, 145, 245, 270 and 276 for treatment of loyalists in Virginia and Connecticut; *cf. Proceedings of Alb. Co. Com.*, i, 30, 133–134, 324.

[3] *Ibid.*, 390.

[4] *Ibid.*, 455. The Provincial Congress made this a provincial law in 1776. *Jour. of Prov. Cong.* (1776), 7–9.

[5] *Proceedings of Alb. Co. Com.*, i, 432, 434.

[6] *Gaine's N. Y. Gazette*, March 27, 1775; *Essex Gazette*, March 21, 1775; Holt's *N. Y. Journal*, March 23, 1775; Moore, *Diary of Am. Rev.*, i, 52; *Am. Archs.*, 4th ser., ii, 1064–1066; *Proceedings of Alb. Co. Com.*, i, 459.

[7] *Ibid.*, 417.

to the Provincial Congress.[1] After being arrested many were
liberated on bail to await trial.[2]

In the early stages of the struggle committees were often
forced to act as local legislatures. In Albany county the
committee resolved, May 18, 1775, that all who refused to
give up arms for the American cause, or sold arms or supplies to "inimical persons," should "be held up to the public
as an enemy to their country."[3] Those refusing public service were put in the same list later.[4] March 6, 1776, the
committee declared every "non-associator" to be an "enemy
to his country,"[5] and a little later no person was allowed to
settle in the county without a certificate that he was a whig
and an associator.[6] No person could leave the county
without the consent of the committee or of Congress.[7] Any
person denying the committee's authority was liable to punishment for the "crime."[8] Like measures were taken in
Dutchess county and a stringent oath was proposed for the
loyalists.[9] It seems that the committee of the county of
New York took the same course.[10] The Westchester county
board was active along similar lines and forced every suspect
to carry a certificate.[11] In all the counties, except Kings,
Queens and Richmond, a like course was followed. Pains
were taken, usually, to have these measures square with the
recommendations of the supreme authority.

Loyalists were arrested for arming to support the British,
or aiding the enemy in any way; for harboring or associating
with tories; recruiting soldiers; refusing to muster; cor-

[1] *Am. Archs.*, 4th ser., vi, 794.

[2] *Proceedings of Alb. Co. Com.*, i, 434.

[3] *Ibid.*, i, 37.   [4] *Ibid.*, 85.

[5] *Ibid.*, 383.   [6] *Ibid.*, 39, 403, 470.   [7] *Ibid.*, 413.   [8] *Ibid.*, i, 443.

[9] *Am. Archs.*, 4th. ser., iii, 457.

[10] *Ibid.*, v, 1491, 1497; vi, 725.

[11] *Ibid.*, iii, 826; Dawson, *Westchester Co.*, 149–151.

responding with loyalists, or with the British; refusing to
sign the association, or violating its provisions; denouncing
or refusing to obey congresses and committees; writing or
speaking against the American cause; rejecting continental
money; refusing to give up arms; drinking the king's
health; inciting or taking part in " tory plots " and riots;
being royal officers; and even for endeavoring to remain
neutral.   Mere suspicion was sufficient to cause seizure, and
this meant at least imprisonment.   On this wide definition
of loyalism, hundreds were arrested, and soon all the jails
were overflowing.   The jails of New York city were filled
very early.   By December, 1775, the Albany committee
had to provide additional quarters and an extra jailor.[1]   By
June, 1776, so numerous were the prisoners there, that the
watch had to be doubled.[2]   Standing guards were ordered
to be kept in Dutchess and Westchester counties.[3]   Albany
and New York city became the great centers where loyalists
were brought together for final disposition.

There was no uniform treatment of loyalists.   Some were
imprisoned,[4] others were sent to the Provincial Congress or
committee of safety for punishment,[5] large numbers were
simply disarmed,[6] many were released on parole or bond,[7] a

---

[1] *Proceedings of Alb. Co. Com.*, i, 360, 364, 426.   [2] *Ibid.*, 433.

[3] *Am. Arch.*, 4th ser., vi, 1415, 1416, 1418.

[4] *Ibid.*, iii, 907, 910, 1016, 1267, 1300, 1303, 1314, 1761, iv, 1030, 1071, 1118,
v, 548, 558, 1428; MS. *Revolutionary Papers*, vi, 195, 203, 207; Dawson,
Westchester Co., 120, 146; *Min. of Prov. Cong.*, iii, 331–333, iv, 48, v, 7–9;
Proceedings of Alb. Co. Com., i, 255, 290, 371, 407, 428, 429, 433, etc.

[5] *Ibid.*, i, 361, 364, 372, 444, 449; *Min. of Prov. Cong.*, iii, 131, 137, 153, iv,
56–57; *Am. Archs.*, 4th ser., iii, 838, iv, 1068, v, 273, 343, 821, vi, 446, 1055,
1383; 5th ser., i, 1467.

[6] *Ibid.*, 4th ser., v, 1491, 1497; Jones, *Hist. of N. Y.*, i., 68; *Proceedings of
Alb. Co. Com.*, i, 365, 369, 394, 396, 416, 418, 421, 459.

[7] *Ibid.*, 369, 371, 384, 401, 406, 416, 421, 429, 430, 433, 435, 439, 441, 443, 449,
460, 467; *Min. of Prov. Cong.*, ii, 54–57, 103–104; *Am. Archs.*, 4th ser., iv, 1118,
1181, 1663, v, 253, 265, 269, 273, 274.

few were reprimanded and let go,[1] others were handed over to the Continental Congress at Philadelphia,[2] numbers were exiled to and imprisoned in Connecticut,[3] Massachusetts,[4] New Jersey[5] and New Hampshire;[6] many were forced to recant or to sign the association, or to take a harsh oath,[7] others were removed to some adjoining county,[8] nearly all were forced to carry certificates, for which they paid a fixed sum;[9] hundreds were published in the newspapers as public enemies and "delinquents,"[10] several were ostracized,[11] some were compelled to give hostages,[12] still others were put to hard labor,[13] and "a few were murdered."[14]   When imprisoned or banished, loyalists had to pay their own expenses. If they were too poor for this, then the province paid the costs.[15]

Neither the Continental nor the Provincial Congress hesi-

[1] *Am. Archs.*, 4th ser., iii, 905, 906; *Proceedings of Alb. Co. Com.*, i, 367, 373, 382, 431.

[2] *Min. of Prov. Cong.*, iii, 923.

[3] *Conn. Jour.*, Nov. 29, 1775, no. 424; Jones, *Hist. of N. Y.*, i, 67, 109–110; *Am. Archs.*, 4th ser., v, 192, vi, 710, 1072; *Cal. of N. Y. Hist. MSS.*, i, 328–333; *Proceedings of Alb. Co. Com.*, i, 456.

[4] Moore, *Diary of Am. Rev.*, i, 52.

[5] *Am. Archs.*, 4th ser., iv, 1498.

[6] *N. H. State Papers*, viii, 379, 389, 393.

[7] *Am. Archs.*, 4th ser., iv, 156, 858–860; 5th ser., ii, 325; *Min. of Prov. Cong.*, iii, 329; MS. *Revolutionary Papers*, vi, 109, 195, 203, 207; Campbell, *Annals of Tryon Co.*, 34–36, 42.

[8] *Am. Archs.*, 4th ser., vi, 647; *Proceedings of Alb. Co. Com.*, i, 290, 454.

[9] *Gaine's N. Y. Gazette*, no. 1272, Feb. 26, 1776; *Jour. of Cont. Cong.* (1776) 7–9; *Am. Archs.*, 4th ser., iii, 826, v, 405.

[10] *Ibid.*, iv, 372–375, v, 518; *Min. of Prov. Cong.*, iv, 123.

[11] *Docs. rel. to N. Y. Col. Hist.* viii, 568, 581.

[12] *Am. Archs.*, 4th ser., vi, 643.

[13] *Ibid.*, v, 1231.

[14] Jones, *Hist. of N. Y.*, i, 109–110.

[15] *Am. Archs.*, 4th ser., iv, 427; MS. *Revolutionary Papers*, vi, 159.

tated to interfere in any county where there was no committee, or where the committee was too weak to cope with a
powerful combination of loyalists.[1] Revolutionary civil authority was always backed up by military force. Such intervention was necessary in Tryon, Dutchess, Westchester,
Kings, Queens and Richmond counties. In the first three
counties the committees and local militia were unable to
deal with the " inimical " effectually, while in the last three
these bodies had practically disbanded by the fall of 1775.

Loyalism in Tryon county had a unique history. The
powerful Johnson family swayed the Mohawk valley. Their
retainers, about 1,000 in number and mostly Scotch Highlanders, were nearly all loyalists. In addition, many others
throughout the county who were indebted to the Johnsons
for favors, chose the royal side.[2] Sir John Johnson was the
leader, ably assisted by Guy Johnson, Colonel Claus and
John Butler.[3] Sir John Johnson and Guy Johnson soon had
tilts with the county committee.[4] The Continental Congress
resolved, December 30, 1775, to send General Schuyler to
secure the arms and stores of the tories in this county, and
" to apprehend their chiefs."[5] With 3,000 men, including
900 Tryon county militia, General Schuyler started for
Johnstown.[6] Sir John agreed to surrender all his arms and
military stores ; to allow his Scotch retainers to give up their
arms, swear neutrality and furnish hostages ; and to try to

---

[1] *Am. Archs.*, 4th ser., iii, 569, 579, 630, iv, 393, v, 45, 466. The Continental Congress ordered the Skeenes of Cumberland county arrested and sent to
Connecticut on parole. *Ibid.*, ii, 1864, iv, 248.

[2] *Am. Archs.*, 4th ser., iv, 828–830; *cf.* Campbell, *Annals of Tryon Co.*, 37.

[3] *Ibid.*, 75.

[4] *Am. Archs.*, 4th ser., ii, 638, 661, 662, 671, 879, 911, iii, 1194, 1245, 1964, iv,
397, 667.

[5] *Ibid.*, iii, 1964; *Jour. of Cont. Cong.*, 310.

[6] Jones, *Hist. of N. Y.*, i, 71, 579.

induce all the loyalists in the county to do the same.   Sir
John was then released on parole.[1]

Hearing later that he was inciting an Indian massacre,[2]
General Schuyler summoned him before the Albany committee.[3] The rumor proved to be false, so he was released.[4]
But shortly after, the reports against Sir John increasing,
Schuyler decided to seize him.   Hence Colonel Dayton was
sent with a letter to the accused, freeing him from his parole,
and with orders to take him a close prisoner before General
Washington.[5] Suspecting this piece of treachery, the titled
loyalist and his Highlanders fled to Canada.[6] In retaliation
Johnson Hall was sacked and Lady Johnson taken as a hos-
tage to Albany,[7] then sent to Fishkill, from which place,
being refused a pass,[8] she escaped to the British.[9] Guy
Johnson, John and Walter Butler and Joseph Brant, with a
crowd of loyalists, had preceded Sir John in their flight to
Canada.[10] For some time Schuyler kept his eye on the remaining tories, and stationed Colonel Dayton on the Mohawk
" until further orders." [11]

Orange county was so seriously disaffected and the
county committee so inactive, that the Provincial Congress
authorized Colonel Hay to arrest the worst tories and send
them to New York city,[12] using the militia, if necessary, for

---

[1] *Am. Archs.*, 4th ser., iv, 827.

[2] *Ibid.*, v, 195, 772.   [3] *Ibid.*, 195, 196.

[4] *Ibid.*, 196; Jones, *Hist. of N. Y.*, i, 584.

[5] *Am. Archs.*, 4th ser., vi, 643.

[6] *Ibid.*, 644, 511, 538; *cf. Sir John Johnson's Orderly Book*, i, 3 note.

[7] *Am. Archs.*, 4th ser., vi, 643, 647, 913; Jones, *Hist. of N. Y.*, i, 76–77, 646.

[8] *Am. Archs.*, 4th ser., vi, 913, 930, 992; *Jour. of Prov. Cong.*, ii, 251, 256, 761.

[9] Jones, *Hist. of N. Y.*, xi, 77–81.

[10] Frothingham, *Montgomery County*, 78.

[11] *Am. Archs.*, 4th ser., vi, 493, 645, 647.

[11] *Ibid.*, 1442; *Gaine's N. Y. Gazette*, no. 1276, Aug. 12, 1776.

the purpose. Dutchess county was fairly overrun with loyalists. The committee was forced to ask the Provincial Congress to arrest the ringleaders.[1]   The militia was repeatedly
called out, and finally the chairman of the county board
begged the Provincial Congress to keep 150 paid troops constantly on guard to suppress the internal foes. This request
was granted.[2]

In Westchester county the loyalists formed a majority of
the population, and were so active and formidable that they
intimidated the local authorities.[3]   An appeal was therefore
made to Connecticut to help disarm the tories. The Provincial Congress also decided to raise an armed police force
of fifty men to keep the peace in the county.[4]   The raid of
Isaac Sears through this county, in November of 1775, was
conducted in a lawless way. The leading loyalists of East
and West Chester were disarmed, and "Parson Seabury,
Judge Fowler and Lord Underhill" were carried off to New
Haven.[5]   This deed was denounced by both whigs and
loyalists, and was repudiated by the Provincial Congress.[6]
General Charles Lee also made a raid on the loyalist farmers
of this region and carried away everything resembling arms.
This was done without the sanction of the committee or of
the Provincial Congress.[7]   Frightened by a "plot . . .
to carry off several of the members" and being "at present

---

[1] *Am. Archs.*, 4th ser., iii, 466.

[2] *Ibid.*, vi, 1415, 1416, 1418, 1425.

[3] Dawson, *Westchester Co.*, 83, note 4, 154–157, 163;   *Am. Archs.*, 4th ser., iii,
1763, iv, 590.

[4] *Jour. of Prov. Cong.*, June 20, 1776; Dawson, *Westchester Co.*, 173, 174.

[5] Jones, *Hist. of N. Y.*, i, 65, 562–566; *Docs. rel. to N. Y. Col. Hist.*, viii, 581;
Am. Archs., 4th ser., iii, 1707; *Conn. Jour.*, Nov. 29, 1775, no. 424; Dawson,
Westchester Co., 128.

[6] *Ibid.*, 132; *Holt's N. Y. Journal*, Dec. 7, 1775, no. 1718.

[7] *Am. Archs.*, 4th ser., v, 272, 273, 274, 304; *Jour. of Prov. Cong.*, Feb. 13,
1776; Dawson, *Westchester Co.*, 123.

too weak " to suppress it, the county committee asked for an armed guard.[1]

Queens county was the stronghold of loyalism in New York.[2] Its inhabitants were a standing menace to the American cause and an encouragement to the British. They caused the Continental Congress, the Provincial Congress and General Washington more anxiety and trouble than the loyalists of any other county. The county committee there did little more than to organize.[3] Therefore all serious cases were brought before the Provincial Congress.[4] The Huntington committee called on that body for aid to quell a tory uprising.[5] Because twenty-six obnoxious loyalists refused to appear before the Provincial Congress when summoned, December 12, 1775, the whole county was " entirely put out of the protection of this Congress " and all intercourse "interdicted."[6] A list of 734 "delinquents" was printed in hand bills and published in the newspapers.[7] The Continental Congress approved of these measures and suggested making them more severe.[8]

So dangerous did the loyalists soon become, however, that the supreme body ordered Connecticut troops from the east and New Jersey troops from the west to enter the county simultaneously, to disarm all who voted against sending deputies to the Provincial Congress, and to arrest and confine obstinate loyalists.[9] The twenty-six

---

[1] *Jour. of Prov. Cong.*, iii, 317–321, 327, 329.

[2] *Am. Archs.*, 4th ser., vi, 725, 1264.   [3] *Cal. of N. Y. Hist. MSS.*, i, 334.

[4] *Min. of Prov. Cong.*, iii, 37, 39, 41; *Am. Archs.*, 4th ser., iii, 887, 889; iv, 1181, 1201.

[5] *Ibid.*, 404; *Min. of Prov. Cong.*, iv, 50.

[6] *Ibid.*, 123.

[7] *Ibid.; Am. Archs.*, 4th ser., iv, 372–375, 435.

[8] *Jour. of Cont. Cong.* (1776), 7–9.

[9] Jones, *Hist. of N. Y.*, i, 68; *Am. Archs.*, 4th ser., iv, 860–861.

loyalist leaders who refused the summons of the Provincial Congress, were also ordered to be seized.[1]   In the end only Colonel Nathaniel Heard with about 900 New Jersey militia entered the county.[2]   In four weeks the whole county was disarmed.   Governor Tryon reported that six hundred had been treated thus in ten days.[3]   Four hundred and sixty-two loyalists were forced to sign an agreement to obey the revolutionary authorities in all instances [4] and nineteen of the leaders were carried to Philadelphia, confined several weeks, returned to New York, held a few weeks longer and then released on parole.[5]   Loyalists in some cases were maltreated and robbed,[6] but Colonel Heard "treated the inhabitants with civility and the utmost humanity." [7]   Some of the chief tories fled.[8]

Meanwhile, General Charles Lee, fresh from "tory hunting" in Rhode Island, proposed his "scheme" to Washington to suppress the loyalists on Long Island.[9]   This was: to disarm all of them, then to force them to deposit one-half the value of their estates with the Continental Congress as a pledge of good behavior.   Those refusing to take the "strongest oath . . . to act defensively and offensively in support of the common cause "—the "desperate fanatics" —were to be sent under guard into the interior.[10]   Washington ordered him to proceed and notified the New York com-

---

[1] *Am. Archs.*, 4th ser., iv, 764, 772.   [2] *Ibid.*, 1639, Jan. 10, 1776.

[3] *Ibid.*, 923; *Docs. rel. to N. Y. Col. Hist.*, viii, 663.

[4] *Am. Archs.*, 4th ser., iv, 858–860; *Cal. of N. Y. Hist. MSS.*, i, 215–218.

[5] *Am. Archs.*, 4th ser., iv, 1118–1119, 1181, 1663, v, 253, 265, 269, 273; *cf.* Jones, *Hist. of N. Y.*, i, 68–69; *Cal. of N. Y. Hist. MSS.*, i, 240, 262.

[6] *Am. Archs.*, 4th ser., iv, 923.   Jones overcolors the facts.

[7] *Ibid.*, 857, 858, 923.   [8] Jones, *Hist. of N. Y.*, i, 108–109.

[9] *N. Y. Hist. Soc. Colls., Lee Papers*, i, 235.

[10] *Am. Archs.*, 4th ser., iv, 806–807, 1095; *Min. of Prov. Cong.*, iv, 612; *N. Y. Hist. Soc. Colls., Lee Papers*, i, 249.

mittee of safety.[1] Lee raised 1,200 Connecticut volunteers
and started for New York, but the Continental Congress
ordered him to stop on the border, while a committee was
sent to investigate the situation.[2]

The committee reported, March 14, 1776, that the defense of southern New York was "totally fruitless" unless
the "professed enemies of American liberty" in Queens and
Richmond counties were rendered harmless. The bonds required were "too ridiculous to be mentioned," and the association forced upon them was null. Hence the committee
advised that, in addition to disarming them, their children
should be taken as hostages.[3] But without waiting for further instructions from the civic authorities, Washington, disappointed at the interference, ordered Lee to arrest all loyalists "notoriously known."[4] Lee at once sent Colonel Wood
to Long Island "to secure the whole body of professed
tories."[5] With him went Isaac Sears, empowered either to
force certain notorious loyalists to take a severe oath or to
carry them to Connecticut.[6] These instructions were carried
out with such severity as "to convert whigs to tories,"[7] and
to cause the Provincial Congress to demand an explanation.[8]

Though disarmed, paroled and banished, the loyalists in
this county were not suppressed, but, as months passed and
British forces were expected, they were reported to be

N. Y. Hist. Soc. Colls., *Lee Papers.* i, 236; *Min. of Prov. Cong.*, iv, 371; *Am. Archs.*, 4th ser., iv, 1095.

[2] *N. Y. Hist. Soc. Colls., Lee Papers*, i, 235; *Am. Archs.*, 4th ser., iv, 943.

[3] *Ibid.*, v, 213–215.

[4] *Ibid.*, iv, 895–896.

[5] *Min. of Prov. Cong.*, v, 3–5.

[6] *N. Y. Hist. Soc. Colls., Lee Papers*, i, 296.

[7] *Ibid.*, 359; Jones, *Hist. of N. Y.*, i, 573; *Am. Archs.*, 4th ser., v, 105, 371–372; *Min. of Prov. Cong.*, v, 59, 60.

[8] *Ibid.*, 66; *Am. Archs.*, 4th ser., v, 372.

" growing worse and worse." [1]   The Provincial Congress, in
June, 1776, urged Washington to disarm and secure them at
once.[2]   Even the Queens county committee was revived, and
resolved that five hundred soldiers be billeted on the loyalists and that all the dangerous ones be sent to the provincial
authorities.[3]   Consequently Washington sent Colonel Cornell to Queens county with 1,000 men.[4]   The loyalists, disarmed by Heard the winter before, " all fled." [5]   A general
hunt followed, some were wounded, " a few were murdered,"
and those who were captured were sent to New York under
guard, and then, without trial, sent to " different parts of
New England." [6]   The arrival of the Howes saved the
county from further punishment.

Richmond county ranked next to Queens in the prevalence
of loyalism.   Because it refused to send deputies to the Provincial Congress, that body declared the county guilty of
" open contempt," consequently published the " delinquents"
in the newspapers and " totally interdicted" the island.[7]
The election of two representatives from the county on January 19, 1776, delayed the execution of the interdict.[8]   A
month later the defiance and insolence of the loyalists forced
the Provincial Congress to ask New Jersey to quell them.
Colonel Heard with seven hundred men arrested the most
dangerous and carried them to New Jersey.[9]   The county
committee, composed of loyalist sympathizers, wholly inactive up to this time, sent three of their number to New
Jersey to demand the release of the captured loyalists, and

---

[1] *Am. Archs.*, 4th ser., v, 450, 1451, 1490, 1491, 1501, vi, 569–574, 1031, 1055,
1320–1321, 1343, 1344, 1347.

[2] *Ibid.*, vi, 533–534, 1427.   [3] *Ibid.*, 1055, 1383, 1394; 5th ser., i, 1466.

[4] Jones, *Hist. of N. Y.*, i, 108–109.   [5] *Ibid.*   [6] *Ibid.*, i, 109–110.

[7] *Am. Archs.*, 4th ser., iv, 435, 1034, v, 283; *Min. of Prov. Cong.*, i, 123.

[8] *Ibid.*, iv, 224, 225, 226, 308, 309, 464.

[9] *Am. Archs.*, 4th ser., iv, 655, 1163, 1498, v, 283.

appealed to the Provincial Congress.[1]   That body requested
the New Jersey authorities to return them for trial by the
local committee, and also asked that the latter body should
report on the cases.[2]   After a brief examination some of
these accused persons were released on the ground of insufficient evidence.[3]   In fact so manifestly lenient was the
local board in dealing with such domestic foes that a council
of war condemned their course as "improper and inef-
fectual."[4]   General Lee's plans for Staten Island were never
carried into execution.[5]   As in the case of Long Island, the
arrival of the British saved Staten Island from further whig
invasion.

It appears that the county committees, organized in every
county except Kings, were far from being uniform in origin,
numbers, method of procedure or activity.   Their power
originated in the right of revolution and in the recommendations of the revolutionary bodies above them.   These committees could determine which were the enemies and which
the friends of American liberty, and could banish the former.
This power was successfully exercised by the county committee, without the intervention of the superior body, in the
counties of Albany, New York, Cumberland, Suffolk and
Ulster.   Albany had most and Cumberland and Suffolk least
to do.   In Tryon, Dutchess and Westchester counties the
committees were very busy and well organized, but so pow
erful were the loyalists that aid was solicited from either the
Continental or Provincial Congress.   In Orange, Queens and
Richmond counties the committees were so feeble and the
"inimical" so strong that it was necessary for the superior
bodies to assume direct control.   To the loyalist all these

---

[1] *Am. Archs.*, 4th series, iv, 1498; v, 28;.

[2] *Ibid.*, v, 293, 309.   [3] *Ibid.*, 102–103.

[4] *Ibid.*, vi, 1436; MS. *Revolutionary Papers*, iv, 109, 111, 189.

[5] *Am. Archs.*, 4th ser., v, 133.

bodies were illegal, and their treatment of him and his fellows the grossest tyranny. For him the only hope of relief now left was in the success of the British arms. For this he and his associates now hoped, prayed, suffered and worked, nor did they doubt that success would crown their efforts in the end.

CHAPTER V

ACTIVITY OF LOYALISTS SUBSEQUENT TO THE ISSUE OF THE DECLARATION OF INDEPENDENCE

EARLY in July, 1776, the British landed on Staten Island and took possession of the "cattle and the tories."[1] This was the beginning of a period of military occupation which ended only with the treaty of peace. Tryon and many "fast friends of government" welcomed the British and reported that "a numerous body" of loyalists was ready to join the army to prove "their loyalty and zeal."[2] The success of British arms was now their only hope, hence they were resolved to aid in bringing it about in every possible way.[3]

The loyalists of Staten Island welcomed General Howe as a deliverer, and placed all their supplies at his disposal.[4] About four hundred militiamen volunarily took the oath of allegiance.[5] Two ships which were sent up the Hudson, secured supplies, and with them twenty loyalists, at Haverstraw.[6] General Howe soon crossed to Long Island. The loyalists there were anxious for his arrival and confident in the expectation of his triumph.[7] The battle of Long Island

---

[1] *Am. Archs.*, 5th ser., i, 20; *Docs. rel. to N. Y. Col. Hist.*, viii, 681.

[2] *Am. Archs.*, 5th ser., i, 105.   [3] *Ibid.*, 1546.

[4] *Ibid.*, 23, 122, iii, 855; *Docs. rel. to N. Y. Col. Hist.*, viii, 681.

[5] *Ibid.;* Clute, *Hist. of Staten Island*, 80; Bayles, *Hist. oj Richmond Co.*, 250; *Am. Archs.*, 5th ser., i, 122.

[6] *Ibid.*, 452.

[7] *Ibid.*, ii, 1183–1184. 1194, 1212, 1213, 1233, 1245, 1247, 1251, 1256, 1259; *Memoirs of L. I. Hist. Soc.*, iii, appendix, 134.

and the occupation of New York city emboldened the loyalists, and led them to believe that there could be but one end
to the conflict. The "disaffected" now flocked by hundreds to the British standards.[1]

Once in possession of southern New York, embracing
60,000 people, General Howe, by a series of proclamations,
restored English rule and the allegiance of the inhabitants.[2]
The courts on Long Island were opened and several whig
estates confiscated.[3] Even force was in some instances used
to make people take the oath of allegiance.[4] The loyalists
at once embraced the opportunity to be reinstated as royal
subjects.[5] Upon Governor Tryon's return to the capital
they wrote him a congratulatory letter professing " the sin-
cerest joy at this happy event," because it was a token of " the
blessings of peace and security under his Majesty's auspi-
cious government."[6] To Lord and General Howe they
reasserted their unshaken loyalty to the king and their
belief that the " constitutional supremacy of Great Britain
over these colonies" was "essential to the union, security and
welfare of the whole empire." Though many loyalists had
been driven or carried away from the city, still 948 persons
signed this address.[7] In a mass meeting of loyalists this
address had been drawn up amid " loud acclamations and

---

[1] *Am. Archs.*, 5th ser., i, 1233, 1506, 1546, ii, 661; *cf. Memoirs of L. I. Hist.
Soc.*, iii, appendix, 96.

[2] Jones, *Hist. of N. Y.*, ii, 116; *Gaine's N. Y. Gazette and Weekly Mercury*,
nos. 1301–1310; *Almon's Remembrancer*, iii, 86; *Doc. Hist. of N. Y.*, i, 474,
gives the population as 53,000 in 1771: *Am. Archs*, 5th series, ii, 282, 1074, 1075,
iii, 855.

[3] Jones, *Hist. of N. Y.*, ii, 117; *Am. Archs.*, 5th ser., ii, 325.

[4] *Ibid.*, 281, 1200.

[5] *Ibid.*, 295, 281, 669, 1159, 1164, 1219–1221, i, 1548, 1564.

[6] *Gaine's N. Y. Gazette and Weekly Mercury*, no. 1304; *Almon's Remembrancer*, iv, 122–123; *Am. Archs.*, 5th ser., ii, 1075, October 16, 1776.

[7] *Ibid.*, 1074–1075.

shouts of applause." "Joy was lighted up in every coun-
tenance on the prospect of returning peace and union with
the parent state." [1]

Expecting a speedy peace, reaction set in all over southern New York. In Queens county 1,293 "freeholders and
inhabitants" sent addresses to the British civil and military
leaders in which they confessed, but lamented having fallen
from "freedom to oppression" through "hopes blasted by
the infatuated conduct of the Congress." [2] Now, however,
they professed allegiance to George III and hoped that " constitutional authority" over the colonies would "be preserved
to the latest ages." [3] "A very large majority . . . stead-
fastly maintained their royal principles," and asked that the
county be declared at peace with the crown. [4] In Kings
county 475 loyalists addressed the king's commissioners,
signifying their wish for a return to the British rule. [5] Even in
Suffolk county, Smithtown, Brook Haven, Huntington,
Southampton, Islip, Easthampton and Southold dismissed
their committees, repudiated all acts of congresses and committees and professed loyalty to "the lawful sovereign."
This restored them to their old footing. [6]

From the region along the Hudson loyalist officials and

[1] *Am. Archs.*, 5th ser., ii, 1158-1163.

[2] This was October 21, 1776. *Almon's Remembrancer*, iv, 198-199, 292, gives
10,184 as the number of signers, but this is evidently a mistake, because a colonial
paper, *Gaine's N. Y. Gazette and Weekly Mercury*, no. 1309, gives the number
1,184; *cf. Am. Archs.*, 5th ser., i, 1212, ii, 1042.

[3] *Am. Archs.*, 5th ser., ii, 1159-1164.

[4] *Docs. rel. to N. Y. Col. Hist.*, viii, 692. They sent a similar address to Governor James Robertson on August 5, 1780; *Rivington's Royal Gazette*, August
12, 1780; *cf.* Arnold's Address to Americans, Oct. 20, 1780, in *Ibid.*, Oct. 28, 1780.

[5] *Gaine's N. Y. Gazette and Weekly Mercury*, no. 1311, Dec. 9, 1776; *Docs.
rel. to N. Y. Col. Hist.*, viii, 692; *cf.* Address to Gov. James Robertson, July 12,
1780, given in *Rivington's Royal Gazette* of same date.

[6] *Ibid.; Am. Archs.*, 5th ser., ii, 252, 505, 1042, 1212, 1219-1221; *Almon's
Remembrancer*, iv, 124-125.

others were constantly fleeing to the British.[1]   The militiamen were disbanded and allowed to keep their arms.[2]   In
Queens county four-fifths of the 1,500 militia were loyal.[3]
Governor Tryon took a tour over Long Island, gave out certificates to loyalists,[4] tendered the oath of allegiance to the
820 militia at Hempstead, in Queens county, and to 800 in
Suffolk county.   Other small districts took the same course.[5]
Westchester, Dutchess and other counties were waiting for
the British army, in order to do likewise.[6]   The loyalists asserted that, were it not for the rebel army, the whole colony
would come out boldly for a return of the "king's peace and
government."   General Howe believed that by appealing to
the "well-affected" American subjects and by promising a
revision of all acts causing grievances, a permanent peace
might be made.[7]

The crown officers, from Governor Tryon down to the
petty justices of the peace, were champions of loyalism, and,
for the most part, were true to their official oaths.[8]   The
Episcopalian clergymen were true to the king's cause almost
to a man.   They made the loyalist cause a holy one.[9]
Early in 1776 they had been forced to close their churches,[10]
but now these were reopened and their communicants were
instructed in the ways of loyalty.

[1] Moore, *Diary of Am. Rev.*, i, 290.

[2] *Am. Archs.*, 5th ser., i, 1564.

[3] Jones, *Hist. of N. Y.*, i, 108.

[4] *Docs. rel. to N. Y. Col. Hist.*, viii, 693.   [5] *Ibid.*, 693–694.

[6] *Ibid.*, 692; *cf. Am. Archs.*, 5th ser., i, 330–452.

[7] *Ibid.*, ii, 398, 1074.

[8] Jones, *Hist. of N. Y.*, ii, 51, 417–421; Clute, *Hist. of Staten Island*, 80, 90;
cf. Flint, *Hist. of L. I.*, 340.

[9] *Gaine's N. Y. Gazette and Weekly Mercury*, no. 1323; *cf.* Address of Epis
copalian clergy to the Howes, March 3, 1777.

[10] *Almon's Remembrancer*, iv, 119.

The process of undoing what rebellion and revolution had accomplished continued after 1776. The governor was kept busy administering the oath of allegiance and granting certificates which would " distinguish the friend from the enemy." [1] The results met with his "warmest wishes." The royal officers helped him. Early in 1777 he reported that over 3,020 had qualified in the city and county of New York, while about 2,600 had done the same in Westchester county and on Long Island and Staten Island. This made a total of 5,620 adult male loyalists in the territory covered by the king's troops. In the capital not more than a hundred refused to avail " themselves of the opportunity of thus testifying their attachment to Government." [2] This work was continued, and additional thousands were added to the number.[3]

The next move was made by the New York city loyalists, in issuing a counter-declaration of independence, declaring null all the powers of the Continental Congress and of all provincial committees, conventions and congresses. It was generally signed.[4] No longer could the representatives of New York claim to have the unanimous consent of the people. The names of the " addressers," of those who took the oath of allegiance and of those who signed this paper, were sent to the British government.[5] These expressions of loyalty were so gratifying to the king that he authorized Governor Tryon to promise grants of land to all loyalists who should help to suppress the insurrection.[6] The executive hoped these acts would arouse intense opposition to the arbitrary and illegal bodies of New York and bring peace.[7] The New York chamber of commerce was very zealous in co-

---

[1] *Docs. rel. to N. Y. Col. Hist.*, viii, 696.

[2] *Ibid.*, 697.   [3] *Ibid.*, 734, 750, 753, 754.

[4] *Ibid.*, 698–699.   [5] *Ibid.*, 705.

[6] *Ibid.*, 704–705; *cf. ibid.*, 695; *cf. Am. Archs.*, 5th ser., iii, 855.

[7] *Docs. rel. to N. Y. Col. Hist.*, viii, 706.

operating with the British army and navy from 1776 to 1783.
General Howe relied upon it to rule the city. In its votes
of thanks to British officers it always spoke of the Americans
as "rebels" and the war as an "unnatural rebellion."[1]

Early in the struggle England began the policy of arming
the loyalists against their rebel brethren.[2] In New York the
plan met with quick response. "Freeing themselves" with
the aid of the royal troops, it was called.[3] As inducements
to enlist, the more active were given good commissions and
others were promised a bounty, the full pay of regulars, 200
acres of land and the estates of the revolutionists after the
war was over.[4] Governor Tryon recognized the necessity
"of raising regiments out of, and giving employment and
protection to, the well-affected part of his majesty's American subjects."[5] Therefore he encouraged the loyalists in
arming, and was the source of many a "tory plot." He believed the whole province would take up arms, if only the
rebel army were driven out.[6] To this end he now bent all his
energies. The British authorities relied on these assertions
made by Tryon and the influential loyalists. It was early
planned, therefore, to "give spirit and vigor to the friends of
government, and incite them to take an active and resolute
part" in recovering New York.[7] Chiefly for that reason,
General Howe was sent to New York.[8]

Before the arrival of the British at New York the loyalists

---

[1] *N. Y. Hist. Soc. Colls.*, 2d ser., ii, part 2, 381–400.

[2] *Cf. Am. Archs.*, 5th ser., i, 122–123, 4th ser., ii, 1755–1776, iii, 6, 1280, 1281,
1282; *Docs. rel. to N. Y. Col. Hist.*, viii, 679, 680.

[3] *Ibid.*, 679.

[4] *Am. Archs.*, 4th ser., v, 1473–1474, vi, 1032, 5th ser., i, 1237; *Docs. rel. to N.
Y. Col. Hist.*, viii, 680.

[5] *Ibid.*, 650.   [6] *Ibid.*, 692.

[7] *Am. Archs.*, 4th ser., ii, 1755, 1776, iii, 1280, 1281, 1282, iv, 699.

[8] *Ibid.*, 5th ser., i. 122–123.

had been arming and enlisting for a year. In the spring of
1775 Lieutenant-Colonel Allan Maclean, aided by Guy Johnson, raised a regiment of " Royal Highland Emigrants,"
composed chiefly of Scotch refugees and old soldiers, and
took them to Canada.[1] About the same time one Grant
was seized in Dutchess county recruiting for General Gage
at Boston. He was released on parole, but fled with some
recruits to the British.[2] Captain Duncan Campbell, sent to
New York for the same purpose, was more fortunate, and
took with him to General Gage enough loyalist volunteers,
mostly from Dutchess county, to help form the regiment of
" Royal Fencible Americans."[3] In June, 1775, the Mac-
Donalds were enlisting loyalist troops in Albany, Dutchess
and Richmond counties,[4] and by August the loyalists, of
their own accord, armed themselves against the revolutionary committee in the first-named county.[5]

Orange county loyalists armed and awaited the arrival of
the British. The Provincial Congress was informed in October of a "conspiracy from Haverstraw to Hackensack to join
the king's troops."[6] The militia at Haverstraw were so disaffected that they refused to allow drafts for the defense of
New York city.[7] Desertions to the English were numerous.[8]

---

[1] *Docs. rel. to N. Y. Col. Hist.*, viii, 562–563; Brown, *Highland Clans*, iv, 242,
307, 308; Smith, *Canada*, ii, 83; *cf.* Ryerson, *Loyalists of Am.*, ii, 262, Maclean's letter is given. Gorneau, *Canada*, ii, 436; *American Annals*, i, 24, 626.

[2] *Min. of Prov. Cong.*, iii, 294, 331–333, iv, 48; *Am. Archs.*, 4th ser., iii, 457–
459, 1314–1315, 1719–1720, 1761, 1900, iv, 187–188, 1117.

[3] *Ibid.*, iii, 1311–1314, 1315; *cf. Docs. rel. to N. Y. Col. Hist.*, viii, 680. Samuel
Woods enlisted about 100 loyalists for Capts. Campbell and Harris. MS.
Transcripts of . . . . Books and Papers . . . . of the American Loyalists, vol. 18, p. 481.

[4] *Min. of Prov. Cong.*, i, 234–244.

[5] *Ibid.*, iii, 274, 294, 331–333, iv, 49; *Am. Archs.*, 4th ser., iii, 457–459, 696,
823, v, 866.

[6] *Ibid.*, iii, 1305, vi, 1032; *Cal. of N. Y. Hist. MSS.*, i, 333; *Min. of Prov.
Cong.*, iii, 274.

[7] *Am. Archs.*, 4th ser., vi, 1442.   [8] *Ibid.*, iii, 841, 907, 908, 913, v, 1369.

Attempts to raise loyalist troops in Albany county were frus-
trated,[1] as elsewhere, only by the vigilance of the revolutionary committee. The Provincial Congress announced, in December, 1775, that Queens county loyalists received arms
from the British warship and were even enlisting their negroes.[2] By May, 1776, they had formed companies, and
Robert Sutton had 700 men equipped to join the English.[3]

Early in 1776 the loyalists about Albany were armed and
awaiting the approach of the British from both north and
south.[4] Small parties were constantly leaving to fight for
the king.[5] In April, J. Huetson was reported to be raising a
regiment of "royal volunteers," and another rumor said that
400 loyalists were *en route* for Canada.[6] When the county
committee asked Robert Van Rensselaer to quell a tory insurrection at Ballstown, his regiment was so disaffected that
he was forced to refuse.[7] In May, 1776, Sir John Johnson,
as has been stated, fled to Canada with 300 Mohawk Valley
loyalists, and was given a colonel's commission to raise two
loyalist battalions of 500 men each, called the "Royal
Greens." This number was soon raised from Tryon, Charlotte and Albany county fugitives.[8] The Mohawk Indians
to a man followed him, and other Indian nations were under
his influence.[9] A party of loyalists left Canajoharie to join

[1] *Proceedings of Alb. Co. Com.*, i, 395, 443, 459, 587.

[2] *Min. of Prov. Cong.*, iv, 47, 50–53; *Am. Archs.*, 4th ser., iii, 403, 404–406,
5th ser., i, 486.

[3] *Ibid.*, v, 1473, 1474, vi, 1321, 1324, 1327, 1328, 5th ser., i, 622; *Docs. rel. to
N. Y. Col. Hist.*, viii, 680.

[4] *Am. Archs.*, 5th ser., iii, 574–575, 585.   [5] *Ibid.*, 586.

[6] *Jour. of Prov. Cong.*, i, 886.   [7] *Ibid.*, i, 888.

[8] *Ibid.*, ii, 493; *Am. Archs.*, 4th ser., iii, 1964, iv, 667, 668, 828, 829, vi, 644,
5th ser., i, 866, iii, 587; *Docs. rel. to N. Y. Col. Hist.*, viii, 651, 663, 664, 683;
Jones, *Hist. of N. Y.*, i, 75.

[9] *Docs. rel. to N. Y. Col. Hist.*, viii, 663; *Am. Archs.*, 4th ser., iv, 260, 5th ser.,
i, 866–867, ii, 1120–1221.

the British, and "multitudes of tories" went from Fort
Dayton.[1] Sir John was ably assisted by John and Walter
Butler, Caldwell, Claus and Brant, and henceforth became
the most bitter and inveterate foe of his former countrymen.[2]

All sorts of horrible "tory plots" were unearthed or in-
vented in every county. In Orange county there was a plan
to join the "ministerial army."[3] From King's district, Queens
county, came the report that the tories had plotted to murder all the whigs.[4] General Washington heard of another
plot to unite all the loyalists of Connecticut and Long Island
for the purpose of seizing or massacring the revolutionists
and joining the enemy.[5] Similar rumors came from New
York city and the counties of Albany, Westchester and Tryon.
The loyalists had established a general system of communication throughout the country.[6] Their post from New York
to Canada was as active as the regular whig post.[7] At Newtown, Long Island, the English flag was hoisted.[8] Threats
were made to raise it in Albany county.[9] The Hickey plot
was a "barbarous and infernal" conspiracy of the loyalists
to murder all of Washington's staff-officers, seize him, blow
up the magazines, arm all loyalists and capture the city upon

---

[1] *Am. Archs.,* 5th ser., ii, 385, 404, iii, 577, 578, 582, 583, 584.

[2] *Ibid.,* i, 1501, ii, 247, 249; MS. *Revolutionary Papers,* v, 249. Sir John
Johnson's Royal Regiment of New York was made up of 800 loyalists, mostly
Scotch and Dutch, and in religion Catholic, Anglican, Lutheran and Presbyterian.
Croil, *A Short Sketch of Canad. Hist.,* 128. The roll of the second battalion of
the King's Royal Regiment is given in Caniff, *The Settlement of Upper Canada,*
in the appendix, 667.

[3] *Am. Archs.,* 4th ser., vi, 1032.   [4] *Ibid.,* 438, 1319.

[5] *Ibid.,* v, 580, 601–604, vi, 455, 471, 477, 482.

[6] *Ibid.,* iii, 889, vi, 1319, 1324, 1328, 5th ser., iii, 574–575, 585; *Min. of Prov.
Cong.,* iii, 37; *cf.* Baird, *Hist. of Rye,* 225–227.

[7] *Am. Archs.,* 4th ser., vi, 1252.

[8] *Ibid.,* 584, 1343, 1344, 1347.   [9] *Ibid.,* v, 343, 345.

the arrival of the British.[1]   All loyalists of southern New
York were believed to be in this plot,[2] and Governor Tryon
was thought to be its instigator.   The committee on conspiracies arrested and tried the mayor of New York and
thirty-five other loyalists.[3]   One of Washington's guards,
Thomas Hickey, was hanged for treason, and with that the
matter dropped.[4]   Rumors of negro and Indian plots and
conspiracies were also rife.[5]   For the most part there was a
solid foundation for these distressing reports.

In Westchester county 500 militia were waiting for the
arrival of British forces to take up arms for the king.[6]   This
was true of every part of the province.   By the time General Howe reached New York not less than 2,500 loyalist
soldiers had already joined the king's forces at various
points, while several times that number were ready to do so
at the first opportunity.   The Americans were constantly
complaining of desertions to the British.[7]

General Howe came to New York expecting much help
from the "friends of government."   He was told on his
arrival that the loyalists were eager to aid him to defeat
their rebellious brethren.[8]   The first loyalist troops raised
by Howe were a provincial corps and a company of horse
on Staten Island.[9]   From this small beginning the number

---

[1] *Am. Archs.*, 4th ser., vi, 1054, 1058, 1431; *Almon's Remembrancer*, iii, 339.

[2] Moore, *Diary of Am. Rev.*, l, 255–257; *Am. Archs.*, 4th ser.,vi, 1152; *Cal. of N. Y. Hist. MSS.*, i, 340.

[3] Moore, *Diary of Am. Rev.*, i, 255–257; *Am. Archs.*,4th ser., vi, 1054.

[4] *Ibid.*, 1058, 1084–1086, 1101, 1119, 1120.

[5] *Min. of Prov. Cong.*, iv, 47; *Gaine's N. Y. Gazette and Weekly Mercury*, March 6, 1775; *Proceedings of Alb. Co. Com.*, i, 29, 105, 175–177, 198; MS· *Revolutionary Papers*, v, 199, 327; *Am. Archs.*, 5th ser., iii, 574.

[6] *Docs. rel. to N. Y. Col. Hist.*, viii, 692, 693–694; *Am. Archs.*, 5th ser., i, 623, ii, 310, 963, 841, 845.

[7] *Ibid.*, 241–243.   [8] *Ibid.*, 622; *cf. ibid.*, ii, 519.

[9] *Ibid.*, 122, 200; *Docs. rel. to N. Y. Col. Hist.*, viii, 681, 705

increased until thousands were in the royal service.   General
Howe offered every inducement in the way of commissions,
bounties, and the pay of regulars to enlist them.[1]   From the
first the "disaffected" swelled his forces by individuals and
by bands.[2]

Governor Tryon early asked the honor of commanding
the provincial loyalists and was appointed " Major General
of Provincial Forces."[3]   On July 8, 1776, he began to raise
1,300 men on Long Island and Staten Island.[4]   By August
16, he had succeeded in raising a "Provincial Corps."[5]
When he made his invasion of Connecticut, sometime later,
he had 2,000 Long Island loyalists under his command.[6]
In Westchester county he raised a troop of Light Horse of
the county's "elite" and made James DeLancey captain,[7]
while in December, 1777, he enlisted 100 men up the Hudson and "swore" 300 more.[8]   Early in 1778 he was given
the command of a regiment of regulars,[9] and in the fall of
the same year, with 1,000 loyalist troops, he went to Suffolk
county, where he suppressed the whigs and forced all of
them to take an oath of allegiance.[10]   His valuable services
continued until 1780, when he returned to England.

Loyalist troops under Tryon took an active part in the
battle of Long Island and were publicly thanked by General
Howe.[11]   At least two companies from New York city were

[1] *Docs. rel. to N. Y. Col. Hist.*, viii, 681, 704–705; *Am. Archs.*, 4th ser., iv, 1776,
v, 1473, vi, 1032, 5th ser., i, 122, 200, 1237, ii, 506, iii, 1490; Moore, *Diary of Am.
Rev.*, i, 288–291; *Docs. rel. to N. Y. Col. Hist.*, viii, 680–681.

[2] *Am. Archs.*, 5th ser., i, 109, 120, 200, 1102, 1109, 1233, 1546.

[3] *Docs. rel. to N. Y. Col. Hist.*, viii, 697–698, 705, 706, 708, 715.

[4] *Ibid.*, 681; *Am. Archs.*, 5th ser., i, 120, 1396.

[5] *Ibid.*, 980; *Docs. rel. to N. Y. Col. Hist.*, viii, 710.

[6] Jones, *Hist. of N. Y.*, i, 177-178.   [7] *Docs. rel. to N. Y. Col. Hist.*, viii, 717–718.

[8] *Ibid.*, 734.   [9] *Ibid.*, 746, 751.   [10] *Ibid.*, 750, 753, 754.

[11] *Ibid.*. 687, 691; *Am. Archs.*, 5th ser., ii, 107, 135, 189, 198, 200, 244, 449, 661,
669, 980.

engaged.[1]   This victory and the easy occupation of the
capital city caused the loyalists jubilantly to "raise their
heads."[2]   Loyalists flocked to the city daily and enlistments
were very numerous.[3]   Eight hundred stands of arms were
sent to Queens County and received "with demonstrations
of joy."[4]   A paymaster-general was appointed, and instructed to keep the accounts of loyalists separate.[5]

Oliver DeLancey was commissioned brigadier general to
raise 1,500 loyalists to defend Long Island.[6]   The whigs
were first subdued and then inducements were offered to
those who would enlist.[7]   One battalion was led by Colonel
Gabriel Ludlow, a second by Colonel George Brewerton, and
the third by General DeLancey.   After some service on the
island two battalions were in 1778 sent to Georgia, the third
remaining at home.   At the close of the war they went to
Nova Scotia.[8]

Major Robert Rogers was commissioned to recruit a regiment for general service.[9]   Drafts were authorized, if necessary.[10]   He began to enlist men in August, 1776.[11]   William
Lounsbury and Richard Miller were both shot in attempting
to raise men for him in Westchester county.[12]   A long list of

---

[1] *Am. Archs.*, 5th ser., ii, 494; Stedman, *American War*, i, 215.

[2] *Am. Archs.*, 5th ser., ii, 661.

[3] *Gaine's N. Y. Gazette and Weekly Mercury*, no. 1304; *Am Archs.*, 5th ser.,
ii, 991.

[4] *Docs. rel. to N. Y. Col. Hist.*, viii, 696, 697.

[5] *Am. Archs.*, 5th ser., i, 980.

[6] *Ibid.*, ii, 345, 494, 504; *Public Papers of George Clinton*, i, 347; *Docs. rel. to
N. Y. Col. Hist.*, viii, 686, 687; Jones, *Hist. of N. Y.*, i, 264.

[7] *Am. Archs.*, 5th ser., ii, 325, 505, 506, 564, 566; *cf. ibid.*, 252, 295.

[8] Jones, *Hist. of N. Y.*, i, 265–268.

[9] *Docs. rel. to N. Y. Col. Hist.*, viii, 686, 687; *Am. Archs.*, 5th ser., i, 1236, ii,
244, 494; *Can. Archs.* (1888), Haldimand Collection, 672, 673.

[10] *Am. Archs.*, 5th ser,, ii, 244.   [11] *Ibid.*, i, 1236, 1556, ii, 310.

[12] *Ibid.*, i, 1236, 1556, ii, 310, 504, iii, 473.

the names of men who were ready to join the "ministerial
army" from that section was sent to Governor Tryon in July.[1]
By December Rogers, with 700 rangers, was making raids
through that county and committing great havoc,[2] forcing
the whigs to appeal again and again for aid.[3] In 1779 Sir
Henry Clinton commissioned him to raise two battalions of
rangers,[4] and he met with considerable success.[5]

In December, 1776, Colonel Fanning was given a warrant
to raise 500 provincials.[6] "We are daily getting the most
authentic intelligence of bodies of men enlisted and armed,"
wrote the committee of safety to General Washington, who, in
turn, wrote to the President of Congress that the British were
pushing their recruiting schemes "with uncommon indus-
try."[7] It was rumored that four or five regiments of loyalists were formed before 1777.[8] A large part of the 6,000
seamen in the metropolis were loyalists.[9] Many who had
been impressed into American service, now deserted and
returned to their allegiance.[10] Washington, in a despairing
letter to Congress, said that the whole army was disaffected.
Many joined the army for bounties and then deserted.[11] The
British had refused to bombard the city of New York because of the large amount of tory property which it con-

---

[1] *Am. Archs.*, 5th ser., i, 623, ii, 841, 845.   [2] *Ibid.*, iii, 473, 1172.

[3] *Ibid.*, ii, 991, iii, 371, 372, 1172; *Public Papers of George Clinton*, i, 463.

[4] *Can. Archs.*, (1888), Haldimand Collection, 673.

[5] *Ibid.*, 674, 675, 676, 677, 678, 679.

[6] *Docs. rel. to N. Y. Col. Hist.*, viii, 694.

[7] *Jour. of Prov. Cong.*, i, 670; *Am. Archs.*, 5th ser., ii, 416, 564, iii, 275; *cj.
ibid.*, ii, 120, 167, 867, 939.

[8] *Ibid.*, ii, 1249; MS. *Revolutionary Papers* (1776), vi. 333.

[9] *Docs. rel. to N. Y. Col. Hist.*, viii, 772.

[10] *Am. Archs.*, 5th ser., ii, 564.

[11] MS. *Revolutionary Papers*, v, 301; *Am. Archs.*, 5th ser., i, 355, 1459, ii, 120,
167, 352.

tained.[1]   Washington was urged to burn it "because two-
thirds of the property of the city and suburbs belong to the
tories."[2]   John Jay and General Greene also urged its destruction.[3]   "That cursed town," wrote another, "from first to
last has been ruinous to the common cause."   But Congress forbade its destruction.[4]

With the capture of all southern New York, the loyalists to the north became bolder and more active.[5]   The
"disarmed and disaffected" in Westchester, Orange, Dutchess and Ulster counties, estimated to be about 2,300, were
waiting for a chance to join Howe, and he was anxious to
enlist them.[6]   Hundreds of negroes fled to the British.[7]
There was a constant fear that the loyalists along the Hudson would organize an armed revolt.[8]   They did spike the
300 or 400 cannon which were found along the course of the
Harlem river.[9]   The county committees were busy arresting
and exiling the loyalists who were enlisting or had enlisted.[10]
Almost the whole population of Livingston manor took an
oath of secrecy and allegiance.[11]   Captain John Duerson
wrote to the Provincial Congress from Dutchess county that
his whole militia company was tory except the lieutenant
and himself, and Lewis Morris complained that out of his
entire regiment not more than a colonel's command was true

---

[1] Sloane, *French War and the Revolution*, 241.

[2] *Scottish Review*, American Loyalists, v, 231.

[3] *Am. Archs.*, 5th ser., ii, 182.

[4] *Ibid.*, 135.

[5] Simms, *Frontiersmen of New York*, 550; *Am. Archs.*, 5th ser., ii, 1173. iii, 205.

[6] *Ibid.*, 597–599, 661.   [7] *Ibid.*, 663.

[8] *Jour. of Prov. Cong.*, i, 669, 670, 757; *Am. Archs.*, 5th ser., ii, 1026.

[9] *Ibid.*, 4th ser., iv, 1068, 1069, 1072, 1073, 1096, 1101, 1102.

[10] *Ibid.*, 5th ser., ii, 979, iii, 265, 467–468, 470–471; *Jour. of Prov. Cong.*, i, 909, 910–911, 918–919.

[11] *Ibid.*, i, 918, May, 1777.

to the American cause.[1] In another district eighty militiamen refused to organize except under officers of the English
government.[2]   So great was the disaffection and so difficult
was it to raise troops, that the neighboring states were asked
to send aid.[3] "Nothing can be more alarming than the
present situation of our state," wrote the Convention to
Washington.[4] On the contrary, the king was very well satisfied with the loyalty of New York.[5] It was declared that,
if America fell, it would be by the death-thrust of the loyalists rather than by the British.[6]

In the campaign of 1777, it was planned that General
Burgoyne should invade New York from the north, and that
Howe should meet him from the south.   At the same time
Colonel St. Leger, with Sir John Johnson and his loyalists,
and Captain Brant and his Indians, was to descend the
Mohawk to meet them.   The loyalists were jubilant at this
plan, and boasted that they alone could capture New York.[7]
At last the loyalists of the Hudson valley were to have an
opportunity to prove their loyalty.   As Burgoyne ap-
proached Albany, hundreds of loyalists joined him.[8]   Col-
onel Skeene, with all the forces he could raise, fought under
British standards.[9] A special committee had to be sent to
Albany in the fall of 1776, to help General Schuyler sup-

---

[1] *Jour. of Prov. Conv.*, i, 654.

[2] *Am. Archs.*, 4th ser., iii, 696.

[3] *Ibid.*, 5th ser., ii, 1026, iii, 589; *Jour. of Prov. Conv.*, i, 669, 670, 757.

[4] *Ibid.*, 669, 670.

[5] *Docs. rel. to N. Y. Col. Hist.*, viii, 704–705, 706, 789,

[6] *Am. Archs.*, 5th ser., ii, 821; *cf. ibid.*, i, 1492. Letter of Convention to Washington, August 9, 1776.

[7] *Ibid.*, 4th ser., vi, 509; *Jour. of. Prov. Conv.*, i, 906.

[8] *Ibid.*, 702–703, 1048, 1057, ii, 497; MS. *Min. of Comsrs.*, i, Apr. 11–20, 1778;
Jones, *Hist. of N. Y.*, i, 198; *cf.* Macauley, *Hist. of N. Y.*, iii, 202.

[9] *Ibid.*, 202; *Jour. of Prov. Conv.*, i, 1101; *cf.* Kellogg, *Hist. of Whitehall.*

press various insurrections.[1]   In May, 1777, uprisings were
reported in the counties of Albany, Tryon, Charlotte, Ulster,
Cumberland, Gloucester and Orange.[2]   General Schuyler
feared that "so much toryism" in the New Hampshire
Grants would greatly aid Burgoyne.[3]   The Tryon county
committee wrote to the committee of safety, July 18, 1777,
"More than half of our inhabitants are resolved not to lift
up arms in defense of this county" against the invasion of
"British troops, tories and savages."[4]   General Heath wrote
to Washington from Orange county that "the tories are
joining the enemy and insulting and disarming the whigs,
stripping them of cattle, effects, etc."[5]   Although the loyalists served Burgoyne nobly on the battlefield and in supplying his army, yet not one word in their behalf was introduced
into his articles of capitulation.[6]   He even blamed them for
his defeat, and after the surrender several thousand of them
were forced either to flee to Canada, or to trust to the mercy
of their victorious enemies.[7]   Chief among those who escaped was "Jessup's Corps" or "Jessup's Battalion," which,
led by two brothers, had fled to Canada in the fall of 1776
and, until organized separately the following spring, had
formed a part of Sir John Johnson's regiment.   Then it
joined Burgoyne, and after his surrender returned to Canada, but was "actively engaged in a bitter partisan warfare"

---

[1] *Am. Archs.*, 5th ser., iii, 561, 563–565, 566, 567, 579, 588, 589; *Jour. of Prov. Conv.*, i, 699, 701.

[2] Cf. *Exam. of Joseph Galloway by Com. of House of Commons*, 23; *Jour. of Prov. Conv.*, i, 912.

[3] *Ibid.*, 1005.

[4] *Ibid.*, 1006, 1007, 1009, 1011, 1017, 1018.

[5] *Ibid.*, 719; *Am. Archs.*, 5th ser., ii, 697, iii, 1169.

[6] Jones, *Hist. of N. Y.*, i, 681–686; *N. Y. Packet*, Oct. 23, 1777; *Jour. of Prov. Conv.*, ii, 490.

[7] *Ibid.*, i, 1048, 1057; De Peyster, *Sir John Johnson's Orderly Book*, 37.

till the conflict ended.[1]   Peeter's corps of loyalists was at
Bennington, and 157 of its number were killed.[2]

St. Leger commanded a loyalist invasion—Sir John Johnson's "Royal Greens,"[3] Butler's "Rangers," a few hundred
regulars, and about eight hundred Indians under Colonel
David Claus and Captain Brant, constituting the small force
of which he was the leader.[4]   Oriskany was a battle between
brothers, fathers, sons, and neighbors.   Hence, in this encounter, to political differences were added hate, spite and
thirst for revenge.   In this "fratricidal butchery" most of the
males of the Mohawk valley perished, and if Tryon county
"smiled again during the war it smiled through tears."[5]

Alexander and John McDonald, Scotchmen of the Roman
faith, left Johnstown with Sir John Johnson in 1776, returned
the next spring, collected a company of Scotch and German
loyalists and escaped with them to Canada. John McDonald
was killed at Oriskany, but his brother with 300 tories fell
upon Schoharie in 1778 with barbarous cruelty, was at Che-
mung the next year with Sir John, and in 1781 committed
inhuman barbarities in the Mohawk valley.[6]

In May, 1780, Sir John Johnson fell upon his "rebellious
birthplace," left a dismal testimony of his visit and escaped
with rich booty and many prisoners.   In August and September he ascended the St. Lawrence, the Oswego, crossed
Lake Oneida, traversed Madison and Otsego counties to the

---

[1] De Peyster, *Sir John Johnson's Orderly Book*, 37–38, note 1. Ryerson
thinks the loyalists numbered twice as many as Burgoyne's army, but is certainly
mistaken. *Hist of American Loyalists*, ii, 147

[2] Thatcher, *Military Journal*, 91, 93.

[3] Called also "The King's Royal Regiment of New York," "The Queen's Loyal
New Yorkers," and "Sir John Johnson's Regiment."

[4] De Peyster, *Sir John Johnson's Orderly Book*, civ.

[5] *Ibid.*, lii–liii; Jones, *Hist. of N. Y.*, i, 217.

[6] De Peyster, *Sir John Johnson's Orderly Book*, 56–57, notes.

Schoharie valley. He devastated it and then crossed again to the Mohawk valley to repeat his destructive work. Attempts to crush him failed. He had with him on this raid his own regiment of "Royal Greens," 200 of Butler's "Loyalist Rangers," and some regulars and Indians.[1]

The enlistment of loyalist troops in New York continued throughout the war.[2] After the surrender of Burgoyne the loyalists who fought on New York soil were engaged under Sir John Johnson in frontier warfare. The others, like Simcoe's "Queen's Rangers," raised in 1776, saw action in the states to the south.[3] In 1779 Willliam Axtell was commissioned colonel of 500 men to be raised in Kings county, and when New York city was threatened, in five days 6,000 loyalists volunteered as militia. They formed 62 companies and were drilled three times a week by the first gentlemen of the state, and served till 1783.[5] There were 2,000 loyal militiamen on Long Island and 400 on Staten Island. In 1781 there were 2,500 armed loyalist provincials in New York city.[6] Loyalist privateers also were fitted out and infested the shores of southern New York and New Jersey.[7]

Judging from the inadequate records, it appears that there must have been at least 15,000 New York loyalists in the British army and navy, and at least 8,500 loyalist militia, making a total in that state of 23,500 loyalist troops. This

---

[1] De Peyster, *Sir John Johnson's Orderly Book*, cxlii, cxlviii;, Roberts, *N. Y. in the Rev.*, xiii–xviii.

[2] *Docs. rel. to N. Y. Col. Hist.*, viii, 793. The Act of Attainder of 1779, and other cruel acts against the loyalists, led many to enlist in the latter stage of the war. *Rivington's Royal Gazette*, Feb. 2, 1780, no. 349.

[3] Surrendered with Cornwallis at Yorktown, 1781. Clute, *History of Staten Island*, 99, 100, 104.

[4] Jones, *Hist. of N. Y.*, 304.

[5] *Rivington's Royal Gazette*, Feb. 9, 1780, no. 350; Jones, *Hist. of N. Y.*, i, 322–323.

[6] *Ibid.*, 348.   [7] *Ibid.*, 300.

was more than any other colony furnished, and perhaps as many as were raised by all others combined. The revolutionary troops from New York numbered only 17,781 regulars, or 41,633 including the militia.[1] New York loyalists fought in every battle on New York soil, and in most of the other battles of the war, and were repeatedly commended for their gallantry.

Those who did not enlist showed their loyalty in other ways. Staten Island raised £500 for the support of the loyalist troops.[2] New York city gave £2,000 in two weeks for the same purpose.[3] For DeLancey's brigade "monies were contributed by the inhabitants of every town upon the island."[4] Kings county contributed £300 for Colonel Fanning's battalion,[5] while Queens and Suffolk collected larger sums.[6] The Quakers furnished clothing and other materials.[7] Wagons, horses, oxen, live stock, wood and farm, garden and orchard products were during a period of seven years contributed to the cause.[8] In 1779, the loyalist ladies of New York city presented a privateer, "The Fair American,"

---

[1] Roberts, *N. Y. in the Rev.*, iv. Among the loyalist troops furnished by New York were the King's Rangers, the Royal American Fencibles, the Queen's Rangers, the New York Volunteers, the King's American Regiment, the Prince of Wales American Volunteers, De Lancey's Battalions, the Second American Regiment, the King's American Dragoons, the Loyal American Regiment, the American Legion, the Orange Rangers, the Guides and Pioneers, the Westchester Volunteers, and the Associated Loyalists. At one time Col. Archibald Hamilton, of New York, commanded 17 companies of loyal militia.

[2] *Docs. rel. to N. Y. Col. Hist.*, viii, 711.   [3] *Ibid.*, 711.

[4] Jones, *Hist. of N. Y.*, i, 265–266.

[5] *Docs. rel. to N. Y. Col. Hist.*, viii, 696.

[6] *Ibid.*, 711. Jamaica alone sent £219 from 189 persons. Onderdonk, *Queens Co. in Olden Times*, 53.

[7] *Docs. rel. to N. Y. Col. Hist.*, viii, 696.

[8] *Am. Archs.*, 5th ser., i, 23, 1103, ii, 416, 506, 564, 566, 825, iii, 674; *Jour. of Prov. Conv.*, i, 1005.

to the British as a New Year's gift.[1]   The "Marine Society" raised an artillery company to defend the city.[2]

In many other ways the loyalists made themselves useful. They acted as armed police.[3]   Most of the spies in the British service were loyalists.[4]   In 1779 they suggested that an independent organization be formed to aid the British, to protect themselves and to requite the whigs for the outrages, confiscations and murders of which they were guilty.   The king and ministry approved of the plan, and ordered Sir Henry Clinton to permit its execution.   Consequently on Dec. 27, 1780, the "Board of Directors of the Associated Loyalists" was organized in New York city.[5]   William Franklin was president and ten directors assisted him, each receiving a salary of £200 sterling a year with rations.   This body continued until Sir Guy Carleton broke it up in 1782. Its object was to unite the loyalists of all the states into three "societies" of "associators," for the purposes of self-preservation and revenge.   One "society," consisting of cavalry, was organized at Kingsbridge, Morrisania and Westchester in order to make incursions against the whigs of that region.   A second "society" was created on Long Island to carry on piratical and marauding warfare on the coasts of Connecticut and eastern New York.   The third "society" was formed in New York city and on Staten Island to harass the Jersey coast and the region along the Hudson.   These "societies" were led by officers who were commissioned by the British commander-in-chief, but who were wholly dependent upon the board.   They were given

---

[1] *Rivington's Royal Gazette*, no. 240, Jan. 13, 1779, July 19, 1780, no. 397.

[2] Jones, *Hist. of N. Y.*, ii, 421–423.

[3] *Docs. rel. to N. Y. Col. Hist.*, viii, 696.

[4] Simms, *Frontiersmen of New York*, 586, 588; Thatcher, *Military Journal*, 99, 409.

[5] *Rivington's Royal Gazette*, December 30, 1780.

arms and vessels by the British, could keep all their captures and were allowed to exchange prisoners for "associated loyalists." They did much damage and kept southern New York in a state of constant turmoil. At the close
of the war most of them went to Nova Scotia.[1]

In New York Great Britain certainly had no reason to
complain of the lack of helpful activity from the loyalists.
Their blood and treasure were freely sacrificed on the altar
of imperial patriotism.

---

[1] Jones, *Hist. of N. Y.*, i, 300, 303, 482; *cf.* Bolton, *Westchester Co.*, i, pp.
xiii, xiv; *cf.* Baird, *Hist. of Rye*, 241.

CHAPTER VI

COMMISSIONERS ON LOYALISTS, 1776–1781

MAY 10, 1776, the Continental Congress recommended the establishment of state governments.[1]   Three weeks later the New York Provincial Congress declared the royal government "dissolved," the government by Congress and committees "unsatisfactory," and ordered the county committees to cause the people to send deputies, on July 9, to New York city, to discuss the "instituting of a new government."[2] The Constitutional Convention thus called was forced to meet at White Plains. Its first act was to ratify the Declaration of Independence.[3] Next it instructed all whig officers to continue to act "in the name of the state of New York."[4]   Civil, and not military, law was declared to be in force.[5]   In August a committee was named to draw up a plan for a new government,[6] but it was not until April 20, 1777, that the constitution it framed was adopted.[7] The election or appointment of local, county and state officers then began, and continued for some months.[8]

[1] *Am. Archs.*, 4th ser., vi, 1671, 1701; *cf. ibid.*, v, 1180, vi, 395, 633, 825.

[2] *Ibid.*, 1332, 1337, 1351; *cf. ibid.* 725, 895, 5th ser., i, 40, 103; *Min. of Prov. Cong.*, v, 650–652, 688.

[3] *Am. Archs.*, 5th ser., i, 1387, 1389, 1391, 1397.

[4] *Ibid.*, 1410.

[5] *Jour. of Prov. Conv.*, i, 729.

[6] *Ibid.*, 552; *Am. Archs.*, 5th ser., i, 1465; Jones, *Hist. of N. Y.*, i, 143, 150, 642.

[7] *Jour. of Prov. Conv.*, i, 892–898.

[8] *Ibid.*, 818, 829, 907, 912, 913, 917, 937, 948, 990, 1007, 1021, 1027, 1053, 1061, 1112; *Am. Archs.*, 5th ser., iii, 687.

The new government, however, did not at once go fully
into operation. In fact it was itinerant and desultory until
1783. The Convention continued in session until May 13,
1777, when it finally dissolved. The continuation of the
government was entrusted to a committee, or council of
safety, previously appointed, with the governor at its head,
until the organization contemplated by the Convention should
be completed.[1] The council of safety continued to act with
" ordinance" power, after the legislature was organized and
was transacting public business,[2] and to take cognizance of
cases involving loyalists even subsequent to the appointment
of a special board for that work.[3] After the formation of a
state government the status of the loyalists was clearly
defined. Consequently their treatment became more uniform and at the same time harsher. The inquisitorial methods
and machinery developed previous to the Declaration of In-
depence were continued by the Constitutional Convention
and by the new state government.

Numerous petitions, both humble and defiant, were sent
by the loyalists to the Convention, to the legislature and
to the three state committees on loyalists. Some begged
for a trial to prove their innocence,[4] a few defiantly demanded death or liberty,[5] several wished to join their families
within the British lines,[6] and many made minor requests.[7]

[1] *Jour. of Prov. Conv..* i, 916.

[2] *Proceedengs of Assembly,* i, 25.

[3] *Jour. of Prov. Conv.,* i, 663, 665, 674, 679; *Am. Archs.,* 5th ser., ii, 673, 677,
683, 687, 711.

[4] *Am. Archs.,* 5th ser., i, 175, 1163, 1481, 1518, ii, 109, 694, 1549, 1551, iii,
1037, 1098, 1320; MS. *Revolutionary Papers* (1776), v, 169, 183; *Public Papers
of George Clinton,* i, 246.

[5] *Am. Archs.,* 4th ser., iii, 268.

[6] *Ibid.,* 1154, 1167, 1204, 1263, 1351, 1379; MS. *Revolutionary Papers,* (1776),
vi, 65, 201.

[7] *Am. Archs.,* 5th ser., i, 1096, 1455.

As a rule these petitions were heard and then answered as the merits in each case deserved. It was said in 1777 that the leniency of the state authorities led all imprisoned loyalists to petition for release.[1]

From all sides came demands to the Convention for sterner measures against these domestic foes. Washington urged their immediate removal from the state,[2] and Gouverneur Morris advocated the same course as being the most effectual.[3] The New York city jails were early filled with tories, mostly from Long Island, and consequently the whigs in general requested that they be sent to safer quarters.[4] The situation was dangerous and something must be done. Prompt action was promised.[5]

The Convention, surrounded by the British and the loyalists, felt it more necessary to define citizenship and treason than to form a constitution. Hence one of the first things it did was to resolve, July 16, 1776, that all persons abiding in the state under its laws owed " allegiance to the said laws," and were "members of the state." Temporary residents held the same relation. All " members" who made war against the state, or adhered to the king or other enemies, or aided them, were "guilty of treason against the state," the penalty for which was death.[6] County and subcommittees were instructed to seize and secure immediately, " all such persons whose going at large at this critical time they should deem dangerous to the liberties of the state." Loyalists might appeal from local to county committees, and all cases were to be reported to the Convention.[7] The county committees were given full power to dispose of imprisoned tories for public protection, but they could employ no "un-

[1] *Jour. of Prov. Conv.*, i, 963, 964, 966.

[2] *Am. Archs.*, 5th ser., i, 255, 351, 1401.   [3] *Ibid.*, 334.   [4] *Ibid.*, 335.

[5] *Ibid.*, 1402.   [6] *Ibid.*, 1403, 1410.

[7] *Ibid.*, 1410.

necessary severity." Traitors, however, were to be dealt with harshly.[1]

On the strength of these acts, Washington urged the committee of New York city to remove "all equivocal and suspicious persons," and justified the act on the ground of international practice and the law of self-preservation.[2] When, early in August, a battle became imminent, believing it "highly improper" to let tories remain where they could do more mischief than in the enemies' camp, he seized them and removed them to Connecticut. But he ordered them to be well treated and their property to be protected, and fully explained to the Convention the reasons for his actions.[3]

The Convention dismissed the committee appointed to execute the resolves of June 5, 1776,[4] and itself took cognizance of all urgent cases. The usual course, however, was to arrest the loyalists, commit them to jail and appoint a special committee to examine them, and then to sentence them.[5] Many were banished to Connecticut.[6] In some cases as a temporary expedient the Convention ordered the officers of the county militia companies, when on the march, to take into their service as fatigue men "all the disarmed and disaffected" men who were from 16 to 55 years of age.[7] It even passed judgment on New Jersey loyalists.[8] So numerous were the complaints about dangerous loyalists, and so many cases were before the Convention, while at the same time a British army was entering the state from the south and another was forming on the north, that it was

---

[1] *Am. Archs.*, 5th ser., i, 1540, August 26, 1776.   [2] *Ibid.*, 330, 448, 452.

[3] *Ibid.*, 917, 981, 989, 1501.   [4] *Ibid.*, 1482, August 7, 1776.

[5] *Ibid.*, 1402, 1546, 1547, 1554, 1557; *Jour. of Prov. Conv.*, i, 855, 856, 882.

[6] *Am. Archs.*, 5th ser., i, 888, 889, 1004, 1391, 1397, 1419, 1441, 1445, 1526, 1529, ii, 593, etc.

[7] *Ibid.*, 1496.

[8] *Ibid.*, 1397, 1415, 1441, 1445, 1446, 1447, 1535.

felt to be necessary to effect a more perfect organization for the purpose of detecting and supressing "such iniquitous practices and conspiracies" of the "parricides." Consequently, on September 21, 1776, a new committee was formed.[1]

This body of seven men now became the head of the inquisitorial system.[2] It was empowered to send for persons and papers, and to seize, imprison or remove all dangerous persons.[3] A body of troops was placed at the disposal of the committee to enforce its will.[4] Money was freely granted to it from the state treasury.[5] Accurate minutes were ordered kept. The chairman and two members were to constitute a quorum. The county committees were made subordinate to it, and were ordered to report all loyalist "machinations and conspiracies."[6] A secret service system was established, and express riders were employed.[7] A treasurer and auditor were appointed, and, as the jails were filled, a commissary became necessary.[8]

The new committee sat daily, and was overwhelmed with work.[9] The Convention and committee of safety turned all tory cases and correspondence over to it.[10] Even prisoners of war were entrusted to its charge. Reports of traitorous plots and schemes came in to it from all directions. In October it was feared that the loyalists would seize the Highland passes and effect a junction with the British; hence, extra precaution

---

[1] *Am. Archs.*, 5th ser., ii, 706, 712, 713, 714, 715, 979, iii, 467; *Jour. of Prov. Conv.*, i, 669, 684; *Public Papers of George Clinton*, i, 359–362.

[2] *Am. Archs.*, 5th ser., ii, 706, 712–714, iii, 249, 467.   [3] *Ibid.*, 467.

[4] *Ibid.*, 238, 251, 257; *Jour. of Prov. Conv.*, i, 669, 684.

[5] *Ibid.*, 687, 707; *cf. Am. Archs.*, 5th ser., i, 1543.

[6] *Ibid.*, iii, 467.   [7] *Ibid.*, 1547, 1549.   [8] *Ibid.*, 1549–1551, 1552–1555.

[9] *Ibid.*, ii, 979, iii, 238; *Jour. of Prov. Conv.*, i, 669.

[10] *Am. Archs.*, 5th ser., ii, 715, 717, iii, 230; *Jour. of Prov. Conv.*, i, 665, 687–689, 756, 758, 760, 775, 784.

was taken."[1]   The local boards were instructed to hunt out
and arrest every tory.[2]   With this vast network of surveil-
lance it was thought that no tory plots could mature, nor any
dangerous loyalists escape, without detection.   Its procedure
was summary, and very similar to that of the previous committee; loyalists were arrested under much the same charges
as formerly.

The first class to be tried consisted of loyalists who had
enlisted with the British,[3] and disaffected militiamen.[4]   Then
other dangerous persons were disposed of.   In four months
at least 500 cases were separately examined.   As many as
thirty-three were considered in one day.   The jails were
crowded and a large number of petitions and letters from
both whigs and loyalists, was sent to the committee.   That
it did such a volume of work, and did it thoroughly and on
the whole fairly, is rather remarkable.

Under the resolution of September 21, no penalty severer
than that of transportation could be inflicted, and this, in
fact, was the form of punishment most frequently resorted
to.   Loyalists were sent west to Pennsylvania,[5] several hundred were sent to New Hampshire,[6] and others to Connecticut[7] and Massachusetts.[8]   This was done at their own expense.   The most vicious and dangerous were confined in
jail after transportation,[9] but the rest were given certain freedom on parole.   Those less feared were imprisoned in the
state or released on parole.[10]   Some were allowed to join the

---

[1] *Am. Archs.*, 5th ser., ii, 991, iii, 238, 257.   [2] *Ibid.*, ii, 883.

[3] *Ibid.*, ii, 979.   [4] *Ibid.*, iii, 265.

[5] *Jour. of Prov. Conv.*, i, 1000; *Am. Archs.*, 5th ser., ii, 979, 1314.

[6] *Ibid.*, iii, 467–468, 469, 470, 471, 825.

[7] *Jour. of Prov. Conv.*, ii, 493, gives a list of loyalists sent to Connecticut at their
own expense; *cf. Am. Archs.*, 5th ser., i, 888, 989–990, 1004, 1391–1392, 1441,
1445, 1526–1530.

[8] *Ibid.*, ii, 1314, iii, 1540–1541.   [9] *Ibid.*, 470–471.   [10] *Ibid.*, 1540–1541.

British, while others were forced to take the oath of allegiance.[1]   Still other penalties were: imprisonment with hard labor,[2] confinement in irons[3] and enforced labor on the barracks.[4]   Those who sought to evade their penalties were treated more harshly.[5]

On October 19, a special committee of twelve was appointed to co-operate with General Schuyler in the north, and it served for a month. Its mode of procedure resembled that of the general committee on tories. It used troops to suppress insurrections at Helleberg, on the Rensselaer manor, the Livingston manor and in Tryon county; and it tried and sentenced loyalists, impressed wagons and drivers and co-operated with the committees of Albany county and with other committees.[6]

Efforts, however, were made to treat the loyalists humanely. When sick, medical attendance was allowed them.[7] Boys were ordered to be mildly treated.[8] A starving loyalist and his family were fed.[9] Again and again the families of loyalists were allowed to join fathers and brothers.[10] Two men were named in each district to grant them passes. If loyalists were found outside their neigborhoods without passes after November 20, 1776, they were subject to arrest.[11] Petitions were willingly heard and efforts were made to give the accused a fair trial.[12] When a Westchester county loyalist,

[1] *Am. Archs.*, 5th ser., iii, 1540.   [2] *Ibid.*, 5th ser., ii, 683, iii, 302.

[3] *Ibid.*, 1547–1549.   [4] *Ibid.*, 302.   [5] *Jour. of Prov. Conv.*, i, 743.

[6] *Am. Archs.*, 5th ser., iii, 561, 563–565, 566, 579, 588, 589; *Jour. of Prov. Conv.*, i, 699–670, 701.

[7] *Ibid.*, 654.   [8] *Ibid.*, 667.

[9] *Ibid.*; *cf. Am. Archs.*, 5th ser., iii, 234.

[10] *Jour. of Prov. Conv.*, 768, 802, 845, 846.

[11] *Ibid.*, 706. About 4000 blank passes were printed. Loyalists had to pay six pence for them. *Cf.* case of Lady Johnson, *Am. Archs.*, 5th ser., iii, 1102, 1158, 1207, 1236.

[12] *Ibid.*, 1354, 1355, 1367, 1390–1391, 1434, 1452.

because of ill-health, asked for a release from prison, a physician was ordered to examine him, and he was sent to a neighboring state.[1]   These instances and others that could be cited, indicate that the principal aim of the whigs was to take from the loyalists, who were dangerous political enemies, their power to work injury.   The desire for personal vengeance or for the infliction of undue or unnecessary punishment also appeared in many cases, but it did not constitute the rule.   The treatment which the loyalists received varied largely with the fortunes of war, and hence with the danger which was apprehended from them.

The committee adjourned December 31, 1776,[2] and reported to the committee of safety a week later.   On February 11, 1777, it was dissolved, and a new committee of three members was appointed to take its place.[3]   This new triumvirate succeeded to all the powers of the former body and carried on its work.[4]   It acted, however, under the instructions of the legislature.[5]   A month later its membership was increased to five,[6] and on August 28 four more assistants were added,[7] making the number nine.

Early in 1777 it was felt that some distinction ought to be made between the dangerous loyalists and those who might be reclaimed.[8]   The commissioners on conspiracies, therefore, were ordered by the Convention to send for all persons not guilty of treason, and to offer them an oath binding them to be faithful citizens of New York state and to reveal all plots against the liberties of America.   Those taking the

---

[1] *Am. Archs.*, 5th ser., i, 1448, 1454.   [2] *Ibid.*, iii, 1555–1558.

[3] *Jour. of Prov. Conv.*, i, 803.   Egbert Benson, Jacobus Swartwaurt and Melancton Smith.

[4] *Ibid.*, 812, 828, 835.   [5] *Cf. ibid.*, 865, 872, 889, 898, 899, 968, *etc.*

[6] *Ibid.*, 827.   Peter M. Contine and Joseph Strong were added.

[7] *Ibid.*, 1050.

[8] *Jour. of Prov. Conv.*, i, 823; *cf. ibid.*, 755, ii, 442–443.

oath were to be discharged and given the "privileges of freemen." Those refusing for six days to take it were to be sent, with their families, wearing apparel and household furniture, to New York city, or to some other city held by the British. Those who refused thus to depart were to be imprisoned and treated as "open enemies of this state," and those who failed to appear before the commissioners were to be considered "as having gone over to the enemy," and their personal property was to be sold for the benefit of the state.[1]

This meant hard work for the commissioners. Money was freely granted for their purposes,[2] but the discretionary power to pardon or to dismiss prisoners placed heavy responsibilities upon their shoulders.[3] Though the Convention was disposed to be lenient,[4] yet on April 21, 1777, it ordered county and local committees to have all loyalists seized.[5] On May 9th, hearing that many loyalists who had joined the British had been deceived and were desirous of returning to their allegiance, the Convention decreed that all "delinquents" who should appear before any magistrate before July 1 and take the oath, should receive "a full and free pardon for all and every treasonable act."[6] A few of the "deluded" accepted the proffer,[7] probably fifty in all up to the beginning of 1778.

When the loyalists of any locality began an uprising, the Convention acted with speed and power. Early in May, 1777, came the rumor that the tories were preparing an outbreak in Dutchess and Westchester counties, on Livingston manor and at points further up the Hudson.[8] Two groups

---

[1] *Jour. of Prov. Conv.*, i, 827, 855–856.   [2] *Ibid.*, 865, 1106.

[3] *Ibid.*, 844, 889.   [4] *Ibid.*, 888.   [5] *Ibid.*, 899.   [6] *Ibid.*, 921.

[7] *Ibid*, 933, 935, 937, 939, 950, 958, 960, 965, 975, 976, 978, 991, 997, 1020, 1021, 1043, 1051, 1070, 1071, 1072, 1074, 1080, etc.

[8] *Ibid.*, 910–911, 918–919.

of three commissioners each were sent out to quell these movements, one to Rhinebeck and Livingston manor and the other to Dutchess and Westchester counties. They were empowered to call out the militia, capture or kill all loyalists found in arms, seize all other loyalists and execute all spies " in terrorem." If possible, the two groups of commissioners were to unite and assist each other.[1] This was the severest action yet taken.[2] When, somewhat later, reports of uprisings in Albany, Tryon, Charlotte, Cumberland, Gloucester, Ulster and Orange counties reached the Convention, even the county committees were instructed to call out the militia and to destroy all who were found in arms against the state.

To hold the large number of loyalist prisoners a well-guarded " fleet-prison " was established on the Hudson. In all parts of the state they were ordered to be arrested and sent to this prison at their own expense.[3] The commissioners on conspiracies were ordered to have all loyalists who were confined in New England jails also sent to the " fleet-prison."[4] A warden, " victualler," commissary and clerk for the prison were appointed to look after them.[5] The loyalists who escaped were to be charged with " felony," and, if proved guilty by the commissioners and a jury, executed at once.[6] Others were to be tried and discharged if found innocent.[7] When the British captured the forts in the Highlands, the prisoners were ordered to be sent to Hartford, Connecticut.[8] On January 2, 1778, they were ordered to be brought back by the commissioners, examined, pardoned if found innocent, or, if found guilty, imprisoned in New York jails.[9]

[1] *Jour. of Prov. Conv.*, i, 909, 910, 911.   [2] *Ibid.*, 912.

[3] *Ibid.*, 908, 927, 967, 988, 991, 1034, 1036.

[4] *Ibid.*, 968.   [5] *Ibid.*, 973–974; *cf. ibid.*, 920.

[6] *Ibid.*, 908.   [7] *Ibid.*, 1054, 1067, Sept. and Oct., 1777.

[8] *Ibid.*, 1063–1064, 1105.   [9] *Ibid.*. 1106.

Shortly after the issue of the Declaration of Independence the Convention, as has been shown, had defined treason and affixed to it the penalty of death.   But as yet there were no courts to try suspected traitors, and it was not deemed wise to entrust such duties to committees.   For this reason many who were suspected or accused of treason "escaped with impunity."   To meet the emergency the Convention resolved, March 31, 1777, that all suspected traitors should be tried "by martial law," and, "if found guilty, should suffer death or other punishment at the discretion of a general court-martial of the continental army," provided, however, that no sentence should be executed till approved by the legislature.[1]

Trials by court-martial soon began.[2]   The Convention, on April 18, 1777, ordered that loyalists in Albany, Orange, Dutchess and Ulster counties should be tried in this manner, and instructed the county committees to furnish evidence.[3] On April 29 the Convention approved three death sentences against loyalist spies, but later commuted one[4]   On May 3 a court-martial sentenced fourteen to death, one to imprisonment during the war and acquitted five.   Of the fourteen the Convention ordered General George Clinton to execute all but two.[5]   When commissioners were sent out to suppress loyalist outbreaks the Convention ordered court-martials to be organized on the spot, as in Albany county and on Livingston manor.[6]   Of seventeen loyalists tried thus at Fort Montgomery, all were released by the Convention but two.[7]   By order of May 12 authority was given to the council of safety or to the governor to pardon loyalists who were under the death sentence.[8]   Executions at the hands of

[1] *Jour. of Prov. Conv.*, i, 856–857, 859; *cf. ibid.*, 898.   [2] *Ibid.*, 884.
[3] *Ibid.*, 889.   [4] *Ibid.*, 904–905.   [5] *Ibid.*, 908–909.
[6] *Ibid.*, 919.   [7] *Ibid.*, 922–926, 929.   [8] *Ibid.*, 928.

courts-martial continued,[1] recantations and pardons, however, being frequent. Imprisonment, branding on the hand,
and fines ranging from $15 to $100 or more were common
forms of punishment, and they were usually approved by
the legislative power.[2]

On May 29, 1777, John Jay reported a plan for the establishment of "courts of oyer and terminer and general jail
delivery," for the trial of cases of treason, insurrection, unlawful congregations, false allegiance, riots and other crimes.[3]
"To awe the disaffected," on September 1, such a court was
ordered held in Tryon county.[4] But the prevailing method
of trying loyalists charged with treason continued to be by
court martial.

Meanwhile the commissioners on loyalists were continually busy. They moved from place to place,[5] and with
their armed forces [6] were occupied in discovering and arresting domestic enemies. Cases of treason were turned over
to courts martial, but those who were guilty of less heinous
offenses were tried, released, imprisoned, fined, forced to
give parole or bond, or compelled to take the oath of allegiance. Since many took the oath of allegiance only to
avoid punishment, and still remained hostile at heart,
the council of safety resolved that those guilty of violating
the oath be "deemed guilty of felony without benefit of
clergy."[7] It was also decided to permit deserters from the

---

[1] *Jour. of Prov. Conv.* i, 969–970, 971–972, 974, 983.

[2] *Ibid.*, 971–972. Other proofs of the death penalty are found in *Revolutionary
Reminiscences*, 131–135, 199; *Jour. of Prov. Conv.*, i, 910, 912, 1085–1086; Jones,
Hist. of N. Y., i, 61, note 1; Dawson, *Westchester Co.*, 165, note 1; Thatcher
Mil. Jour., 79, 99, 409; Greenleaf, *Laws of N. Y.*, i, 26–38; *Public Papers of
George Clinton*, i, 391, 580, 584.

[3] *Jour. of Prov. Conv.*, i, 922–926, 929.

[4] *Jour. of Prov. Cong.*, i, 1053.   [5] *Ibid.*, 1030, 1034.

[6] *Ibid.*, 872, 1030, 1045.   [7] *Ibid.*, 1040.

British to take the oath,[1] but since, in spite of promises of
of pardon, many of the loyalists clung to the British, and
their families were only a burden to the state, every district
committee was empowered to send the " families of traitors
and rebels, with provisions, wearing apparel and bedding, to
them."[2]   Some individual loyalists were treated in like
manner.[3]

It was felt to be especially necessary to suppress domestic
foes before coping with Burgoyne, who was coming down from
the north.   From every side loyalists were joining him.   Believing that many could be reclaimed, the commander of the
northern army was authorized to pardon all who surrendered
and took an oath of allegiance before October 1, 1777.[4]
This was looked upon as a wise, humane act, but comparatively few loyalists gave heed to the call.

The first month of 1778 saw an effort made for the appointment of a third " committee for detecting and defeating
conspiracies,"[5] but it was not until April 3, 1778, that it was
actually created.[6]   The powers of the committee were renewed
from time to time until August 30, 1781.[7]   This board was
larger, and it was in existence longer, than either of the two
former ones.[8]   It met for the first time April 13, and began
work at once.   By this time methods of procedure and
forms of punishment had been well established by precedent or law.   As formerly, a company of rangers was em-

---

[1] *Jour. of Prov. Cong.*, i, 1050.   [2] *Ibid.*. 1078.

[3] *Ibid.*, 1093.   [4] *Ibid.*, 1040; *cf. ibid.*, 1005, 1006–1011.

[5] *Votes and Proceedings of the Assembly*, i, 38, 39, 41, 45.

[6] *Jour. of Assemb.*, i, 106, 107.

[7] *Ibid.*, ii, 21, 24. 25, 27, 28, 51, 53, iii, 22, 29, 30, 33, 36, 41, 47, 117.   *Cf.
Laws of N. Y.*, i, 257. MS. *Min. of Comsrs.*, ii, 89–90, and June 30, 1780 (no
page).

[8] *Ibid.*, i., 1.   John McClung, James W. Master, Cornelius Humphrey, William Willis, P. N. Wynkoop, Samuel Stringer, Jeremiah Rensselaer, Matthew
Vescher, Isaac D. Fonda, John M. Beekman, Hugh Mitchell and Stewart Dean.

ployed to assist in its work.[1] Money was supplied by the state.[2] A clerk was appointed and correspondence was carried on constantly with the other committees throughout the state, with the legislature and with the governor.[3] This committee took cognizance of robberies,[4] counterfeiting[5] and murder,[6] as well as of toryism ; it acted under all the laws which applied to former committees, and enjoyed all their privileges. Most of the sessions of this body were held at Albany. Beginning in 1778, the legislature passed a series of acts regulating the treatment of loyalists.[7]

The first work of the committee was to try the prisoners in the various county jails. The district committees were asked to furnish evidence against them, and the committees of Tryon and Charlotte counties were invited to meet with the general committee. Altogether over a thousand loyalists were tried and sentenced during the three years' existence of this board of commissioners. The charges against them ranged from mere suspicion to the gravest treason. In a single month, April, 1778, one hundred and fifty-five cases were heard—most of the parties being accused of having been with the British. The penalties were far from uniform ; over six hundred were released on bail, varying from £40 to

---

[1] MS. *Min. of Comsrs.*, i, 35, 106.

[2] *Ibid.*, i, 1, 50, ii, 89–90. *The State Treasurer's Book* shows that £55,789 was paid to these committees from 1777 to 1781—£6,857 in 1777, £28,430 in 1778, £9,946 in 1779, and £10,556 in 1781,—or about $139,500.

[3] *Ibid.*, i, 27.

[4] *Ibid.*, 74, 77, 78, 90, 95, etc.   [5] *Ibid.*, 223, 224.

[6] *Ibid.*, 71, 74. The legislature even ordered the committee to care for the poor, and to send the families of tories who were with the British to join them. *Ibid.*, 282.

[7] *Jour. of Assemb.*, I, 90, 92, etc. Greenleaf, *Laws of N. Y.*, i, 17, 22, 26, etc. On October 27, 1778, the Assembly passed an act which offered rewards varying from $300 to $1,200 each for the arrest of fourteen dangerous loyalists. *Jour. of Assemb.*, ii, 26.

£5,000;[1] some were closely confined;[2] a few were freed on promise of good behavior; and many were dismissed upon taking an oath of allegiance.[3]

After July, 1778, the oath of allegiance was made the supreme test. Many loyalists stubbornly refused to take it— about forty in July of 1779 alone. Most of them were former royal officers, lawyers, physicians and merchants.[4] If violent and abusive, they were put in close confinement; if moderate, they were sent to the British.[5] Rather than leave their homes, not a few recanted.[6] Some of the obnoxious, who had bad records behind them, were not permitted to take the oath, even though they petitioned for it.[7] These professed loyalists were used also to effect exchanges.[8] It was not uncommon for the neighbors of a loyalist to petition that he might be paroled instead of banished.[9] As late as 1782 the loyalists renounced allegiance to king George III and pledged their faith to the state of New York. Since the committee was not then in session,[10] the oaths were taken in

---

[1] In 1778 six were released on £40 bail, twenty on £50, one hundred and three on £100, eighteen on £200, one on £250, nine on £500, and one on £1000. In 1779 two were put on £50 bail, thirty-six on £100, two on £150, twenty-five on £200, one on £400, one on £300, sixteen on £500, one on £600, four on £1000, and three on £5000. In 1780 one hundred and fifty were forced to secure £100 bail, thirty-one £200, one £400, sixteen £500, and three £1000.

[2] In 1778 about seventy-five were imprisoned, the next year the number sent to jail was nearly eighty, and in 1780 perhaps fifty were committed to close confinement.

[3] In 1778 sixty-two were released upon taking the oath of allegiance. The number in 1779 was only about forty, and in 1780 about fifty. MS. *Min. of Comsrs.*, i, 240, has a copy of an oath signed by twenty loyalists. On page 242 there is another oath signed by sixteen.

[4] MS. *Min. of Comsrs.*, i, 108. See list given there.

[5] *Ibid.*, 108, 117, 122, 123, 124.   [6] *Ibid.*, 122.   [7] *Ibid.*, 127, 128.

[8] *Ibid.*, 158, 172, 176; Greenleaf, *Laws of N. Y.*, i, 43.

[9] MS. *Min. of Comsrs.*, i, 210–211.

[10] The commissioners were authorized to act till the war was over, but the war really closed in 1781.

the presence of a justice of the peace.[1]   As the war drew to
a close and it became apparent that the colonies would gain
their independence, many a loyalist, whose natural conservatism, principles of loyalism, religion, material interests or
hope of reward had led him to champion the royal side, was
converted to the American cause.   No doubt many of these
changes were sincere, but others were prompted solely by
base and selfish motives.[2]

The Declaration of Independence of itself made no change
in the county committees save to increase their power,[3] and
after the organization of the state government they were still
continued. They were uniform in authority and procedure, but
in nothing else. They often acted as county governments,
while they continued to be vital parts of the inquisitorial
machine. In organization they remained about the same
as in 1775 and 1776. They had their presidents, clerks,
doorkeepers, treasurers, and could control the militia.
They received instructions from the legislature, convention, committee or council of safety, or commissioners on
loyalists.[4] In turn they gave orders to local bodies. Both
county and district committees were elected by the people,
but in case they neglected to choose them, superior bodies
were ordered to appoint them.[5] The expenses of these committees were paid by the state.[6] Sub-committees were appointed for special work, like carrying on correspondence.[7]
Until the first committee was appointed, in September, 1776, to

---

[1] MS. *Min. of Comsrs.*, i, 240.

[2] *Cf. Rivington's Royal Gazette*, July 7, 1779, which has a "hit" on loyalists
who changed from one side to the other.

[3] *Proceedings of Alb. Co. Com.*, i, 462–466.

[4] *Cf. Am. Archs.*, 5th ser., i, 1413, 1539, ii, 339.

[5] *Jour. of Prov. Conv.*, i, 1096.

[6] *Am. Archs.*, 4th ser., 1458–1459, 5th ser., i, 1413.

[7] *Cf. Proceedings of Alb. Co. Com.*, i, 17.

have general charge of the loyalists, the county committees were kept unusually busy. When in doubt about what course to pursue, the superior bodies were consulted,[1] and these could always veto the acts of the local boards.[2] In fact, the county committees had power only to arrest loyalists and institute preliminary hearings.

In the five southern counties the committees disappeared with the British occupation, and were never revived. In the northern counties they continued after July 4, 1776, but were overshadowed by the various state boards of commissioners. When an efficient civil government, both state and local, was established, the county committees gradually disappeared. The records of their proceedings after the close of 1776 are very meagre. The Albany county committee, however, was kept rather busy in counteracting the "desperate designs" and the "tory plots" which were being unearthed continually.[3] The jails were full, and many loyalists were sent to Connecticut.[4] So overworked was this committee that the special committee sent to help General Schuyler was ordered to co-operate with it in suppressing the "disaffected."[5] Troops had to be used to quell them.[6] It was reported in 1777 that the loyalists took a sacred oath to remain neutral till the British arrived. Many were "wavering in their principles." On Livingston manor they outnumbered the whigs three to one.[7] Coxsackie, Cattskill, Lunenberg, Groetenboght, Kings and Helleberg districts were especially

---

[1] *Jour. of Prov. Conv.*, i, 890–891, ii, 497: *Am. Archs.*, 5th ser., i, 1146, 1408, 1484, 1523.

[2] *Ibid.*, 1453, 1472–1473.

[3] *Jour. of Prov. Conv.*, i, 666, 671, 694; *Am. Archs.*, 5th ser., i, 338, 357, 500, 888, ii, 1143, 1169, 1206.

[4] *Ibid.*, i, 888, 889.

[5] *Ibid.*, iii, 231, 266; *Jour. of Prov. Conv.*, i, 671, 688, 694.

[6] *Ibid.*, 666, 671, 706.

[7] *Am. Archs.*, 5th ser., iii, 231, 266; *Jour. of Prov. Conv.*, i. 671, 706.

disaffected.[1] The slaves could not be trusted and the Indians were feared.[2] Parties were joining the British all the time.[3] The people were afraid to molest them.[4] The county chairman complained that it was better to be a tory than a whig, since tories were treated so leniently.[5]

The committees in Charlotte and Cumberland counties were not very active. In the former county there were loyalists on Onion river, at Skeenesborough and about Crown Point, but little more was done than to proclaim them as public enemies.[6] The few cases tried in the latter county were by jury, with appeals to neighboring or higher bodies.[7] The tories in Dutchess county, the hot-bed of " dangerous insurrection," disarmed the whigs and awed the committee. That body told the Convention that it would take a standing army to enforce the acts of Congress.[8] Cortland manor was very disaffected; the county militia could not be trusted, whig officers feared for their lives, drafting was impossible, and New Hampshire and Connecticut troops had to be called in.[9] The inactivity of the district and county committees in Dutchess county was severely denounced.[10]

Orange county continued under General Heath. Some loyalist officers fled to the British, others were publicly exposed, and a few were sent to the committee of safety.[11]

---

[1] *Jour. of Prov. Conv.*, i, 694-695, 706, 707.

[2] *Am. Archs.*, 5th ser., iii, 266, 574–575.

[3] *Ibid.*, 586.   [4] *Ibid.*, 1076.

[5] *Ibid.*, 574-575; *Jour. of Prov. Conv.*, i, 890–891.

[6] *Am. Archs.*, 5th ser., i, 128, 239, 358, 488.

[7] *Ibid.*, ii, 216–219.   [8] *Ibid.*, i, 1408, 1413.

[9] *Ibid.*, 1404, 1408, ii, 1026, iii, 205, 238, 239; *Jour. of Prov. Conv.*, i, 654, 666, 757, 758, 766; MS. *Revolutionary Papers*, vi, 359.

[10] *Am. Archs.*, 5th ser., ii, 352.

[11] *Jour. of Prov. Conv.*, i, 648, 667, 688, 719; *Am. Archs.*, 5th ser., iii, 1169; *Cal. N. Y. Hist. MSS.*, i, 351; Moore, *Diary of Am. Rev.*, i, 290.

The committee of Tryon county had a hard role to play. It permitted some tories to return and treated others leniently, though they were constantly guarded.[1] Ulster county was comparatively free from loyalists. The Claverack committee, however, petitioned the Convention in 1777 for a company of rangers "to quell the disaffected."[2] The committee in Westchester county was constantly occupied.[3] The people were badly disaffected and the harshest measures were taken to render them harmless.[4]

Thus it appears that after 1776 the local committees, though still in existence in the counties not held by the British and occupied by them until the war closed, gradually waned in their powers and activity. They were the most effective as factors in dealing with loyalism when centralized power was weak, when laws and precedents remained to be made, and when loyalists were rendered harmless only through the activity of local patriotic sentiment as expressed in an organized committee. But as a strong state government was formed and laws were passed to deal with the tories, and general committees were created to enforce the laws, the powers of the local committees were gradually absorbed by the superior bodies. With the full establishment of civil government and the opening of courts, both state and local committees disappear.

[1] *Am. Archs.*, 5th ser., i, 132, ii, 247, 249, iii, 228–229, 526; *Jour. of Prov. Conv.*, i, 663.

[2] *Ibid.*, 898; *Am. Archs.*, 5th ser., i, 125, 791, 1079, 1113, 1146, 1404, 1405, 1518, ii, 688, iii, 1046.

[3] *Ibid.*, i, 354, 855, 1411, 1412, 1443, 1444, 1447, 1448, 1454, 1456, 1523, 1526, ii, 597–599, 683, 1523, 1526.

[4] *Am. Archs.*, 5th ser., i, 337, 355, 626, 1030, 1556, ii, 258, 310, 373, 384, 597–599, 829, 841, 845, 854, 963; *Jour. of Prov. Conv.*, i, 670, 766–767.

CHAPTER VII

CONFISCATION AND SALE OF THE PROPERTY OF LOYALISTS

THE idea of confiscating the property of the loyalists was a growth. It developed with the conviction that they were traitors, and was intended to be both a retribution and a punishment. It was a blow at individuals rather than at a cause or a party. Aside from the wanton fury of mobs, there was at first a decided effort made to preserve loyalist property. When the Provincial Congress ordered loyalists to be disarmed, great care was taken to have the arms appraised and marked, so that they, or their value, could be returned at the close of the war.[1] Washington caused the dangerous tories on Long Island to be removed, but took pains to preserve their property.[2] When the Albany county committee authorized the arrest of Sir John Johnson, instructions were given to seize all military stores, but not to injure his property. Even his papers were not to be molested.[3] But after his flight, Colonel Dayton, acting on his own responsibility, sacked Johnson Hall and appropriated " his cattle, his negroes, his horses, hogs, sheep and utensils of husbandry." [4] In the Continental Congress a resolution to retaliate so far as possible for the seizure of American vessels by confiscations was tabled.[5] But as time passed the

---

[1] *Min. of Prov. Cong.*, iii, 73-76, Sept. 16, 1775; *Am. Archs.*, 4th ser., v, 1638, 1646, iv, 1628-1629.

[2] *Ibid.*, 5th ser., i, 1501, August 12, 1775; *cf. ibid.*, 4th ser., v, 1696.

[3] *Ibid.*, vi, 642.   [4] Jones, *Hist. of N. Y.*, i, 76.

[5] *Am. Archs.*, 4th ser., v, 1696.

policy adopted in this matter became more severe, until all the property of loyalists, personal and real, was confiscated and sold for the benefit of the state.

In the confiscation of property England herself set the example. In 1775 parliament ordered all American ships and cargoes on the high seas to be seized and confiscated.[1] Upon the arrival of Howe at New York in 1776 confiscations were made on Staten Island,[2] Long Island[3] and Manhattan Island.[4] Again and again the loyalists were promised the estates of their rebellious brothers after the war was over.[5] At first only movable property was taken, but later real estate as well.[6] These acts, together with the boastings and threats of the loyalists, gave the revolutionists ample occasion, if not justification, for their conduct.

The first act implying confiscation in New York was passed August 3, 1775. It provided that those who supplied the British should be disarmed and pay double the value of the supplies. A denial of the authority of any revolutionary body should entail the loss of arms. Those who enlisted or armed themselves " against the liberties of America," should be " confined in safe custody," and both their real and personal property should be turned over to a person appointed by the nearest committee to be held in trust.[7] Many arms were thus confiscated from the loyalists and properly recorded.[8] This act was taken as authority for more sweep-

[1] *Am. Archs.*, 4th ser., v, 843. 16 Geo. III, c. 5. *Cf. ibid.*, 1696.

[2] *Ibid.*, 5th ser., ii, 325.   [3] *Ibid.*, 325, 506.

[4] *Docs. rel. to N. Y. Col. Hist.*, viii, 692.

[5] *Ibid.*, 680; *Am. Archs.*, 4th ser., v, 1473, vi, 1032, 5th ser., i, 1237.

[6] *Docs. rel. to N. Y. Col. Hist.*, viii, 692; *Am. Archs.*, 5th ser., ii, 325; *cf. Memoirs of L. I. Hist. Soc.*, iii, 96, appendix.

[7] *Min. of Prov. Cong.*, ii, 314-319.

[8] *Ibid.*, iii, 113-114, 116-117. New York anticipated the Continental Congress by five months in this procedure. *Almon's Remembrancer*, i, 221-223. In New York city 58 loyalists were deprived of guns, pistols, cutlasses, swords and ammunition appraised at £203 in 1775. *Cal. of N. Y. Hist. MSS.*, i, 259-261.

ing confiscations, where the exigencies of the case seemed to demand it.   To make good the bonds of escaped tories, their estates were seized.[1]   In Albany county loyalists' property was sold to pay for the military service they should have rendered.[2]   The Provincial Congress ordered two sloops on the Hudson, used by the "disaffected," to be captured. Dobb's sloop was burned, and Berg's sloop was sold at vendue for the benefit of Congress.[3]   The New York committee proposed to declare all goods imported in violation of the association to be forfeited.[4]   In August, 1776, the Convention used the houses of the chief loyalists in New York city as hospitals.[5]   Such were the early examples of the appropriation and confiscation of loyalist property.

Treason was defined by the resolutions of the Continental Congress of June 24, 1776,[6] while at the same time it was declared that all the property of those who adhered to the king or abetted him in his unjust war against the states should be liable to seizure.[7]   These resolutions were supplemented some weeks later by the acts of the New York Convention, explaining allegiance, citizenship and treason.   The status of the loyalists having been clearly defined, and all doubts about the political issues removed, New York was soon ready to take the necessary legal steps to supplement the inquisitorial

[1] Dawson, *Westchester Co.*, 174–177.

[2] *Min. of Alb. Com. Co.*, i, 389.

[3] *Am. Archs.*, 4th ser., iii, 569, 900, 907, 908, 910, 1016, 1267, 1300, 1303.

[4] *Ibid.*, iv, 692. As early as July 11, 1775, the New York committee named a sub-committee of six to attend to " the sale of two bales and two trunks of goods, the property of Benjamin Booth, imported in the ship Lady Gage . . . from London in Dec. last; also to attend the sale of boxes and goods, the property of Grey and Blakie." *Am. Archs.*, 4th ser., ii, 1645.

[5] *Ibid.*, 5th ser,, ii, 1499.

[6] *Am. Archs.*, 4th ser., vi, 1431, 1720; *cf. Gaine's N. Y. Gazette and Weekly Mercury.* no. 1293, for a discussion of " Citizenship."

[7] *Am. Archs.*, 5th ser., i, 1590, resolution of July 24, 1776.

program by sequestrating, confiscating and selling their property in a systematic manner for the benefit of the state.

Subsequent to July 4, 1776, confiscations became more numerous. This was work which fell naturally to the local committees. In Orange county large stores of household goods and other articles, also horses and oxen, belonging to William Bayard and other disaffected persons, were seized.[2] A list of the estates of the tories was made out in Albany county.[3] In Westchester county the farms, stock, tools, crops and furniture of loyalists were seized and sold before December 6, 1776.[4] In Orange county, and no doubt elsewhere, commissioners were appointed to secure the " perishable effects " of absconded tories.[5] When Colonel Hitchcock took a loyalist's horse, the committee of safety ordered him to keep it until the legislature took action respecting such property.[6] When Thomas Barclay joined the British, the same committee caused his hay, forage, stock and grain, except so much as was necessary to support his family and slaves, to be seized; but it was appraised, sold and the value deposited in the state treasury until more definite action should be taken.[7]

These cases became so numerous that it was felt that some additional administrative regulation was necessary to cover them, hence a committee was named to report an "ordinance for securing all estates and effects" of absconded tories.[8]

---

[1] *Am. Archs.*, 5th ser., i, 1403, 1410.

[2] *Jour. of Prov. Conv.*, i, 679; *Am. Archs.*, 5th ser., iii, 347.

[3] *Ibid.*, 364.

[4] *Ibid.*, 364; Dawson, *Westchester Co.*, 120; *Hist. MSS. Miscl. Papers*, xxxv, 397.

[5] *Am. Archs.*, 5th ser., iii, 1248. General Arnold also seized the effects of tories at Montreal. *Ibid.*, 4th ser., vi, 976.

[6] *Jour. of Prov. Conv.*, i, 679.   [7] *Ibid.*, 720–721.

[8] *Ibid.*, 730, 731–733, 755; *Am. Archs.*, 5th ser., iii, 347.

Meanwhile the " commissioners on conspiracies " were ordered
to seize the effects, money and crops of loyalists who broke
their paroles.[1] The ordinance, as reported by the committee,
on February 22, 1777, and adopted, provided that six commissioners should be ordered to sell the personal property of
loyalists who had gone to the British and to keep the money
till orders were received from the state legislature.[2] Local
committees were instructed to prepare lists of such property.[3]

Finally, on March 6, 1777, the Convention took decisive
action. Three paid commissioners of sequestration, who were
continued in service for seven years, were appointed for each
of the counties except those in control of the British, and
excepting also Gloucester and Cumberland counties.[4] They
took an oath to perform their duties honestly, fearlessly and
impartially. Two constituted a quorum. They were authorized to seize all the personal property of those who
joined the British, and after ten days' notice sell it at public
vendue. The entire proceeds were to go into the state
treasury, and their expenses were to be paid by the state.
The families of loyalists were allowed to retain their wearing
apparel, the necessary household furniture, and provisions
for three months. The purpose of this measure was, by
using such property for the advantage of the new state, to
prevent it from going to waste or serving as supplies for the
enemy.[5]

These committees began their work at once. To make
their work more effectual the act of March 6 was soon supplemented by others. The Albany county commissioners
resigned, and the Convention appointed ten commissioners
to replace them.[6] When the committee of Claverack district in

---

[1] *Jour. of Prov. Conv.*, i, 760, 769, 777–778, 804, 810.

[2] *Ibid.*, 811.   [3] *Ibid.* 821, 827.

[4] The committees for these two counties were appointed later. *Ibid.*, 861, 907.

[5] *Ibid.*, 826.   [6] *Ibid.*, 956, 967, May 30, 1777.

Renslaerwyck complained that the county commissioners had not done their duty, the council of safety ordered it to act in their stead and with like powers.[1]   A new commission of two members was created for Orange county, north of the mountains.[2]   The Convention filled vacancies again and again.   The commissioners received orders from the Convention and the legislature to appropriate the property of certain loyalists,[3] to lease all lands yearly at moderate rates, giving the homeless whigs the preference;[4] to sell all personal property,[5] to administer oaths to witnesses and punish them for contempt;[6] to send all gold and silver to the state treasurer,[7] to pass on the validity of sales made by loyalists before their flight,[8] to suppress frauds,[9] and " to enter any houses and places wherein they shall have reason to suspect any of the goods, chattels and effects are concealed, and to break open any building or dig up any soil " to secure them.[10]   The estates of traitors who had been executed were also put under their jurisdiction.   No private sales were allowed.[11]   Suspecting that the commissioners were not doing their duty or were over-zealous, the legislature appointed a committee of six in 1779 to inquire into the conduct of the commissioners of Albany, Charlotte, Tryon, Dutchess, Ulster, Orange and Westchester counties.[12]   So severe were the commissioners in Westchester county that even General Putnam complained

---

[1] *Jour. of Prov. Conv.*, i, 1079.   [2] *Ibid.*, 1112, Jan. 8, 1778.

[3] MS. *Assembly Papers, Forfeited Estates*, vol. 25, p. 5-7; *Jour. of Prov. Conv.*, i, 826, 1052.

[4] *Ibid.*, 856, 883, 899, 930. April 17, 1780, John Younglove and George Palmer reported 26 loyalist farms rented at a total income of £551, and 11 farms for £638 in 1779. MS. *Audited Accounts A*, in Surveyor General's Office.

[5] *Jour. of Prov. Conv.*, i, 872.   [6] *Ibid.*, 1056, Nov. 10, 1777.

[7] *Ibid.*, 1090, 1112.   [8] *Ibid.*, 930.   [9] *Ibid.*. 930.   [10] *Ibid.*, 1092.

[11] *Jour. of N. Y. Assemb.* (1777), 87, 92, 93, 99.

[12] *Ibid.*, iii, 19, 40, 71, 79.

of their conduct.[1]   These commissioners were kept busy until after the war closed, and in order to hasten their work, the state gave them a bonus of ten per cent. on all sales made after March 11, 1784.[2]

The most complete minutes of the sales now accessible are for Dutchess county, and will serve as a sample of what was done in all the counties.   The commissioners for that county sold the personal estate of Beverly Robinson on April 21, 1777.   It consisted of live stock, farm implements, household articles, barn and cellar fixtures, grain, fruits, hay, clothing, books and numerous other articles, which were sold for £680.[3]   Further confiscations and sales followed.   At Fredericksburg the personal effects of twenty-six loyalists sold for £1,637.   In Paulding's precinct £2,133 was realized from the property of twenty loyalists.   In Southeast precinct the property of eighteen loyalists brought £800.   In Rumbout precinct the personal estates of thirty-four loyalists were disposed of for £2,985.   The personal effects of fourteen Poughkeepsie loyalists brought £1,630, and £4,906 was secured from thirty-six loyalists in Charlotte precinct.   In Rhinebeck precinct £3,762 was raised from the personal possessions of forty-two loyalists, while Beekman's precinct returned £1,017 from the belongings of nine loyalists, and Northeast precinct reported £15,144 from sixty-seven loyalists.   Between 1777 and 1780 the sum of £24,694 was realized from the sale of the personal property of 262 loyalists in the county.[4]   By November 22, 1781, this

[1] *Jour. of Prov. Conv.*, i, 1031, Aug. 15, 1777.

[2] *Laws of N. Y.*, i, 232.

[3] MS. *The Personal Estate of Beverly Robinson*, etc., of 116 pages, in the library of N. Y. State.   The book seems to have been larger, because there are references to page 119.

[4] The MS. *The Personal Estate of Beverly Robinson*, etc., has in it all the names of the loyalists whose estates were confiscated, and an itemized account of the sales.

amount had increased to £75,352,[1] and by May, 1783, the total of £99,771 had been paid to the state treasurer from Dutchess county.[2]

This record was repeated in most of the other counties. From June 30, 1777, to July, 1781, the commissioners for Ulster county collected £32,082.[3] Tryon county raised £27,815 between August 31, 1777, and July, 1781.[4] The sales in Westchester county during the period from July 1, 1777, till May, 1784, amounted to £43,880.[5] The sum of £18,494 was realized in Albany county between March 14, 1778, and May, 1782.[6] Only £360 was turned into the treasury between August 29, 1778, and February, 1779, from Charlotte county.[7] The Orange county commissioners sold personal property to the value of £38,193 between Septem-30, 1778, and March, 1783.[8] The personal possessions sequestrated and sold in seven counties brought to the state treasury £260,595.

Of sales of personal property there are no returns before 1783 from the strongholds of loyalism, New York city, Long Island and Staten Island, for the very sufficient reason that these places were till that time in the possession of the British. After the treaty of peace and the evacuation of these regions, the zeal for discovering and selling this class of property had abated. Loyalists who chose to remain under the new order of things were not molested, while most of those who emigrated either removed or sold their personal effects. It seems, however, from petitions which were sent to England asking for compensation for losses, that after the evacuation

---

[1] MS. *State Treasurer's Book*, 1775–1796, p. 77.

[2] *Ledger from 1775 to 1793*. in State Comptroller's office, p. 106, 199.

[3] *Ibid.*, 106.   [4] *Ibid.*, 107.   [5] *Ibid.*, 107, 172.

[6] *Old Ledger* of State Treasurer from 1775 to 1793, in comptroller's office, 131, 136.

[7] *Ibid.*, 150.   [8] *Ibid.*, 146; *cf. State Treasurer's Book* for 1775–1796.

of southern New York some of the loyalists did lose their
personal property.[1]   The report made to the English commissioners on loyalists' claims by E. Hardy, the agent sent
to New York, March 5, 1784, gave the names of fourteen
loyalists from New York city who requested compensation
for an aggregate loss in personal property of £15,006.[2]   No
doubt loyalists on Long Island and Staten Island suffered
similar losses.[3]   Using these known figures as the basis
for a conservative estimate of the total amount of money
realized by the state from the sale of this class of property, it can be safely said that the sum was £300,000.   The
loss to the loyalists, however, would at least approximate
£600,000.[4]

It is very difficult to convert these sums into hard
money, because of the great fluctuations in the value of currency.   When the sales began in 1777 bills of credit could
be exchanged easily for specie at a small premium,[5] but by
March 15, 1780, the ratio between paper money and coin

---

[1] William Axtell had his home and furniture on Broadway sold.   Sabine, 198.
The personal property of Andrew Elliott in Bowery Lane was sold at auction Sept.
1783.   *Ibid.*, 404.   In this same year the furniture of John Tabor Kempe was
sold in New York city.   *Ibid.*, 601.

[2] MS. *Transcript of . . the Books and Papers of . . . the American Loyalists*,
vol. I, 369–371.   James Houghston, Uriah Wright, Tertullus Dickinson, Thomas
Spragg, Samuel Dickinson, Joshua Curry, Nathan Whitney, James Dickinson,
Jesse Sturges, Ezekiel Welton, Robert Thorne, Jesse Powell, Simon La Roy and
Joshua Gidney.

[3] Jesse Oaks, of Suffolk co., reported a loss of $1,485, and Capt. Samuel Hallett,
of Hallett's Cove, estimated his loss at $10,730.

[4] This estimate is based on the fact that the loyalists' claims for losses were
about double the amounts for which their property sold.

[5] At the outbreak of the revolution $6 in specie was worth only $7.50 in bills.
This ratio lasted until the fall of 1777.   Hart, *Hist. of Paper Money in Am. Cols.;*
Gouge, *Paper Money and Banking in the U. S.*, 26.   From 1775 to 1781 New
York issued £464,000 in paper money, but most of it was successfully redeemed
by taxation.

was 40 to 1.[1]   After 1781, however, efforts were made to
have payments for forfeited property made in gold or silver,
or the equivalent in currency.[2]   The monetary standard
used by New York in issuing bills of credit was the Spanish
silver dollar.[3]   Since a pound in currency was equal to
$2.50, the sums given above can easily be reduced to dol-
lars.[4]   By assuming that the sales made in 1777 and those
made after 1781 were for specie, or its equivalent in currency,
the amount of standard money realized from these sales was
nearly $222,000.[5]   Taking the legal rate of exchange of
June, 1778, which was 2.6 to 1, as an average for the year,
the sales of that year amounted to $56,350 in Spanish silver.
In June, 1779, the ratio was 13 to 1, and, by using that as
the average for the year, the state received but $2,060 in
hard money.   The ratio for 1780 and 1781 was about 40 to
1, and would reduce the $315,000, which was received for
loyalist property, to a little less than $8,000.   The total in-
come from the sale of confiscated personal effects, reduced
to Spanish silver dollars, would be almost $390,000.[6]   This

[1] The scale of the depreciation of paper money was fixed by law in New York.
Laws of N. Y., i, 261, 377, 328; Hickcox, *N. Y. Bills of Credit*, 98; Phillips,
Hist. Acct. of Paper Cur., i, 33.

[2] *Laws of N. Y.*, i, 378.

[3] The Spanish silver dollar had in it in 1772 417 grains. Chalmers, *Hist.
of Cur. in the Br. Cols.*, 392.

[4] At this ratio the total amount realized, for instance, from the sale of sequestrated personal property in Dutchess county, would be nearly $250,000, while the
total loss in the state, from the loyalists' standpoint, would be about $1,500,000.

[5] From Tryon, Ulster, Dutchess and Westchester counties £27,457 was received
in 1777, and from Westchester, Albany, Orange and Dutchess counties £61,338
after 1781.

[6] Since coin became very plentiful in the colonies after 1780, according to
Phillips, *Hist. Account of Paper Currency*, ii, 173, it is possible that some of the
property which was purchased was paid for in hard money.   In that case this sum
should be increased.   These estimates are based upon the supposition that the payments were all made in depreciated currency.   Prices of the time indicate the low

sum was turned into the treasury of the state and used to meet the expenses of war. If translated into bullion values of the present day these figures would not be changed very materially.[1]

Although efforts were made after 1781 to have all business in the state transacted on a specie basis, it was not until the Act of May 12, 1784, was passed that the relative value of the various kinds of money was determined. Gold and silver were to be accepted at their "legal and current values." The bills of credit of New York and the continental paper money were to be taken at the rate of one silver dollar for $120 in currency. Other special certificates and warrants were to be received on more favorable terms.[2]

The office of commissioner of sequestration, created March 6, 1777, was abolished May 12, 1784, and orders were given to the commissioners to render an account of their transactions and to turn all moneys and records over to the state. Their powers and duties then devolved on the commissioners of forfeiture. They were released from all obligations and were guaranteed protection against suits for damage.[3] So thoroughly had their work been done during the seven years of their existence that by 1784 comparatively little confiscated personal property remained to be sold.

The confiscation and sale of the personal property of loyalists was followed by a like disposition of their real estate. This course was followed partly in response to popular clamor. Between August 3, 1775 and October 22,

---

value of paper money. A pair of trousers sold for £35, a pair of boots for £17, a grindstone for £260, a cow for £164, a negro for £260, a bed for £76, a looking glass for £21, and an ox-cart for £144.

[1] *Cf.* Sumner, *The Financier and the Finances of the Am. Rev.* ii, 36; Bolles, *Finan. Hist. of U. S.*, i, 31; A pound "sterling" in this chapter does not mean British money, but simply the standard money of the colony, or $2.50.

[2] *Laws of N. Y.*, i, 740-741.   [3] Greenleaf, *Laws of N. Y.*, i, 45, 156, 159, 279.

1779, the houses and lands of pronounced loyalists were seized and held in trust by the state.[1]   The products from these estates were sold, and the rents went into the state treasury.   The question of what should finally be done with forfeited lands was raised as early as 1776.[2]   On October 15, 1778, James Jay reported in the New York assembly the need of "an act to confiscate and make sale of all real and personal estates of such inhabitants and others who have forfeited the same to the state."[3]   A bill was reported February 26, 1779, declaring "the sovereignty of the people of this state" over all such possessions.[4]   It was passed, but the council of revision declared it to be repugnant to the "plain and immutable laws of justice," because it deprived inhabitants "of their just rights" and put the possibility of the "grossest oppression" in the hands of the commissioners. They objected to the punishment of persons without trial by jury, and the indictment of absentees for high treason.   They complained that there was no provision for the return of property to the innocent, no definite instructions to the commissioners, no provision for debts due citizens of New York by the loyalists, and that even persons who were dead when the act was passed were declared guilty of high treason and a decree of confiscation was issued against their property.[5]

A new bill was then prepared and became a law, October 22, 1779.[6]   The act declared that fifty-nine persons were *ipso facto* guilty of felony; that they should be attainted and their property forfeited to the state;

[1] This was the general rule.   There were exceptions.   Dec. 10, 1776, the committee of safety ordered part of the estate of Thomas H. Barclay sold.   It was sold for £1,603 Jan. 2, 1777.   No doubt there were other cases.   MS. *Assemb. Papers, Forfeited Estates*, vol. 27, p. 35; MS. *Transcript . . of the Books and Papers of . . the American Loyalists*, vol. 17, p. 38.

[2] MS. *Revolutionary Papers*, v, 143, 211.

[3] *Jour. of Assemb.*, ii, 7, 40, 46, 58, 64, 67, 74, 78, 79, 81.

[4] *Ibid.*, 83, 85, 98.   [5] *Ibid.*, 99, 102-106.   [6] *Ibid.*, iii, 19-29, 57, 80.

if found within the state, they were to be executed. The list included two governors,[1] seven councillors,[2] two supreme court justices,[3] one attorney-general,[4] twenty-four "esquires"[5] and two of their sons,[6] one mayor of New York city,[7] two knights,[8] four gentlemen,[9] nine merchants,[10] one minister,[11] one farmer[12] and three women.[13] They were scattered over eleven counties.[14] Further, the act directed that the grand jurors of any supreme court or courts of oyer and terminer, or "general and quarter sessions of the peace," were empowered, on the oath of one credible witness that any person dead or alive was guilty of loyalism, to bring in an indictment against such person.[15] If he failed to appear after

[1] Dunmore and Tryon.

[2] John Watts, Oliver De Lancey, Hugh Wallace, Henry White, John Harris Cruger, William Axtell and Roger Morris.

[3] George Duncan Ludlow and Thomas Jones.

[4] John Tabor Kempe.

[5] William Bayard, Robert Bayard, James De Lancey of New York city, Guy Johnson, Daniel Claus, John Butler, Frederick Philipse, James De Lancey of Westchester, David Colden, Daniel Kissam, Sr., Gabriel Ludlow, Philip Skene, Benjamin Seaman, Christopher Billop, Beverly Robinson, Beverly Robinson, Jr., Malcom Morrison, Abraham C. Cuyler, Peter Dubois, Thomas H. Barclay, John Rapalje, George Muirson, Richard Floyd and Parker Wickham.

[6] Andrew P. Skeene and Frederick Philipse.

[7] David Matthews.

[8] Sir John Johnson and Sir Henry Clinton.

[9] Robert Kane, Robert Leake, Edward Jessup and Ebenezer Jessup.

[10] James Jauncey, George Folliot, Thomas White, William McAdam, Isaac Low, Miles Sherbrook, Alexander Wallace, John Weatherhead and Henry Lloyd.

[11] Charles Inglis.

[12] John Joost Herkimer.

[13] Mrs. Charles Inglis, Mrs. Susannah Robinson and Mrs. Mary Morris.

[14] Orange, Cumberland and Gloucester were omitted.

[15] The sheriff of Westchester county called loyalists indicted for high treason to appear to traverse it or have their estates confiscated, August 25, 1783. They failed to appear, and their estates were forfeited. MS. *Transcript of . . Books and Papers of . . . American Loyalists*, i, 336.

four weeks' advertising in the newspapers, he was to be declared guilty, and to forfeit all his property. Those who were pardoned, or who had taken the oath of allegiance, were not included. Such of the accused as were brought to the bar should have a fair trial. High treason in this act was interpreted to mean all it included in English law. In addition, persons in territory not in possession of the British on July 9, 1776, who voluntarily joined the enemy, or who broke paroles and went over to the British, or who were allowed to go to the British on condition of returning but who failed to observe the condition, were declared guilty of high treason. Those who lived in southern New York solely to protect their property, and did not aid the enemy, were exempt. The confiscation of property should not prevent the trial and execution of traitors. All conveyances of property by traitors after July 9, 1776, were presumed to be fraudulent. All lands and rents of the crown were likewise declared forfeited.[1]

This act of attainder was passed largely through personal spite, and in order to secure property.[2] The Dutchess county whigs, to the number of about 450, had petitioned the legislature for harsh measures.[3] The act was drawn up by John Morin Scott and James Jay. It was opposed by many persons for its manifest unfairness. Though passed in 1779, it did not go into complete effect until four years later.[4] Then it was put into force regardless of the fifth article of the treaty of peace.[5] John Watts and James De Lancey

---

[1] Greenleaf, *Laws of N. Y.*, i, 26–38; Jones, *Hist. of N. Y.*, ii, 510–523; *cf. Jour. of Assemb.*, iii, 112–114, 122, 125, 139, iv, 26, 36, 39, 47, 49, 50, 59, 61, 63, 79, 86, 88, 92, v, 25, 26.

[2] *Cf.* Jones, *Hist. of N. Y.*, i, 153, ii, 269–306.   [3] *Ibid.*, 528.

[4] *Ibid.*, 530, 538; *Senate Journal*, 115, 148, 156, 159, 166, 202, 215; *cf.* Jay, *Life of Jay*, i, 112–113.

[5] Jones, *Hist. of N. Y.*, ii, 538.

went to England in May, 1775, and there remained, while Governor Dunmore, Governor Tryon and Sir Henry Clinton had never been anything but British subjects, yet their property was declared forfeited. All the attainted were Episcopalians.

The governor was authorized by the above act to appoint " commissioners of forfeiture " for " the great districts of the state." Seven were named—two for the southern district, embracing New York city and county, Long Island and Staten Island ; one for the middle district, including the Hudson River counties ; one for the eastern district, taking in Vermont and Washington county ; and three for the western district, made up of Albany and Tryon county, and the Mohawk valley.[1] They were authorized to sell all lands and houses confiscated and forfeited, and to grant deeds which should be valid against all claims. The sales were, as a rule, public, and held after due notice in the newspapers. The commissioners might divide the estates so as to sell them better, but the sale of parcels of over 500 acres was discouraged. Sales were to be made in the counties where the lands were located, though the commissioner of the middle district was allowed to dispose of estates in New York city.[2] Buyers were protected in every way and tenants were always given preference.[3] Mortgages given before the Declaration of Independence were to be considered valid, but all issued after that date were to be investigated before claims arising from them were allowed. Good debts against forfeited estates were audited and paid, and those due such estates were collected. One-third of the purchase money must be

[1] Greenleaf, *Laws of N. Y.*, i, 127–149; Jones, *Hist. of N. Y.*, ii, 543; *cf. Laws of N. Y.*, ii, 310.

[2] Greenleaf, *Laws of N. Y.*, i, 309.

[3] *Ibid.*, 53, Act of May 4, 1784; *cf.* Act of Nov. 24, 1784; *Laws of N. Y.*, i, 422, 489.

paid down and the rest within nine months. In the southern
district the commissioners were paid for their services 1 ¼
per cent. of all sales, but elsewhere they received twenty-
four shillings per day while actually employed.[1] Great care
was taken to prevent their speculating in lands.[2] Maps and
field books were made, records were kept, reports of sales
were frequently sent to the governor, and deeds were regis-
tered in the office of the secretary of state or of the county
clerk. In all the districts except the southern, the commissioners began work before the treaty of peace, though the act
of attainder was not put immediately into execution. On
March 10, 1780, the commissioners were instructed to begin
sales at once.[3] Laws were passed at frequent intervals to
regulate the traffic.[4] Lands might be leased and rents were
to be collected.[5] All property was appraised before being
sold.[6] The office of "commissioner of forfeitures" was
abolished September 1, 1788, when all the work was turned
over to the surveyor-general.[7] By 1782 the state had confiscated loyalist property in land valued at £500,000, hard
money.[8]

John Hathorn, Samuel Dodge and Daniel Graham were
appointed commissioners of forfeiture for the middle district,
but by the later act of May 12, 1784, the number was reduced to one.[9] The sale of loyalist property in that district

---

[1] The Act of March 10, 1780, allowed them $30 a day and actual expenses,
This was in currency.

[2] Greenleaf, *Laws of N. Y.*, i, 127–149.

[3] *Laws of New York*, Act of March 10, 1780.

[4] *Ibid.*, i, 381–383, 422, 489, 621.

[5] *Ibid.*, i, 381–383, 751. In Dutchess co. 100 cleared acres rented for £30 in
currency a year.   [6] *Ibid.*, 753.   [7] *Ibid.*, 822.

[8] MS. *Transcript of . . Books and Papers . . of the . . American Loyalists,*
i, 39.

[9] Greenleaf, *Laws of N. Y.*, i, 26–38, 127–149.

began June 15, 1780, and within a year amounted to £337,-
000 in currency from lands forfeited by Beverly Robinson,
George Folliot and Charles Inglis.[1]   The large estate of
Roger Morris, amounting to 50,850 acres, was offered for sale
April 20, 1781, and by June 30, 1785, 39,100 acres were disposed of for about £260,000, mostly in specie or its value
in bills of credit, but it was not until 1819 that the surveyor
general declared that all was sold.[2]   William Bayard's estate
brought to the state £7,542 for 1722 acres.[3]   The surveyor
general continued the sales after 1788.   From 1785 to 1808
the records are very meagre, but it is quite likely that sales
were made right along.   Between 1808 and 1819 about
$10,000 worth of loyalists' property in Sullivan, Orange
and Ulster counties, forfeited by James DeLancey, Oliver
DeLancey and John Weatherhead, was sold.   Altogether
$1,523,000 was received in this district in currency and
specie from the sale of loyalist real estate.   The sales in
1780 and 1781 were probably in currency, while those made
later were in coin or its equivalent.   On this basis the total
sum reduced to Spanish silver dollars would be $575,000, or
£226,400 sterling.

The three commissioners of forfeiture for the western district, John Lansing, Christopher Yates and Jeremiah Van
Rensselaer, began to sell forfeited lands May 17, 1780, and by
April 30, 1781 they had sold £477,396, or $1,193,000, worth
in paper money from the estates of thirteen loyalists.[4]   Be-

---

[1] MS. *N. Y. State Treasurer's Book*, 138–145.

[2] MS. *Abstract of Sales of Forfeited Lands*, etc., in the office of the surveyor
general; MS. *Putnam Co. Lands Claimed by John Jacob Astor*.

[3] MS. *Assembly Papers, Forfeited Estates*, vol. 26, p. 321; *Laws of N. Y.*, i, 555.

[4] MS. *An Account of Monies . . for Forfeited Lands . . in Assemb. Papers*.
Henry White, Edward Jessup, A. C. Cuyler, Guy Johnson, James De Lancey, Rob-
ert Leake, Sir John Johnson, David Colden, Daniel Claus, James Green, Malcom
Morrison, Moses Holt and Alexander Crookshank. Simms, *Frontiersmen of
N. Y.*, 248, 257, estimated Sir John Johnson's estate at 50,000 acres.

tween August 10, 1780 and May 9, 1781, the state treasurer received £9,343, or $23,400, in specie or its equivalent from the sale of the lands of four prominent loyalists.[1]   The act of May 12, 1784, gave a new impetus to the sales, and soon the estates of twenty-two loyalists were divided into small lots and sold to several hundred persons for £328,500, or $821,000 in hard money.[2]   On November 8, 1785, 243,480 acres in this district remained unsold. This land, which was valued at £150,000, or $375,000 in standard money, was gradually sold.[3]   In 1788 the legislature ordered the surveyor general to sell the estates of four loyalists, and sales were made at intervals for some years.[4] Converting the total amount of sales into standard money, the sales in this district produced about $1,250,000 or £500,000 sterling.

The three commissioners for the eastern district were reduced by the act of May 12, 1784, to one, Alexander Webster. Up to that time they had sold 2,329 acres forfeited by Oliver DeLancey, 4,067 acres forfeited by Philip and Andrew Skeene, and 2,000 acres forfeited by Edward and Ebenezer Jessup. In the standard money of the day these lots were worth about $50,000.[5]   From October 12, 1784 to

[1] MS. *Assembly Papers, Forfeited Estates*, vol. 26, 108–113; MS. *N. Y. State Treasurer's Book*, 120. Sir John Johnson, Oliver De Lancey., Guy Johnson and John Butler.

[2] MS. *Report of Comsrs. of Forfeiture.*   John Butler, Sir John Johnson, Henry White, G. Banker, Waldran Blauw, John Weatherhead, Hugh Wallace, J. Merkel, Joshua Shell, John Brown, Duncan Cameron, Patrick Carrijan, Stephen Tuttle, John Docksteeder, Wilson and Abels, Caleb Peck, John Watts, Robert Hoxley, Daniel Claus, William R. Wowen and Henry Cosby.

[3] MS. *Assemb. Papers, Forfeited Estates*, vol 26, p. 104.

[4] A MS. *Account Book*, no. 2, in the surveyor general's office, is apparently a supplemental list of sales amounting to £34,500, or $86,000; *cf. Laws of N. Y.*, i, 828.   The lands of Oliver De Lancey, James Jauncey, Goldsbrow Banyor were ordered to be sold in 1788.

[5] In 1785 Edward Jessup alone estimated his losses at £11,173. *Can. Archs.*, (1881), 720; MS. *Report of Sales by the Comsrs. of Forfeiture of the Eastern District*, 12th May, 1784, in *Assemb. Papers, Forfeited Lands*, vol. 26, pp. 100, 108–113.

August 29, 1788, the estates remaining of these same persons, and of John Tabor Kemp, John Rapelje, David Jones, Michael Hofnagle and Jonathan Jones, aggregating 62,000 acres, brought only £40,000, or $100,000, to the state.[1] Later sales probably increased this amount considerably. The sums given above were equal to £60,000 sterling.

The tory property in the southern district could not be touched till the British evacuated. The commissioners, Isaac Stoutenburg and Philip Van Cortlandt, were instructed to do nothing with property, real or personal, within the enemy's lines.[2] The most valuable possessions of the loyalists in the state were in this district. "Two-thirds of the property of the city of New York and the suburbs belongs to the tories," wrote an observer.[3] All the wealthy landowners in Queens and Richmond counties were loyalists, and a few of the richest in Kings and Suffolk counties were in the same class. On April 6, 1784, Isaac Stoutenburg was ordered to sell exclusively for gold or silver forfeited property in the metropolis and Kings county to the amount of £20,000.[4] At that time he gave public notice of the sale of the estates of Hugh Wallace, George Folliot, Frederick Philipse, John Harris Cruger and others.[5]

From June 16, 1784 to December 24, 1787, the commissioners executed 339 conveyances in the city and county of New York. The property of only twenty-six loyalists, however, was sold during that time, and the amount realized was

---

[1] MS. *Commissioners of Forfeiture, Eastern District*, in surveyor general's office; *cf.* Greenleaf, *Laws of N. Y.*, i, 276–279.

[2] *Ibid.*, i, 26–38.

[3] *Am. Archs.*, 5th ser., ii, 182.

[4] At this time silver was valued at one hundred times the face of a paper bill. *Laws of N. Y.*, i, 621; Jones, *Hist. of N. Y.*, ii, 501.

[5] MS. *Transcript . . of the Books and Papers . . of American Loyalists*, vol. 1, p. 345.

nearly £200,000. James DeLancey's property alone, consisting of farms, and houses and lots, brought to the state about £120,000.[1] This was the largest sum realized from a single individual in the district, while the smallest amount secured was £40, from the sale of five lots and a house and lot belonging to John Grigg, of Kinderhook.[2] The losses of other loyalists ranged somewhere between these extremes, but in no case did the sum realized from the sale of a loyalist's estate equal the amount of his claim for compensation. The property of eight of these loyalists was sold because of "conviction" of treason,[4] while the rest were "attainted." At least five of them lived outside of the county of New York.[5] The petitions sent to the British government, asking

---

[1] Jones, *Hist. of N. Y.*, ii, 544–556, says his estate sold for £93,769, or $234,-200. De Lancey himself valued his estate at £56,782 sterling, and his annual income at £1,200. MS. *Transcript . . of Books and Papers . . of the American Loyalists*, vol. 2, p. 72, and vol. 11, p. 78, etc.

[2] MS. volume of *Forfeited Estates*, in the recorder's office of New York city.

[3] The property of Henry White, Sr., was sold for £22,536. The possessions of James Jauncey brought to the state treasury £8,445, but he judged his loss to be £12,920. MS. *Transcript . . of Books and Papers . . of the American Loyalists*, vol. 11, p. 78. Only £8,195 was realized from the property of William Bayard, while he estimated his loss at £100,000 on one occasion and £65,274 on another. *Ibid.*, vol. 4 and vol. 11, p. 78; *cf. Can. Archs.* (1886), p. 554, no. 154, 215. Oliver De Lancey's houses and lots went for £5,710, but he, like William Bayard, owned land all over the state, and estimated his loss at from £60,000 to £78,000. *Ibid.*, vol. 4, and vol. 11, p. 78. Roger Morris placed his loss at £61,891, while only £3,010 was secured for his property in the metropolis. *Ibid.* Like differences between the sales in New York city and the loyalists' claims for losses was true in the case of Thomas White, Waldron Blauw, Robert Bayard, Thomas Jones, John Watts, Sr., Joshua T. D. St. Croix, Frederick Phillipse, Edward Ward, Isaac Low, John Weatherfield, John Harris Cruger, Alexander Wallace, Joshua Gidney, Robert McGinnis, William Axtell, James Leonard, David Matthews and Beverly Robinson. *Ibid.*

[4] Joshua T. D. St. Croix, Waldron Blauw, Joseph Leonard, Edward Ward, Roger Morris, Joseph Gidney, Robert McGinnis and John Grigg.

[5] Frederick Phillipse, Beverly Robinson, Roger Morris, Thomas Jones and John Grigg.

compensation for losses of property in New York city on account of loyalty, show the names of at least eight loyalists who were not mentioned in the records of the commissioners, with an aggregated loss of about £30,000.[1] The English commissioner on loyalist claims, E. Hardy, who was sent to New York to receive testimony and make an examination, also reported the names of fourteen loyalists, who claimed a total loss of property worth approximately £14,000.[2] The list of compensated claims has in it the names of still other loyalists from New York city.[3] A tract of confiscated property was set aside by the commissioners of forfeiture for the residences of the officers of the state.[4] Counting in all property confiscated in this county, not less than £264,000 sterling must have been realized for the benefit of the state.

Outside of New York city the records of the sales of the loyalists' property in the southern district are not very complete. The act of 1779 "attainted" loyalists in Richmond, Kings, Queens and Suffolk counties, and many others were " convicted " of treason and thus forfeited their possessions. In Kings county the commissioners sold the

[1] Benjamin Booth, Lloyd Danbury, Stephen De Lancey, David Fenton, Thomas Hughes, Archibald Kennedy, Mrs. Dr. Magra, and Thomas Miller. MS. *Transcript . . of the Books and Papers . . of the American Loyalists*, vol. 4 and vol. 11, p. 78.

[2] James Houghton, Uriah Wright, Tertullus Dickinson, Thomas Spragg, Joshua Curry, Nathan Whitney, Christopher Benson, James Dickinson, Ezekiel Welton, Robert Thorne, Jesse Powell, Simon Le Roy, Joshua Gidney and Theophylact Bache. *Ibid*.

[3] MS. *Transcript , . of Books and Papers . . of the American Loyalists*, vol. 11, p. 78.

[4] A house and lot in the west ward, belonging to William Axtell, was set aside for the secretary of state, and a house and lot of Henry White, in the east ward, was made the residence of the governor. *Laws of N. Y.*, i, 759. The legislature authorized the commissioner of this district to give Thomas Paine a farm of 300 acres, forfeited by the conviction of Frederick Devoe, and located in the township of New Rochelle, Westchester County. *Ibid.*, 751. John McKesson was also given a house and lot in the east ward, forfeited by James Jauncey, on account of his great service to the state. *Ibid*.

estates of thirteen loyalists.[1] Not less than fifty-two loyalists in Queens county lost their lands in the same way.[2] The
sale of confiscated property began in Queens county on
November 19, 1784, and within four months £14,265 was
received for the estates of nine loyalists.[3] Since the minutes
of the further sales are lost it is impossible to say how much
was actually turned into the state treasury from this county,
but no doubt the sales continued for several years, and the
sum realized was many times that given above. In Suffolk
county the commissioners sold the property of three loyalists during July and August, 1784, for £8,554.[4] In Rich-

---

[1] Theophylact Bache, who lost but £488, and was able to save the rest of his property by remaining in the state, Benjamin James, Augustus Van Cortlandt, John Rapalje, who said his loss was £40,000, Whitehead Cornell, John Cornell, William Cornell, Miles Sherbrook, Colonel Richard Floyd, James Hubbard, Stephen Thorn, Abraham Rapalje and William Axtell, who estimated his loss at £25,710. *Ibid.*

[2] Richard Hulet, Thomas Cornell, Stephen Huett, Joseph Beagle, John Kendall, John Bodin, John Hulet, Isaac Denton, Charles A. Moorsener, David Beaty, Gabriel Ludlow, who asked £6,500 as compensation for his losses, Thomas Jones, whose losses amounted to £44,600, Archibald Hamilton, David Colden, Richard Colden, George D. Ludlow, who estimated his loss at £7,000, Whitehead Hicks, Samuel Clowes, George Folliot, who believed his loss to be £13,144, Samuel Doughty, David Kissam, Gilbert Van Wyck, John Townsend, John Polhemus, Benjamin Whitehead, John Shoales, Nathaniel Moore, Samuel Hallett, who lost £6,000, William Weyman, Thomas Hicks, Benjamin Lester, David Colden of Flushing, Dow Vandine, Henry Floyd, Joseph Ford, Israel Youngs, Isaac Youngs, Plum Weeks, Johannes Barnet, Thomas Place, Jr., John Hewlett, John Kissam, Joseph Thorne, Stephen Thorne, Thomas Thorne, Stephen Hewlett, Hewlett Townsend, Jacob Moore, John Moore and Arthur Dingey. The first thirty-four names were taken out of the MS. *N. Y. Assemb. Papers, Forfeited Estates*, vol. 25, pp. 268, 272, 292, 301, 316, and vol. 27, pp. 211, 327, 383. The last eighteen names are given in Onderdonk, *Queens Co. in Olden Times*, 66, 67.

[3] Johannes Polhemus, Dow Vandine, David Colden, Daniel Kissam, Gabriel G. Ludlow, Henry Floyd, George Folliott, Joseph Ford and George D. Ludlow. Onderdonk, *Queens Co. in Olden Times*, 67.

[4] Parker Wickham, Richard Floyd and George Muirison. MS. *Abstract of Certain Lands . . . Forfeited*, etc., in Old Civil List Book in Suffolk county clerk's office.

mond county tory property met a similar fate. Although there were many loyalists on Staten Island, still there are few records extant giving the sales of forfeited estates.[1] It is very difficult even to approximate the total amount realized from the sales of forfeited estates in the southern district outside of the metropolis, but using the few figures preserved and considering the relatively large number of loyalists whose property was sold, the total amount must have reached £200,000 in hard money. This sum would make the total for the southern district £464,000 in standard money, or $1,160,000 in Spanish silver.

In 1788 the sale of forfeited estates was entrusted to the surveyor-general of the state.[2] He was ordered to dispose of the lands at the capital after eight weeks' notification in the principal newspapers of the state.[3] Sales were made in this way until several decades of the nineteenth century had passed away. In 1802 a bonus of twenty-five per cent. was allowed to persons who should discover any unsold lands belonging to attainted or convicted loyalists.[4] Between 1803 and 1805 the property of five loyalists sold for nearly $14,000.[5] The work of these two years was probably repeated during the entire period from 1788 to 1808, after which sales continued at rare intervals for another decade.[6]

---

[1] Mrs. and Miss Dawson had 300 acres confiscated. MS. *Transcript . . of Books and Papers . . of the American Loyalists*, etc., vol. 4. The MS. *Court Records* of Richmond co. show that the estates of Peter Alexander Alaire and John Christopher were sold as late as 1788. All of Christopher Billop's lands on Staten Island were confiscated. Sabine, 229. Both he and Benjamin Seaman were included in the general act of attainder.

[2] *Laws of N. Y.*, i, 822, Act of March 21, 1788.

[3] Webster, *Laws of N. Y.*, i, 307.   [4] *Ibid.*, ii, 47.

[5] MS. deeds marked *Lott and Magin Patent*, in surveyor-general's office. Isaac Low, Sir John Johnson, Frederick Philipse, Beverly Robinson and Roger Morris.

[6] *Ibid.* There are many bundles of sales, deeds, claims, appraisements, certificates, etc., in the surveyor-general's office at Albany.

The English historian, Lecky, says that " Two-thirds of
the property of New York was supposed to belong to the
tories."[1] If this statement be intended to include the crown
lands, as well as the forfeited estates, it is undoubtedly true.
Approximating the total sales from the partial sales which
are left, it seems fair to conclude that the state received
one million two hundred and sixty thousand pounds in
standard money, or three million one hundred and fifty
thousand dollars in Spanish coin, from the sale of forfeited real estate. The total loss for personal and real
estate would be nearly three million six hundred thousand
dollars.[2]

During a period of fifty years after the peace of 1783 the
New York legislature was disturbed more or less by questions concerning forfeited estates. Suits were brought to
recover property.[3] For some years the legislature was
flooded with petitions from persons whose claims against loyalists had not been satisfied, from those who had been forcibly prevented from returning home when captured by the
British, from the heirs of loyalists, from repentant loyalists
and from the widows of loyalists. These petitions met
with varying degrees of success.[4] Purchasers also petitioned
the assembly for the removal of various grievances.[5] Whigs

---

[1] Lecky, *Hist. of Eng. in XVIII. Cent.*, iii, 479; *cf. Parl. Hist.*, xviii, 123–129;
cf. Am. Archs., 4th ser., i, 773, 957.

[2] In the claims submitted to the government of Great Britain, asking compensation for losses, the total amount was considerably larger than this sum received by
the state.

[3] MS. *Assemb. Papers, Forfeited Estates*, vol. 26, p. 16, John Waters, a Tryon
county loyalist, returned and sued John Thayer for selling his property, and re-
covered £976. Thayer then petitioned the legislature to reimburse him.

[4] *Ibid.*, volumes 25–29.

[5] *Jour. of Assemb.* (1781), 26, 27, 50, 51, etc.; MS. petition of several hundred
tenants of Roger Morris against John Jacob Astor.

were given permission to bring damage suits against loyalists who had injured their property during the war,[1] but in 1797 claims against forfeited estates were ordered barred in five years.[2]   Some of the loyalists who were indicted for treason appeared before the supreme court, and, by employing shrewd lawyers, saved their estates.[3]   Others, like Theophylact Bache, saved their property by the help of influential relatives or friends on the whig side. Small owners, who returned after the war, were in most cases able to recover their estates.

Although the confiscation and sale of loyalist property was primarily a punishment for treason against revolutionary authority made good by war, still there was a result growing out of it of greater importance than the acquisition of property to the value of about $3,600,000 by the state.   That result was the weakening of the feudal element in the social system of New York.   The revolution was thus a democratic movement in land-tenure as well as in political rights.   The ownership of the greater part of the lands of the state by a few aristocratic landlords like the De Lanceys, the Johnsons, the Skeenes, John Tabor Kempe, the Jessups, Beverly Johnson, Roger Morris and others, now began to give way to ownership by their dependants and tenants. Large manors, patents and estates were to an extent cut up into small lots and sold on easy terms to the common people. Although it was not uncommon for the widow or son of a

[1] *Laws of N. Y.*, i, 499, 700, Act of March 17, 1783. Loyalists who used whig houses had to pay eight years' rent. Prosecutions were made against them for cutting timber and other things. Over $1,000,000 were thus claimed for damages. Jones, *Hist. of N. Y.*, ii, 251, 252, 255. In 1784, Ebenezer Allen, a loyalist who furnished supplies for Burgoyne, was prosecuted by the state for damages, and a judgment was rendered in favor of the state for £375.   *Can. Archs.* (1888), 716.

[2] *Laws of N. Y.*, iii, 73.

[3] Onderdonk, *Queens Co. in Olden Times*, 64, 66–67.

loyalist to buy in his property,[1] yet it was not the rule. The property of James De Lancey, for instance, in the southern district, went to about 275 different persons, and the 50,000 acres forfeited by Roger Morris in Putnam county were sold to nearly 250 persons. The large tracts in the central and northern parts of the state were divided into farms of from one to five hundred acres and sold to poor farmers. The whole movement was leveling, equalizing and democratic, and left permanent social results in the new state.

[1] In New York city the property of John Watts, Sr., was purchased by John Watts, Jr., and Robert Watts. Eleanor Blauw bought the estate of Waldron Blauw. Anna White took the lot of her attainted husband. Rachel Weatherhead did the same for John Weatherhead. Henry White, Sr.'s, property was bid in by Henry White, Jr. Such cases appeared in every district.

CHAPTER VIII

THE EMIGRATION OF LOYALISTS

ALTHOUGH the war virtually ended in 1781, the fate of the loyalists was not definitely determined until the treaty of peace in 1783. They had staked all upon the success of the British arms, and had stubbornly opposed every suggestion of concession or compromise. Lord North's terms of peace were suicidal in their eyes.[1] Nothing short of complete victory and a restoration of the old colonial government would satisfy them, because nothing less than that would restore their own political power, save their property and punish their rebellious persecutors. The re-establishment of British supremacy after the Declaration of Independence was absolutely essential to loyalist prosperity. To the very last, in England and America, they urged war and insisted that the revolutionists were on the verge of defeat. When the English cause was lost, and with it their own, they attributed it entirely to wicked ministers and shamefully incompetent generals. The treaty of peace, therefore, sounded the death-knell of their fondest hopes.[2] Little could they expect from their triumphant kinsmen, and henceforth they were forced to rely upon the gratitude and generosity of the mother country for which they had sacrificed native land, property, comforts and life itself.

[1] Wharton, *Dip. Corresp. of the Am. Rev.*, i, 317–324.

[2] One loyalist wrote that nothing was left them but "the consciousness of having done their duty." *Can. Archs.* (1888), 834, Sherwood to Mathews, March 10, 1783; "Everything looks gloomy for the loyalists," he wrote at another time. *Ibid.*, 838, April 19, 1783.

In concluding the treaty of peace with the victorious United States, the English government made an honest effort to provide for those loyal subjects in America who had lost all for the crown and the empire.[1] Shelburne really expected that the loyalists would be protected by the treaty, though he was far from being satisfied with its terms,[2] while the American envoys knew that the provisions respecting the loyalists would never be carried out. The fourth article stipulated that creditors on each side should " meet with no lawful impediment " to recover all good debts in sterling money. By the fifth article, it was agreed that the Congress of the United States should " earnestly recommend " to the states the restoration of the rights and possessions of " real British subjects," and of loyalists who had not borne arms against their countrymen. All other loyalists were to be given liberty to go into any state within twelve months to adjust their affairs and to recover their confiscated property upon paying the purchasers the sale-price. The sixth article stated that no future confiscations should be made, that imprisoned loyalists should be released, and that no further persecutions should be permitted.[3]

The Americans regarded the loyalists with greater aversion than they did the English, and looked upon them as both fools and traitors. Although victorious, they could not forgive, much less forget, the course of their former friends and neighbors, who had disagreed with them honestly and fearlessly about what was best for America. Congress sent the

[1] The loyalists who knew the hostility of their victorious countrymen thought that the terms would not be enforced. *Can. Archs.* (1895), xiii. *Cf.* Instructions to Carleton about the restoration of loyalist property, *ibid.* (1885), Feb. 16, 1783; *cf. ibid.* (1887), 164, for the case of Van Allen, who went to Albany to collect his debts, May 31, 1783.

[2] *Parl. Hist. of Eng.*, xxiii, 411.

[3] Wharton, *Dip. Corresp. of the Am. Rev.*, vol. 6, 96. *Parl. Hist. of Eng.*, xxiii, 354.

"recommendations" to the states, but professed to have no power to enforce them. New York felt no obligation to re-restore "tory" lands and to receive their owners as fellow-citizens. These provisions of the treaty were repudiated and the legislature declared that forfeited and sequestrated property ought not be returned, since England offered no compensation for property which had been destroyed.[1] Loyalists who returned under the treaty of peace were insulted, tarred and feathered, whipped and even "ham-stringed."[2] The grand jury indicted before the supreme court about a thousand of the richest loyalists for treason.[3] Although every effort was made to drive the loyalists out of the land, to prevent their return and to effectually suppress those who did come back as well as those who remained, still the loyalists were so numerous in some sections that they were able to carry on a bitter political contest.[4] In 1783 they voted for governor and other officers.[5] But an effort was soon made to deprive them of the franchise and thus to greatly diminish their influence. The act of May 12, 1784, declared that all who had held office under the British, or helped to fit out vessels of war, or who had served as privates or officers, or had joined the British, or had left the state, to be guilty of "misprison of treason" and disqualified from both franchise and office.[6] This is said to have excluded from voting two-thirds of the inhabitants of New York city, Richmond and Kings counties, one-fifth of those of Suffolk county, nine-

---

[1] *Journal of Senate* (1784), p. 14; Jones, *Hist of N. Y.*, ii, 494.

[2] *Ibid.*, ii, 244, 505; *Can. Archs.* (1888), 840, 841, 843 (1890), 158 (1889), 72, 77.

[3] Jones, *Hist. of N.Y.*, ii, 251.

[4] Onderdonk, *Queens Co. in Olden Times*, 71.   [5] *Ibid.*, 62.

[6] Jones, *Hist. of N. Y.*, ii, 248; Greenleaf, *Laws of N. Y.*, i, 127; *Laws of N. Y.*, i, 772. For a description of the three parties in New York in 1784, *cf.* Jay, *Life of Jay*, ii, 145.

tenths of Queens county, and all of the borough of Westchester. When a tax of £150,000, payable in gold and silver,
was levied in 1785, the whigs escaped easily, and the burden
fell upon the loyalists.[1] By this and other measures the
former domestic foes, though tolerated, were eliminated as a
factor in New York politics.[2] In 1782, debts due loyalists
were cancelled, provided one-fortieth was paid into the state
treasury.[3] Local committees resolved that the loyalists who
were returning to their homes should not be tolerated,[4] and
the people in general were determined not to allow loyalists
to return.[5] The most obnoxious loyalist lawyers were for
some years refused the right to practice law.[6] That barrier
was not removed until April 6, 1786, and then only on condition that they take an "oath of abjuration and allegiance." [7]

Of the New York loyalists, some never left the state,
others fled but returned, and still others became permanent
exiles. The first class was very large and the least obnoxious of the three. It was composed of two groups—those
who at heart were true to the crown and empire, but had
outwardly conformed to the will of congress and to the committees, and those who were avowed loyalists, having refused to sign the "association," to obey the revolutionary
bodies, and who gave secret aid to the British, but who
never took up arms against the Americans. As early as

[1] *Can. Archs.* (1890), 314; *cf. Laws of N. Y.*, i. 707; Jones, *Hist. of N. Y.*, ii,
249–250.

[2] *Ibid.*, 502–503.

[3] *Jour. of Assemb.*, v, 59–60, 73–76, 88–89.

[4] *Can. Archs.* (1888), 791, 839, 841. " The committees through the country
are determined not to allow the return of loyalists." *Ibid.*, 840. Report of John
Cobham, June 3, 1783.

[5] *Ibid.*, (1888), 840, 841, 843, (1890), 158.

[6] *Laws of N. Y.*, i, 772, Oct. 9, 1779.   *Ibid.*, ii, 237.

1776 many under the first head took the oath of allegiance.[1] After the war they were looked upon as genuine whigs. When the tide began to turn against the English in 1778, many of the second group took the oath of allegiance and became citizens of the state.[2] Severe laws and the harsh measures of the commissioners on conspiracies, had a like effect.[3] The lot of these persons was not a hard one. Those whose worst crime was open loyalty, who had been arrested, imprisoned, exiled, or paroled, but never charged with treason, were found in every community, and, although subjected to more or less abuse, were for the most part allowed to remain after the war was over, and to keep their property. While never fully forgiven, in time they came to be looked upon as true Americans, and were given full political rights. Even some who were strongly suspected, and no doubt were guilty of treason, were allowed to remain because of the intercession of friends or attorneys. The act of May 12, 1784, gave a special permit[4] to twenty-seven loyalists to remain in the state. Thousands in southern New York were not molested, because they plead loyalty under stress of British occupation, and were willing to abide by the results, and because no local committees could disprove their assertions. They constituted an undoubted majority, so strong that hostile feeling in the localities was not strong enough to mark them for revenge. Still it was complained, January 3, 1785, that " those in New York whose estates have not been

---

[1] *Can. Archs.* (1888), Haldimand Collection, 642.

[2] *Ibid.*, (1889), 113, May 7, 1778; *Laws of N. Y.* (1886), i, 252.

[3] *Ibid.*, 370.

[4] Greenleaf, *Laws of N. Y..* i, 127–159. Cadwallader Colden, Richard Harrison, David Colden, John Watts and others begged the New York Assembly, Feb. 4, 1784, to remove the sentence of banishment against them, but it was then refused. MS. *Transcript . . of Books and Papers . . of the American Loyalists* i, 345.

confiscated are so loaded with taxes and other grievances that there is nothing left but to sell out and move into the protection of the British government." [1] If the petitions of loyalists to the crown for compensation for property losses through loyalty be taken as a basis for comparison, the proportion of loyalists who emigrated from the counties above New York city, as contrasted with those in the southern part of the state, was as 439 to 27. During the war loyalists in the northern counties were so harshly treated that they left the state voluntarily, or they were forcibly removed. They fled to Canada, or to New York, in large numbers. In the metropolis, however, and on Long Island and Staten Island, the loyalists remained unmolested during the contest. When peace came the fury of persecution had subsided; consequently, most of them were willing to accept the new order of things. These facts account for the difference in the proportion.[2]

The loyal refugees who returned to their homes were not so numerous as either the loyalists who never departed, or those who, having departed, never came back; still such individuals appear in all parts of the state. The families of many who had gone to Canada, Nova Scotia or England, continued to reside in New York, preserving their property or endeavoring to recover it, and they thus helped to draw the refugees back. Kind relatives, neighbors and friends induced others to return. Genuine love for their native land led many to retrace their footsteps and brave the indignity of their victorious communities. The wilds of Nova Scotia and Canada,[3] the cool reception in England and the refusal

---

[1] *Can. Archs.* (1890), 314, Augustus Von Horne's letter.

[2] MS. *Transcript . . of Books and Papers . . of the American Loyalists*, vols. 17–22. Albany furnished most of the 466 petitioners, then came Westchester, Tryon, Dutchess, Charlotte, Orange and Cumberland counties in the order named.

[3] *Can. Archs.* (1889), 79; *cf. ibid.* (1886), 411.

of the British government adequately to reward their loyalty
sent many a disappointed "friend of government" back to
New York to begin life anew.   Phrases such as " the fatal
day when I left home," "all I desire is to return and lay my
bones in that dear soil," and "I am not welcome here," are
found in their letters.[1]   Peter Van Shaack and loyalists of
his integrity and character, who both denounced the arbitrary
program of Great Britain and feared the results of independence, who wished to remain neutral, and who, when forced
to decide between two evils, went to England "under the
stress of double allegiance" to await the end of the war—
these persons were welcomed back by all but the extremists.
Peter Van Schaack returned in 1784, and by the act of May
12 was restored to full citizenship.[2]   On March 31, 1785,
thirty loyalists returned to Queens county from Nova Scotia.[3]
Similar bands came back to Westchester,[4] Dutchess, Albany,
Tryon and other counties.   New York city was a great
haven for returned loyalists.   There they could move easily,
lose their identity and gain a new foothold.   Philip R. Frey,
Hendrick Frey and Adrian Klock, of Tryon county, were
loyalists of another type.   They joined the British and
served in the king's army, returned after peace was made
and were unmolested.[5]   Few, however, of this character
were thus favored.   "Many tories came back after the war,
but their former neighbors . . . usually made the atmosphere so close for them that not a few fled precipitately back
to Canada, some with and some without scourging, while

---

[1] Wharton, *Dip. Corresp. of Am. Rev.*, i, 313.

[2] Van Schaack, *Life of Peter Van Schaack*, 403; Greenleaf, *Laws of N. Y.*, i,
127–149.

[3] Onderdonk, *Queens Co. in Olden Times*, 68.

[4] Baird, *History of Rye*, 265; *cf.* Case of William Hunt, of North Castle, who
was sued and imprisoned as a " Cow Boy."   Sabine, *American Loyalists*, 557.

[5] Simms, *Frontiersmen of N. Y.*, 99, 100, 344: Sabine, *American Loyalists*, 448.

here and there one was suffered to remain, though unhon-
ored and hardly noticed by those who had been their warmest friends before the war." [1]   In 1784 the Albany jail was
reported to be full of tories, who were whipped and perse-
cuted.[2]   The statement was made in letters from Canada
that the loyalists were "daily coming in from the states to
avoid persecutions." [3]   One Becraft, a Schoharie tory, who
had taken part in the cruel border warfare, came back, was
whipped nearly to death by ten men and warned never to
return.[4]   Abraham C. Cuyler, ex-mayor of Albany and
major of a loyal battalion, returned to Albany, but soon fled
to Canada.[5]   Alexander Hamilton, as counsel, gave it as his
opinion, when Cuyler applied for leave to return to New
York to recover his property under the protection of the
treaty of peace, that it would be very dangerous personally
and that there was no prospect of the restoration of his
property.[6]   The inhabitants were urged to avoid returned
loyalists "as persons contaminated with the most dreadful
contagion," and to let them remain, as they justly merit,
"vagabonds on the face of the earth." [7]

The third class, those who expatriated themselves forever,
was very numerous and included the flower of the loyalist
party.   They continued true British subjects, though exiled
to various parts of the world.   They were found in England,
Ireland, Scotland, Nova Scotia, in various parts of Canada
and even in the islands of the sea.[8]   Many of them were driven
out by persecution, others fled through fear, but most of

---

[1] Simms, *Frontiersmen of N. Y.*, 344.

[2] *Can. Archs.* (1888), Haldimand Collection, 840, 841, 844.

[3] *Ibid.* (1886), 429, May 31, 1784; *ibid.* (1887), 367.

[4] Sabine, *Loyalists of the Am. Rev.*, i, 223.   [5] *Ibid.*, 356.

[6] *Can. Archs.* (1895), State Papers, Cape Breton, I, Feb. 13, 1784; *ibid.* (1887),
xiv.   [7] *Ibid.* (1887), 242–243, April 17, 1783.

[8] Bahamas, Newfoundland, etc.

them left at the close of the war because their cause had
been lost.   They loved British institutions, were true to their
oaths of loyalty, dreaded the scorn and contempt of their
victorious brothers, hated republicanism, loved adventure,
and wished to help preserve the integrity of the British empire.[1]   Some received offices, pensions and lands from the
British government.

The flight of New York loyalists began as early as 1774
and continued during ten years,[2]   The causes of this movement varied with different groups and at different periods.
To escape the vengeance of a New York mob, Dr. Myles
Cooper, president of King's College, was forced to leave in
May, 1775.   In company with several other Episcopal
clergymen, he went to England and never returned.[3]   Representatives of the other professions, lawyers and physicians,
also to an extent took the same course.   The loyalist soldiers who joined the British in Canada and Boston in that
year, formed another group.[4]   When the war closed they
settled in various parts of the British dominions.   Rich
merchants, like James Jauncey and William Bayard, formed
another group that retired to England early in the contest.
Closely allied with them were the great land-owners, like

---

[1] "No loyalist of principle could endure to live under the imperious laws of
Washington and his minions," declared a "friend of government," March 10,
1783. *Can. Archs.* (1888), 834.

[2] One Alpheus Avery was forced to flee from Westchester county in 1774 because
he was a "tory." He entered the British navy and later asked for compensation.
But it was decided that he had no claim. MS. *Transcript . . of Books and
Papers . . of American Loyalists*, vol. v.

[3] Moore, *Diary of Am. Rev.*, i, 82. Dr. T. H. Chandler was one of them. Sabine, *American Loyalists*, 166.

[4] *Docs. rel. to N. Y. Col. Hist.*, viii, 562, 563, 680; *Min. of Prov. Cong.*, i, 234–
244, 886, iii, 274, 294, 331–333, iv, 48; *Am. Archs.*, 4th ser., iii, 457–459, 1305,
1311–1315, 1719, 1761, 1900, iv, 187, 1117, vi, 1032; *Cal. of N. Y. Hist. MSS.*,
i, 333.

James De Lancey[1] of New York city, who crossed the ocean never to return.   Still another body of voluntary exiles were the royal officials.   They began to leave America in 1775, but the larger part remained in New York city or Canada until the struggle ceased, when nearly all went to Great Britain.[2]   Supplementing these five classes were the common people—the farmers, mechanics, laborers and small tradesmen—who began to emigrate in 1776, continued the process throughout the war, and departed in large numbers after 1783.

Early in 1777 the Convention ordered the " commissioners on conspiracies" to compel loyalists either to take the oath of allegiance, or to remove with their families within the British lines.[3]   This marked the beginning of legally enforced exile by the wholesale for the crime of loyalism, and the measure was vigorously enforced.[4]   A second law strengthened the act in April, 1778, and made banishment perpetual after Jnly 18, 1778.[5]   Neutrality was impossible, for every person had to announce his political principles and allegiance.   All loyalists who refused to perjure themselves for the sake of safety were banished and forfeited their property. Many swallowed their convictions, took the required oath, and remained unmolested.   The test was severe and separated the wheat from the chaff.   By July, 1778, about a thousand loyalists were receiving provisions in Canada—209 at St. Johns, 208 at Montreal, 196 at Machiche, 126 at

[1] Sabine, *Loyalists of the Am. Rev.*, i, 367.

[2] *Ibid.*, 661.   The case of John Tabor Kempe, the attorney general, is a good example.

[3] *Jour. of Prov. Conv.*, i, 827, 855.

[4] MS. *Min. of Comsrs. on Conspiracies*, i, 108, 117, 122, 123, 124; *Jour. of Assemb.*, iii, 16, 29, 36; *Can. Archs.* (1888), 776.

[5] Greenleaf, *Laws of N. Y.*, i, 22–24; *cf.* Van Schaack, *Life of Peter Van Schaack*, 485–487; *cf. Can. Archs.* (1888), 780, Carleton to Van Schaick, Oct., 1780; *ibid.*, 782, Clinton to Haldimand, March 27, 1781.

Pointe Claire, 87 at Sorel and 27 at Chambly.[1]   This number included men, women and children,[2] but no soldiers. No doubt there were more who cared for themselves.   The number banished to New York city must have been larger. With the decline of British power after 1778, the laws against loyalists increased in severity.   The act of attainder of 1779 put fifty-nine of the wealthiest under the ban, and forbade their return under penalty of death.[3]   Between 1779 and 1783 hundreds were "convicted" of treason and banished by decree of the supreme court of the state.   The failure of both the imperial and loyalist cause, and the refusal of the states to enforce the provisions for loyalists in the treaty of peace, produced the final great exodus.

The New York loyalists for the most part went to one of three places — England, Nova Scotia or Canada.   They began to cross the Atlantic in 1775, and continued to do so for a decade.   Those who took this course were persons in high civil office, like John Tabor Kempe, Judge Thomas Jones, William Axtell, Andrew Elliot and Abraham C. Cuyler; military officers of advanced rank, like Oliver DeLancey, John Harris Cruger and Archibald Hamilton; men of wealth, like James DeLancey and James Jauncey; Anglican clergymen, like Dr. Myles Cooper and Dr. Thomas B. Chandler; and professional men, like Peter Van Schaack.   They represented the aristocracy, and before and after the treaty of peace went to England to secure safety and compensation.

Two classes of loyalists went to England before 1783 — those who went under "stress of double allegiance" to wait for the end of the war as neutrals, and those who went as champions of the royal cause, driven from America for their loyalty.[4]   Their number is uncertain, and was limited by the

[1] *Can. Archs.* (1888), Haldimand Collection, 732, 734, 742.   [2] *Ibid.,* 742.
[3] Greenleaf, *Laws of N. Y.,* i, 26–38.
[4] *Cf.* Wharton, *Dip. Corresp. of Am. Rev.,* i, 317–324.

inconvenience and expense involved. Certainly not more than two thousand took this course.[1] Many returned in want to British North America,[2] and a few found their way back to the States.

The emigrants to Nova Scotia included not a few of the aristocratic type, but consisted mostly of disbanded loyalist soldiers, farmers, small merchants and traders, lawyers, physicians, clergymen and persons of various trades and of no trades. From and after 1776 small parties of loyalists found their way there.[3] In September, 1782, General Guy Carleton wrote to Lieutenant-Governor Hammond at Halifax that 600 wished to embark for Nova Scotia, and that another large company desired to leave in the spring, but that he could send only 300. Prior to 1783, 500 loyalists from New York were residing at Annapolis.[4] When terms of peace were concluded the metropolis was crowded with loyalists from all parts of the United States. The British government was under obligation to provide for them. To transplant them in undeveloped parts of the British empire in America seemed to be the best course. General Guy Carleton, who was in command at New York, was alert and active in their behalf. The loyalist historian, Judge Jones, says that 100,000 had left the city when it was finally evacuated,[5] but this number is probably an exaggeration.

---

[1] Haight, *Before the Coming of the Loyalists*, 16, quotes this: " Sir Guy Carleton also sent to England a numerous train of loyalists, who accompanied the fleet."

[2] *Can. Archs.* (1890), 321, July 31, 1793. Judge George Duncan Ludlow said that there were not more than 30 loyalists in London. MS. *Transcript . . of Books and Papers of . . American Loyalists*, i, 34.

[3] *Can. Archs.* (1894), Massay to Germain, June 27 and Oct. 6, 1776, 351, 354.

[4] Raymond, *The U. E. Loyalists*, 35; cf. *Can. Archs.* (1894), 400, Hammond to Lords of Trade, May 9, 1782; *ibid.*, 401, Carleton to Hammond, Oct. 26,1 782; *ibid.*, 402, Parr to Townshend, Jan. 15, 1783; *ibid.*, Parr to Nepeau, Jan. 22, 1783; cf. *ibid.* (1886), 549, no. 417, and 550, no. 460; cf. Murdock, *Hist. of Nova Scotia*, iii, 8.

[5] Jones, *Hist. of N. Y.*, ii, 260, 504.

An account of the territory from Annapolis to St. Mary's bay was sent to New York January 14, 1783.[1] Plans now began for a grand exodus. The departure was orderly. Advance agents were sent ahead to choose sites and report. The rich formed companies and chartered ships, while the poor, upon application, were transported by the British government. There was some difficulty in securing an adequate supply of boats,[2] and the newspapers of the day are full of notices of the departure of vessels. By March, 1783, "numbers of loyalists" arrived at Nova Scotia,[3] and land surveys began for them.[4] On April 26 a fleet of twenty vessels carried 7,000 from New York city,[5] and, on May 18, landed them at St. Johns. Men, women, children and servants were in the company. The fleet returned to transport others, and by August 23 Governor Parr wrote that "upwards of 12,000 souls have already arrived from New York," and that as many more were expected.[6] By the end of September he estimated that 18,000 had arrived, and stated that 10,000 more were expected from New York. These were located chiefly at Halifax, Annapolis, Cumberland Bay,[7] St. John and Port Roseway.[8] The St. John settlement was the most numerous.[9] On October 4 the governor thought they num-

---

[1] This was sent by Amos Botsford and other advance loyalist agents. Murdock, *Hist. of Nova Scotia*, iii, 13–15.

[2] Onderdonk, *Queens Co. in Olden Times*, 63; *Gaine's N. Y. Gazette*, Sept. 8, 1783.

[3] *Can. Archs.* (1894), Letter of March 12, 1783, to Lord President, 404.

[4] *Ibid.*, 404, Parr to Townshend, May 13, 1783; *ibid.* (1888), 578.

[5] (1894), 404, Parr to Townshend, June 6, 1783; *cf.* Baird, *Hist. of Rye*, 265; *Can. Archs.* (1888), 578, Patterson to Haldimand, May 8, 1783.

[6] *Ibid.*, (1894), 406, Parr to North, Aug. 23, 1783; *ibid.* (1888), 578; Murdoch, *Hist. of Nova Scotia*, iii, 19.

[7] Amherst.

[8] Shelburne. *Cf. Can. Archs.* (1888), 578, Parr to Haldimand, May 20, 1783.

[9] *Ibid.* (1894), 407, Parr to North, Sept. 30, 1783.

bered 20,000,[1] and by December 16 about 30,000.[2] From these centers settlements soon spread in all directions—to Guysborough, Stormout, Baddeck, St. Peters, Louisburg and other places. Most of the 3,000 negroes in New York city settled at Shelburne.[3]

As early as November 30, 1782,[4] Prince Edward Island was pointed out as a desirable location, and the landholders there offered to cede one-fourth of their lands to the loyalists.[5] By January 10, 1785, however, only 200 had arrived,[6] and the number who settled there probably never exceeded 300. Cape Breton seemed to be an attractive place.[7]   Abraham C. Cuyler asked for a grant there for himself and 500 families, and received it.[8]   Most of the settlers on that island went, with government aid, from Canada,[9] and by the fall of 1784 630 families with 3,150 individuals were located there.[10]

Emigration to Nova Scotia continued after the beginning of 1784. Within the period of one year, Shelburne grew into a city of 1,400 houses and 12,000 people.[11]   At the mouth of the St. John a city of between 2,000 and 3,000

---

[1] *Can. Archs.* (1894), Parr to Nepeau, Oct. 4, 1783.

[2] *Ibid.*, 409, Parr to Shelburne, Dec. 16, 1783; cf. *Kingston and the Loyalists of 1783*; cf. Tuttle, *Hist. of Dom. of Can.*, 327.

[3] *Cf.* Raymond, *The U. E. Loyalists*, 32; cf. *Can. Archs.* (1895), 25, Carleton to Dundas, Dec. 13, 1791; cf. *ibid.* (1894), 478, 489.

[4] *Ibid.*, (1895), Prince Edward Island, 33.   [5] *Ibid.*, 34, 50, 52.

[6] *Ibid.*, 43, cf. Kingsford, *Hist. of Canada*, vii, 221.

[7] *Can. Archs.* (1894), 405, Parr to North, July 6, 1783.

[8] *Ibid.* (1895), Cape Breton, 1, Feb. 21, March 11, 1785; cf. *ibid.* (1883), 111 (1885), 286, 310, 311.

[9] *Ibid.* (1886), 448, 450, 452, 453, 64, (1887), 165, 363, (1888), 753, (1890), 144.

[10] *Ibid.* (1885), 286, (1888), 753, 754; cf. Kingsford, *Hist. of Canada*, vii, 221; cf. Brown, *Hist. of the Island of Cape Breton*, 391, 392.

[11] *Can. Archs.* (1894), 409, 413, 417.

houses had sprung up by November 15, 1784.[1] Loyalists were settled for 150 miles up the course of that river.[2] On January 15, 1784, Governor Parr reported the " arrival of a considerable number of refugee families." [3]   In July of that year a body of New York Quakers who had been " plundered and ruined," asked permission to join their brethren.[4] About 300 poverty-stricken loyalists reached Halifax from England in August, and more were then expected.[5] In December an officer spoke of the " multitude of loyalists arrived and arriving." [6]   The few emigrants in 1785 did not materially change the total number. The estimates of the whole number of loyalists who settled in Nova Scotia vary from 28,347 [7] to 40,000.[8] England furnished as many as 33,682 rations, and on November 30, 1785, was still feeding 26,317 refugees.[9] On Nov. 24, 1783, Sir Brook Watson, the commissary-general of New York, reported 29,244 refugees,[10] while Governor Parr's estimate was 30,000.[11] Counting all loyalists in Nova Scotia proper, New Brunswick, Cape Breton and Prince Edward Island, it must be concluded that not less than 35,000 found new homes in these regions.[12] Of these, prob-

---

[1] Can. Archs. (1894), 417, (1895), 2, New Brunswick Papers. [2] Ibid. (1895), 2.

[3] Ibid. (1894), 412; ibid. (1888), 579.

[4] Ibid. (1894), 412, Parr to Sidney, July 24, 1784; ibid., 426, 444.

[5] Ibid., 422, August 10, 1784; ibid., 423, August 26, 1784; ibid., 424, Sept. 1, 1784; cf. Murdock, Hist. of Nova Scotia, iii, 34–35. Of them 41 died. They were destitute of clothes and food.

[6] Can. Archs. (1894), 429, Campbell to Sidney, Dec. 29,

[7] Ibid. (1884), p. xl, (1895), 36. Col. Robert Morse's description of Nova Scotia.

[8] Ibid. (1875), Prince Edward Island Papers, 36, Stuart to Nepeau, May 14, 1784.

[9] Ibid. (1894), 438, Campbell to Sidney.

[10] Cf. New Brunswick Magazine, i, 96, 101.

[11] Can. Archs. (1894), 413, 423, Parr to North, Feb. 4 and Aug. 13, 1784. This was the estimate of Rev. John Breynton in his report to the Soc. for the Prop. of the Gospel.

[12] Cf. Jones, Hist. of N. Y., ii, 507; cf. Murdock, Hist. of Nova Scotia, iii, 23, 34.

ably 30,000 came from New York, and more than 20,000 were, we may believe, inhabitants of that state.[1]

With the exception of about 200 families, who went to the Bahama Islands, the remainder of the loyalists of New York removed to Canada. The emigration northward began in 1775 and continued for several years after the war ceased. Seven general routes were taken; first, by the way of the Hudson, Mohawk, Wood Creek, Lake Oneida and the Oswego to Lake Ontario;[2] second, up the Hudson, Mohawk, West Canada Creek and Black River to Sackett's Harbor; third, up the Hudson, across the Mohegan mountains, down the Moose and Black rivers to Sackett's Harbor, or down the Oswegatchie to Ogdensburg; fourth, up the Hudson, over the mountains and down the Racket river to the St. Lawrence; fifth, up the Hudson, down Lake George and Champlain and the Sorel to Montreal; sixth, by the way of the Atlantic and the St. Lawrence river; and seventh, across western New York.[3] Journeys were often made in the winter with sleighs, when whole neighborhoods united for the enterprise.[4] In general three classes of loyalists settled in Canada—the loyal provincial troops, those who were driven from their homes by persecutions during and after the war, and the voluntary exiles. Before July 4, 1776, those who went to Canada were almost entirely of the first class, but after that event refuges of the other two classes found their way thither.[5] With the increased activity of the inquisi-

---

[1] Some loyalists left Nova Scotia and went to Canada or to the south. *Can. Archs.* (1895), 61. Others got large land grants, sold them and returned to the U. S. *Ibid.* (1894), 418.

[2] This was a favorite route to Upper Canada. Ryerson, *Loyalists in America*, ii, 188–189.

[3] *The U. E. L. Centennial* (1884), address by Hon. G. W. Allen, 57–58; Caniff, *Hist. of the Prov. of Ontario*, 132. This was the common route to Lower Canada.   [4] *Ibid.*, 143.

[5] On Dec. 2, 1776, a party of loyalists reached Quebec, and temporary relief

torial boards, the passage of harsher laws against traitors, and the surrender of Burgoyne, many loyalists were driven to Canada, while others felt it wisest to go in order to avoid trouble.[1]

By 1778, counting loyalist troops and men, women and children who were refugees, not less than 3,000 had found their way to Canada.[2] " Refuges are increasing daily," wrote an official at Quebec on November 1.[3] " Helpless friends of government" were on their way to Niagara.[4] Until 1783 they were constantly arriving.[5] By 1782 they were so numerous that monthly returns were made of them.[6] With the treaty of peace came a great rush to the north. On June 4, 1783, Sir Guy Carleton wrote to General Haldimand that " 200 families wish to go to Canada ;"[7] and a month later eight companies of loyalists, organized as militia, had embarked.[8] They intended to settle in the county of Frontenac. By the middle of August they reached Quebec.[9] Part of them were from Tryon county.[10] On August 8 a second company embarked for Canada,[11] and arrived there Septem-

---

was given. *Can. Archs.* (1885), 250, 251, Sir Guy Carleton to Gen. Phillips, Nov. 29 and Dec. 2, 1776. All of them took an oath of allegiance. *Ibid.*, 253.

[1] Letter of Col. John C. Clark, given in Ryerson, *Loyalists in America*, ii, 217; Caniff, *Hist. of the Prov. of Ontario*, 61–67. Also *Scraps of Local History*, in Ryerson, ii, 224.

[2] *Can. Archs.* (1883), 83, (1888), 742, shows that there were 853 loyalists at six places.   [3] *Ibid.* (1886), 404, no. 294.

[4] *Ibid.* (1886), 544, 549, (1883), 56, 113, 203, (1887), 246, 247, 249, 352, 355, 365, 369, 372, 373, 378, 460; *ibid.* (1888), 619, 627, 685, 687, 688.

[5] *Ibid.*, 365.   [6] *Ibid.* (1883), 83, Oct. 6, 1778.

[7] *Ibid.* (1887), Haldimand Collection, 535, 563, Carleton to Haldimand from New York, June 4, 1783.

[8] *Ibid.*, 534, 563, Carleton to Haldimand, July 4 and 6, August 8.

[9] *Ibid.*, 564. Return of Aug. 14 and 16, 1783, at Quebec.

[10] *Ibid.* Return of Aug. 17, at Quebec.

[11] *Ibid.* Carleton to Haldimand, Aug. 8, 1783.

ber 6.[1]   On September 8 a third company, under Captain
Michael Grass and Captain Van Alstine, with loyalists from
Rockland, Orange, Ulster, Westchester, Dutchess and Columbia counties, set sail for Upper Canada.   They reached
Quebec a month later, wintered on the Sorel, and settled on
Quinté Bay.[2]   It was reported that 3,000 more loyalists
wished to go to Canada.[3]   Four families, disappointed in the
new region, returned to New York city.[4]   Alexander White,
a former sheriff of Tryon county, led a large party to Upper
Canada to settle between Glengarry and Quinté Bay.[5]   This
is a sample of the many small groups of loyalists who went
to the Canadian wilderness to carve out homes and begin
life anew.   The English population in Lower Canada[6] increased from comparatively few in 1782, to about 20,000 in
1791, and was due very largely to the influx of loyalists.[7]
In March, 1784, 1,328 "friends of government" were being
fed at Quebec.[8]   On the seigniories of the Sorel, in eight
townships at the Long Sault, in five townships at Cataraqui,
at Point Mullie in the vicinity of Montreal, Chambly, St.
Johns and the Bay of Chaleurs were settled in 1784 5,628
men, women and children.[9]   Probably there were at that

---

[1] *Can. Archs.* (1887).   Return of Sept. 6, 1783, at Quebec; *ibid.*, Sept. 15.

[2] *Cf.* Haight, *Coming of the Loyalists*, 6; *cf.* Ryerson, *Loyalists in America*, ii,
188, 287; Caniff, *Hist. of Prov. of Ontario*, 132, 422, 449; *Can. Archs.* (1887), 436.

[3] *Ibid.*, 433, Riedesel to Haldimand, June 5, 1783.

[4] *Ibid.*, 564, Haldimand to Carleton, Sept. 15, 1783.

[5] He advertised his expedition in *Gaine's New York Gazette*, June 7, 1783, no.
1655.   *Can. Archs.* (1888), 959, Maurer wrote to Mathews, June 17, 1784, " Loyalists are daily coming in across the lake."

[6] *The Constitutional Act*, 31 George III., chap. 31, made the Ottawa river the
boundary between Upper and Lower Canada in 1791.

[7] Ryerson, *Loyalists in America*, ii, 287, note.

[8] *Can. Archs.* (1883), 115, (1885), 320, 369, (1888), 744.

[9] *Ibid.* (1891), 4–20, gives a complete list of names and places of settle
ment; *cf. ibid.* (1888), 753, 754, (1883), 115

time many more loyalists in Lower Canada, who had as yet
made no definite settlement.   By 1791 the loyalist population did not fall far short of 10,000 in the region below
Cataraqui.

It is estimated that in 1783 10,000 loyalists reached Upper
Canada,[1] that the next year the population had doubled, and
by 1791 was 25,000.[2] These numbers are certainly too
large. Perhaps 17,000 would be a more reliable estimate
for 1791.[3] They settled along the entire course of the upper
St. Lawrence, the northern shore of Lake Ontario, the western banks of the Niagara river and on the Canadian side of
Lake Erie.[4] In 1789 there was a "great influx of Americans" to the fertile regions of upper Canada.[5] The "Old
United Empire List" and the "Supplementary List," preserved in the department of crown lands at Toronto give the
names of the heads of about 6,000 loyalist families.[6] Most
of the names are those of soldiers. Including the wives and
children of these, together with other loyalists in Canada
whose names are not included in the "lists," a total of probably 20,000 would result, of whom perhaps 15,000 were formerly inhabitants of the empire state.

The period of the dispersion of the loyalists covered the
twelve years subsequent to 1775.   During that time possibly
60,000 persons of the defeated party went, either from or

---

[1] Ryerson, *Loyalists in America*, ii, 287, note.

[2] *The United Empire Loyalists' Centennial* (1884), 93, address by Hon. J. B.
Plumb.

[3] Pitt gave 10,000 as the population in 1791; *cf. The United Empire Loyalists'
Centennial* (1884), 27, address by Sir Richard Cartwright; *ibid.*, 109, address by
William Kirby; *cf.* Sir Richard Bonnycastle, *Canada Before 1837*, i, 24–25; *Can.
Archs.* (1890), 236.

[4] Harris, *United Empire Loyalists*, 9–10; *Can. Archs.* (1890), 168.

[5] *Ibid.* (1886), 583, no. 284.

[6] *The United Empire Loyalists' Centennial* (1884), 129–333, has the complete
"Lists" reprinted; *cf. Can. Archs.* (1883), 206.

through New York, to various parts of the British dominions, and of this number about 35,000 had been inhabitants of the former province of New York.

Beyond question New York was the stronghold of loyalism, and had more adherents to the British flag than any other state.[1] Thousands of the most influential loyalists could be named, because they have left themselves on record in British army and navy lists, in loyal addresses, in the minutes of inquisitorial boards, in the forfeiture and sale of their property and in petitions to the British government. Still other thousands are known to have been loyalists collectively, though not individually. It is impossible, therefore, to give the exact number of loyalists in New York.[2]

The loyalist party, as an active organization with a definite part to play, varied in the number of its adherents with the changing scenes of the revolution. In 1775 and the early months of 1776, before the edict of separation had been decreed, at least ninety-five per cent. of the people professed loyalty to the king, empire and British constitution. The remaining five per cent. embraced those ardent republicans who openly advocated independence. The Declaration of Independence made loyalty to the king or to the Continental Congress, the issue on which party lines were finally formed. After that great event it was still believed that a majority of the "honest-hearted people in New York" were on the king's side.[3]

The whigs were wont to believe that the open loyalists alone, whose nature, interests and convictions led them to defiant declarations against the revolution and to action for

---

[1] *Am. Archs.*, 4th ser., iv, 359.

[2] *Ibid.*, vi, 789. "The movements of this kind of people . . . are more easy to perceive than describe," wrote Washington to Congress, June 10, 1776.

[3] *Can. Archs.* (1888), 855. "Cald" to Johnson, Sept. 20, 1776; *cf.* Moore, *Diary of Am. Rev.*, ii, 449.

the established government, constituted the party.   They
formed but a minority, however, and were supplemented by
the secret loyalists, who were so timid and cautious that they
either remained as neutral as possible, or else played a false
part by professing to support the revolution when at the
same time they were acting secretly against it.   The loyalists
always insisted that they formed a large majority in New
York and that an honest vote would prove it.   Great Britain
believed that the loyalists outnumbered the whigs.[1]   Galloway asserted that " more than four-fifths of the people " preferred a constitutional union with England, and in 1779 he
declared that nine-tenths of the colonists would vote for it.[2]
While these figures are exaggerated, yet the loyalists constituted no small part of the population.   From first to last New
York city was overwhelmingly tory.   Early in 1776 it was
reported that all the leading inhabitants were at heart with
the crown, and that at least 2,000 of them could be pointed
out.[3]   From the arrival of the British until their evacuation,
this city was the center of loyalism in America.   Washington
declared that most of the people on Long Island were loyalists and ready to help the British,[4] and it was said that there
were only forty-five whigs on Staten Island.[5]   Southern New
York had, it appears, a large majority of loyalists before its
occupation by royal troops, and it was but natural that
loyalist sentiment should increase during the seven years of
British occupation.   There was not a single county above

---

[1] Letter in *Holt's N. Y. Journal*, April 27, 1775; declaration in *Rivington's Gazette*, March 9, 1775; London letter in *ibid.*, March 16, 1775; *Am. Archs.*, 4th ser., iv, 587, vi, 1338.

[2] *Examination of Joseph Galloway*, etc., 12; Galloway, *Letters to A Nobleman*, etc., 21.

[3] *Am. Archs.*, 4th ser., iv, 587, vi, 1338.

[4] *Ibid.*, iv, 1066, 1095, vi, 725, 1324, 1338; *Min. of Prov. Cong.*, iv, 371; *Docs. rel. to N. Y. Col. Hist.*, viii, 663; Stiles, *Hist. of Kings Co.*, i, 32.

[5] *Gaines' N. Y. Gazette*, Oct. 21, 1776; *Docs. rel. to N. Y. Col. Hist.*, viii, 681.

New York city that did not have a powerful faction of loyalists within its borders.[1] In many localities they actually outnumbered their opponents, and certainly one-third of the inhabitants along the Hudson and Mohawk rivers were of the loyalist political faith. It seems fair to conclude, therefore, after averaging the loyalists of southern New York with those of the regions to the north, that one-half of the population upheld the doctrine of loyalism.[2] In other words, out of a population of 185,000, 90,000 were loyalists, of whom 35,000 emigrated and 55,000 accepted the inevitable and became valuable members of the new state.

[1] *Am. Archs.*, 4th ser., iii, 826, iv, 187, 188, 828, 830, v, 39, vi, 1385, 1415; Dawson, *Westchester Co.*, 83, n. 4, 154; Howell, *Hist. of Alb. and Schenect. Cos.*, 393.

[2] John Adams thought that New York would have joined the British had not the example of New England and Virginia deterred her. *Works of John Adams*, x, 63, 110. Judge Thomas McKean believed that one-third of all the colonists were loyalists, *ibid.*, 87. Alexander Hamilton declared that not half of the people were whigs in 1775, and that one-third still sympathized with the British in 1782, Winsor, *North America*, vii, 185, 187. Gouverneur Morris thought that it was doubtful whether more than one-half the people of New York " were ever in really hearty and active sympathy with the patriots," Roosevelt, *Gouverneur Morris*, 36. In 1782 it was still reported that more were for the king than for Congress, *Can. Archs.* (1888), 925. Sabine concluded that " in New York the whigs were far weaker than their opponents."

CHAPTER IX

TREATMENT OF THE LOYALISTS BY GREAT BRITAIN

AFTER a losing contest of eight years and a treaty of peace through which 35,000 New York loyalists lost their wealth and homes and were scattered over the remaining parts of the empire, they were forced to throw themselves upon the generosity of the British government. The nature of their claims and the character of imperial compensation remain to be considered.

From the outbreak of the revolution the policy of Great Britain was to use the loyalists to help subdue it. Therefore loyalism was encouraged by fair promises and inducements. To the loyal colonial volunteers, who entered the British service in increasing numbers from 1775 to 1783, large tracts of land at the close of the war were offered, in addition to the clothing, rations and pay of regulars.[1] This promise was faithfully kept. Loyalist officers were well treated, and many a New Yorker secured a good appointment in the royal army or civil service in recognition of merit in the effort to suppress rebellion. Many others were given good pensions[2] or half-pay.[3] Loyalists not in military service were promised protection against their rebellious brothers and compensation in case of loss through loyalty. In this way their moral and material assistance was sought in the contest. Hence the governor was ordered "to offer

---

[1] *Can. Archs.* (1890), 80, Germain to Carleton, Mch. 26, 1777; *ibid.* 87, 96. (1888), 745, (1883), 75.

[2] *Ibid.* (1886), 432. [3] *Ibid.*, 431; *Parl. Reg.*, vol. 35, 209.

every encouragement" to loyalists,[1] and the king's royal
commissions proposed "due consideration" for the "merito-
rious service" of all who in any way aided in the efforts to
quell the insurrection.[2]

As early as November 18, 1775, the British government
ordered the governor of Florida to receive and protect all
"friends of government." A proclamation to this effect
was printed and publicly circulated in New York city.[3]   But
it was not enforced, because Governor Tryon was able to
protect obnoxious loyalists until the arrival of the royal
forces in the summer of 1776. New York city, after its occupation by the British, became the loyalists' Mecca.[4] Thither
they went from all parts of the state for protection and suc-
cor.   They had implicit trust in the power of the British
to give them both.   To the very last they confidently believed that the revolution would be crushed, and that they
would be victors.[5]   They endured abuse, lost their real and
personal property and suffered enforced or voluntary exile
all the more easily because they were certain of retribution
and ample restitution.

There was a marked difference between the treatment of
loyalists by the civil and military authorities of Great Britain.   Loud and bitter were the complaints made by loyalists
concerning the cruelty, robbery, insults and ill treatment
they suffered from the British army.   The whigs were called
"rebels," but the tories were sneered at as "damned traitors

---

[1] *Parl. Reg.* (1775), i, 186.

[2] *Annual Reg.* (1776), Proclamation of the Howes in June.

[3] *Am. Archs.*, 4th ser., i, 340–341.

[4] *Can. Archs.* (1885), 181, Hutcheson to Haldimand, July 10, 1776; *ibid.*, 182,
Aug. 8, 14 and 26, 1776, and Jan. 1, 1777.   Five loyalist governors were there at
once.

[5] *Docs. rel. to N. Y. Col. Hist.*, viii, 781.

and scoundrels.'"[1]   On Long Island the loyalists were plundered of crops, cattle, horses and even household goods.[2] On Staten Island " the tories were cruelly used," plundered and maltreated, until they were even willing to poison the British.[3]   Those who went with the whigs and then deserted were well-treated,[4] while the loyal farmers who voluntarily gave liberal supplies to the British, were later harshly ordered to continue it.[5]   It was not uncommon to impress loyalists into military service.[6]   Those who went to Halifax in 1776 were told that they must take up arms, or get no relief, and some were even forced to work in coal mines.[7]   It was reported that Sir Guy Carleton whipped all loyalists who refused to arm.[8]   For inciting desertion loyalist soldiers were given 1000 lashes.[9]   Burgoyne grumbled about them, said they had been overrated, and attributed his defeat largely to them.[10]   Because of the barbarities of the British, many loyalists refused to join them.[11]   The harshest loyalist tirades were written against the unjustifiable conduct of British military officers.[12]

---

[1] *Am. Archs.*, 5th ser., ii, 1276; *cf. Rivington's Royal Gazette*, Jan, 30, 1779, no. 244; *ibid.*, May 22, 1779, no. 276.

[2] Jones, *Hist. of N. Y.*, i, 114–118, 136.

[3] *Am. Archs.*, 5th ser., i, 1110, 1112, 1532; *cf.* Wharton, *Dip. Corresp. of Am. Rev.*, i, 303.

[4] *Rivington's Royal Gazette*, Jan. 30, May 1, and May 22, 1779, no. 276, etc.

[5] *Ibid.*, Sep. 10, 1778, Mch. 13, 1779, Jan. 23, 1779, no. 242, etc.

[6] *Can. Archs.*, (1886), 594, no. 69; *Public Papers of George Clinton*, i, 548; *Am. Archs.*, 5th ser., i, 1112.

[7] *Ibid.*, 46, 98.

[8] *Can. Archs.* (1888), 774, Phillips to Carleton, Apr. 11, 1776.

[9] *Ibid.* (1885), 191, 256.

[10] *Ibid.* (1883), 75, 76, 77, (1888), 746, 748, (1890), 86.

[11] Wharton, *Dip. Corresp. of the Am. Rev.*, i, 22–24; Jones, *Hist. of N. Y.*, i, 138, 201, 341, ii, 136, 137; *cf. Am. Mag. of Hist.*, vi, 421.

[12] *Cf.* Jones, *Hist. of N. Y.*

Relying upon the promises made by the king's agents and on their own expectations, loyalists early asked for material aid from the civil power. In 1776 it was written that there was not a province in America " which does not afford shoals of petitioners hanging about the treasury." In fact, the administration was "unable to answer the numerous demands."[1] Those fleeing to England for loyalty's sake were either given positions or granted temporary annuities.[2] In New York city, from the time of Howe's arrival till the treaty of peace, loyalists were received with open arms by the royal agents. Many were given lucrative civil or military offices, and all refugees received more or less aid.[3] The deserted lands and houses of the revolutionists in southern New York were given, leased or rented to them.[4] They were allowed to cut timber, and build houses on vacant lands.[5] Subscriptions were taken for the needy, who were ordered to go in a body to the police office for aid.[6] The " associated refugee loyalists," organized to make themselves self-supporting, held lotteries to raise money.[7] As late as March 10, 1783, suffering loyalists were asked to apply for their allowances.[8] Governor Tryon wished to institute an office of in-

[1] *Am. Archs.*, 5th ser., i, 149, Oliver to Winslow, July 10, 1776; *cf. ibid.*, ii, 1317.

[2] *Docs. rel. to N. Y. Col. Hist.*, viii, 569. April 5, 1775, Drs. Cooper and Chandler were voted an annual allowance of £200.

[3] *Ibid.*, 568, 773–774, 799, 809. James Rivington was made royal printer at £100 a year. *Can. Archs.* (1883), 71; *Rivington's Royal Gazette*, Jan. 30, March 10, 1779, and Dec. 23 and 28, 1780. Christopher Billopp was made policeman of Staten Island.

[4] *Ibid.*, Feb. 17, 1779, no. 249; *Docs. rel. to N. Y. Col. Hist.*, viii, 774, 809.

[5] *Rivington's Royal Gazette*, Feb. 17, and March 24, 1779.

[6] *Ibid.*, March 13, 1778, no. 256.

[7] *Ibid.*. Nov. 13, 1779, Dec. 27, 1780, etc.; *Docs. rel. to N. Y. Col. Hist.*, viii. 769–770.

[8] *Gaine's N. Y. Gazette*, March 17, 1783, no. 1639.

quiry " to examine and register all loyalists coming into the
British lines and to take cognizance of their losses and sufferings." [1]   Lord George Germain expected New York to
compensate loyalists for their losses, when the rebellion
should be stamped out.[2]   Through these various helpful
measures the British officials hoped to lighten the burden
of the loyalists and to lessen the expense to government.[3]

The many loyalists who went to Canada, and the few who
went to Nova Scotia before 1782 were given food and shelter
until some definite provision could be made for them.   Sir
Guy Carleton wrote to General Phillips from Quebec that
temporary relief would be given all New York refugees.[4]
Those who joined Burgoyne and fled north after his surrender were well cared for.[5]   By July 1, 1779, there were
853 loyalists, excluding soldiers, in Canada receiving provisions at seven different points,[6] and this number rapidly
increased.   Comfortable houses and barracks were provided,
or else huts were built for them.[7]   Some were allowed to
settle on estates as tenants.[8]   Machiche was set aside as a
refuge for the wives and children of loyalists in the British
service.[9]   The general policy was to receive all loyalists,
help the needy, encourage the men to enlist in the army,
and make all as self-supporting as possible.   Hence the
women were given washing to do,[10] and the men were sup-

---

[1] *Docs. rel. to N. Y. Col. Hist.*, viii, 771, Tryon to Clinton, July 26, 1779.

[2] *Ibid.*, 768, Germain to Robertson, July 9, 1779.

[3] *Ibid.*, 801, Robertson to Germain, Sept. 1, 1780.

[4] *Can. Archs.* (1885), 250, (1888), 744.

[5] *Ibid.* (1886), 387, 393, 399, 407, 528, 544, 594, 655–659, 660, 663, (1888), 648, 687, 732, 734, 742.

[6] *Ibid.* (1886), 404, no. 294.   [7] *Ibid.* (1886), 401, Oct. 1, 1778, (1888), 732.

[8] *Ibid.* (1886), 403, Oct. 7, 1778; *cf.* Caniff, *Hist. of Prov. of Ontario*, 156.

[9] *Can. Archs.* (1888), 726, Jan. 22, 1781.

[10] *Ibid.*, (1888), 688, June 25, 1780.

plied with other work.[1]   Still fuel, beds, and household
goods were furnished them,[2] clothing was given,[3] and occa-
sionally money was paid them as pensions.[4]   Arms were refused, however.[5]   Their claims were usually submitted to,
and passed on by, a board appointed for that purpose.[6]   In
1782 Townshend ordered General Haldimand to provision
the loyalists, make out a list of them, and return an account
of their losses.[7]   Officers were detailed to watch and guard
them, and monthly reports of their condition were made.[8]
England's policy of strict economy in dealing with them, and
the scarcity of supplies, caused much suffering among them,[9]
as was natural under the circumstances of war; still her
treatment was just and generous, and the complaints were
comparatively few.   It was believed by both loyalists and
Englishmen that, when the revolution was crushed, the expenses incurred would be paid by the rebellious colonies.

The refusal of New York to comply with the terms of
peace relating to the loyalists threw 35,000 of them upon
the British government for temporary support.[10]   Compensation had been promised them and now they demanded it,
not as charity, but as justice.   The vast majority of the
loyalists had lost but little property.   Many who went to
Nova Scotia took their personal effects with them, and some
even tore down their houses to take the material to the wil-

[1] *Can. Archs.* (1888), 627, 651, 724, 727, 732, 745, 749, 977.
[2] *Ibid.* (1886), 405, Nov. 19, 1778.
[3] *Ibid.* (1888), 648, 734.
[4] *Ibid.* (1888), 729, 734, 750.
[5] *Ibid.* (1888), 722.
[6] *Ibid.* (1888), 748, 750, (1886), 418, (1887), 106, 108.
[7] *Ibid.* (1885), 284, Feb. 28.
[8] *Ibid.* (1888), 685, 721, 725, 736, 745, (1886), 402.
[9] *Ibid.* (1886), 544, (1888), 658, 725, 726, 736.
[10] *Ibid.* (1886), 552, no. 50.

derness for new homes.[1]   Not a few were able to dispose of
their property before leaving.[2]   Those who went to Canada
after 1783 drove their live stock before them and took as
much personal property as they could carry, while others
returned for their goods.[3]   Losing little of value through
loyalism, most of the unfortunates demanded no more of the
crown than land and supplies for starting again in life.   The
minority of the loyalists, composed of the wealthy, who
had lost all their possessions, offices and established incomes
for the sake of the unity of the empire, demanded indemnity
in British gold.

England accepted the responsibility.   To the loss of her
colonies and the war debt was added this extra burden.
All loyalists were to be treated as fairly and equitably as
possible.   To the masses, therefore, lands, tools, provisions
and seeds were given in British North America   To influential citizens, army officers, royal officials and loyal
churchmen were given larger land grants, lucrative positions
in the army, state or church, or pensions.   Actual losses
were made good in proportion to services rendered.   All
who suffered in their " rights, properties and professions "

---

[1] Sabine, *Loyalists of Am. Rev.*, i, 288; *cf. Gaine's N. Y. Gazette*, Aug. 29, 1783,
and Sept. 8, 1783.   The Board of Commissioners had to be consulted before it
could be done.

[2] Onderdonk, *Queens Co. in Olden Times*, 61–63.   This was in accord with the
treaty of peace.   Jones, *Hist. of N. Y.*, i, 266–268.   The papers are full of sales,
auctions, etc., of loyalists about to leave.   Israel Young, of Queens co., sold his
farm of 500 acres before going to Nova Scotia.   MS. *Transcript of . . Papers . .
of the American Loyalists*, vol. 17, p. 192.   Christopher Billopp sold his estate on
Staten Island in 1782.   He had 1078 acres valued at £15 an acre.   He sold it for
£8000, but lost, he claimed, $5000 by it.   *Ibid.*, vol. 4.   Benjamin Seaman sold
his estate on Staten Island before leaving.   Sabine, ii, 272.   Henry Mellows went
to New York to sell his property after the war.   MS. *Transcript of . . Books and
Papers . . of the American Loyalists*, vol. 18, p. 65.   C. W. Apthorp remained in
New York city to sell his property before going to Canada.   *Ibid.*, vol, 17, p. 581.

[3] *Can. Archs.* (1886), 412;   Caniff, *Hist. of Prov. of Ontario*, 143.

for the sake of loyalty were recognized as having a claim to compensation.[1]   Before evacuating New York city, Sir Guy Carleton was instructed to collect the loyalists' debts in accordance with the treaty of peace.   He created a commission to examine all loyalists' claims, above £10, contracted after November 1, 1776, to hear all parties, call witnesses, ascertain the exact sums due each claimant and collect them.   The commissioners sat for seven months, drew their pay, but compelled the payment of no debts.   The loyalists protested in vain.   Evacuation took place, and they lost the honest debts due them.[2]

By inducing loyalists to settle in Canada or Nova Scotia, Great Britain made good her promise to reimburse them, and, at the same time, was developing rich parts of the empire in a much-needed direction.   As early as May 9, 1782, loyalists applied for lands in Nova Scotia.[3]   Governor Parr advised that each family be given 500 acres of land, every single man 300 acres, and that 2,000 acres for a church, and 1,000 acres for a school be set aside in each township.[4]   It was estimated that there were 12,000,000 acres of ungranted, cultivable lands in Nova Scotia in 1783.[5]   Surveying began in the spring of that year, and by October it had cost £3,000.[6]   Seven surveyors plotted the land for a distance of 150 miles up the St. John; six men did the same work for the district of Shelburne, Port Mouton and the coast between the two; five surveyed Annapolis, Bason, St. Mary's Bay, Clare, Conway

---

[1] *23 George III.*, ch. 80.

[2] Jones, *Hist. of N. Y.*, ii, 266–268; *Gaine's N. Y. Gazette*, April 2, 1783.

[3] *Can. Archs.* (1894), 400.

[4] *Ibid.* (1894), 401, Parr to Townshend, Oct. 26, 1782; Lawrence, *Footprints,* etc., p. 1–2.

[5] *Can. Archs.* (1894), 403, April 23, 1783.

[6] *Ibid.* (1894), 404, 405, June 7, 10 and 24, 1783; Murdock, *Hist. of Nova Scotia*, iii, 23.

and Bear River. Passamaquoddy Bay and the coast east to the
St. John were divided by four surveyors, while one man did
the work at Newport, and another at Dartmouth.[1]   Prior to
April 10, 1784, this work had cost £1,838 more, and 1,000,-
000 acres had been surveyed and divided into lots.[2]   It was
still in progress in November.[3]   The surveying was not adequate to the demand, and occasioned considerable discontent.[4]   Escheated estates[5] and a quarter of the lands of the
Acadia Land Company were opened to settlers.[6]   There was
little uniformity in the size of grants.[7]   The ordinary lot was
200 acres [8] for each individual, with an additional two hundred
acres for non-commissioned army officers, and fifty acres for
privates.[9]   Carleton urged the granting of 5,000 acres to each
of fifty-five field officers, but the home government restricted
the number to 1,000.[10]   Loyalists were exempt from fees and
quit-rents for ten years.[11]   By August 10, 1784, grants for
nearly 5,000 families, or 20,120 persons, had passed the seal,[12]
and others followed, until every loyalist had his farm. Lands
were granted as late as June 20, 1792.[13]

Provisions for one year were supplied to loyalists when
they left New York, and upon reaching Nova Scotia they

---

[1] *Can. Archs.* (1894), 408, Oct. 21, 1783.

[2] *Ibid.* (1894), 417; Murdock, *Hist. of Nova Scotia*, iii, 31.

[3] *Can. Archs.* (1894), 427, Parr to Sydney, Nov. 15, 1784.

[4] *Ibid.* (1894), 417, April 11 and 16, 1784.

[5] *Ibid.* (1894), 407, Aug. 28, 1783.

[6] *Ibid.* (1894), 406, Aug. 8, 1783; *ibid.*, 407, Sept. 23, 1783.

[7] *Ibid.* (1894), 407, Aug. 28, 1783.

[8] *Ibid.* (1895), 13, July 4, 1787.

[9] *Ibid.* (1894), 406, Aug. 8, 1783.

[10] *Ibid.* (1894), 414, 416, 417, 418.

[11] *Ibid.* (1894), 406.   [11] *Ibid.* (1894), 423.

[13] *Ibid.* (1895), 27. In 1790 2000 acres were granted to Isaac Wilkins, 2600
acres to Major Philip Van Cortlandt, etc. Murdock, *Hist. of Nova Scotia*, iii, 94.

were to be fed until the "instructions for granting lands" could be carried out.[1] In 1784, a few could care for themselves, but the governor urged a continuation of food for the needy.[2] To prevent frauds and abuses a board was formed to examine the claims of the loyalists for provisions; [3] yet it was reported on November 30, 1785, that 26,300 men, women and children were still "entitled to provisions which they fully merit." [4] It was not until June of 1786 that rations were cut off,[5] but the action was not final, for as late as September 22, 1792, relief was given to loyalists in distress.[6] Clothing, medicine, and other supplies, were also furnished.[7]

General Carleton, in sending the refugees to Nova Scotia, recommended that they be given " materials and artificers for building."[8] Governor Parr, without authority from home, promised them boards for houses to the value of £1,000,[9] and by February 4, 1784, lumber amounting in value to £4,500 had been thus distributed.[10] The supply stopped in November of that year,[11] after more than another £1,000 had been distributed in building materials.[12] Nails, window glass, shingles and bricks, and carpenter tools were also supplied. The king ordered iron work for grist and saw-mills, tools for the woods and farms, boats and tents and necessary implements of husbandry to the value of £5,500, to be sent out

---

[1] *Can. Archs.* (1894), 404–406, 408; *cf.* Lawrence, *Footprints*, etc., 1–2.

[2] *Can. Archs.* (1894), 413, 414, 416.

[3] *Ibid.* (1894), 417, April 20, 1784.   [4] *Ibid.* (1894), 438.

[5] *Ibid.* (1894), 443, 447.   [6] *Ibid.* (1895), 27; *New Brunswick Papers.*

[7] Raymond, *The U. E. Loyalists*, 11.

[8] *Can. Archs.* (1894), 401, Oct. 26, 1782; *cf.* Lawrence, *Footprints*, etc., p. 1–2.

[9] *Can. Archs.* (1894), 402, Jan. 15, 1783; Murdock, *Hist. of Nova Scotia*, iii, 12.

[10] Murdock, *Hist. of Nova Scotia*, iii, 19–23; *Can. Archs.* (1894), 413.

[11] *Can. Archs.* (1894), 427, Nov. 15, 1784.

[12] *Ibid.* (1894), 418, May 1, 1784, (1895), 43.

and distributed among the loyalists.[1]   They were further assisted in agriculture with grains and seeds.[2]   "Many thousands of loyalists have taken refuge in the province, to whom
assistance has been given," wrote an officer.[3]   Although
there was some discontent,[4] chiefly over the delay in surveys, the apportionments, and the various supplies, still
within two years what had been the wilds of Nova Scotia,
began to give evidence of a healthy civilization.[5]   The people cleared and settled their lands, built their homes and
formed villages—"all seemingly happy and contented."[6]   On
January 2, 1785, Governor Parr wrote, "The loyalists are at
last contented and getting on exceedingly well in clearing
and cultivating their lands."[7]   And so well pleased was the
king with their prosperity, that he immediately ordered a
retrenchment in expenses.[8]   For surveys, lumber, tools and
seeds certainly not less than $100,000 had been spent.[9]
For transportation, clothing, provisions during at least two
and a half years, and governmental expenses, probably
$4,500,000 additional was required to make the colony pros-
perous and self-supporting.   About two-thirds of this expen-
diture was in behalf of New York loyalists.

The treatment of loyalists in Canada after the treaty of
peace was similar to that which they experienced in Nova

---

[1] *Can. Archs.* (1894), 411, (1895), 43; *cf.* Perley, *Early Hist. of New Bruns.*, 20.

[2] *Ibid.* (1894), 412, Jan. 3, 1784.   [3] *Ibid.* (1888), 578, May 20, 1783.

[4] *Ibid.* (1894), 413, 414, 415, 416, 417, 419, 422, 423, 424, 426, 429, 443, 447; Murdock, *Hist. of Nova Scotia*, iii, 29, 31.

[5] *Can. Archs.* (1894), 413, 414, 421, 427.

[6] *Ibid.* (1894), 422, 426.   [7] *Ibid.* (1894), 430.

[8] *Ibid.* (1894), 431, March 8, 1785.

[9] By August 11, 1784, the expenses for land grants and surveys alone amounted to £10,345.   Murdock, *Hist. of Nova Scotia*, iii, 33.   Major Studholm spent £6,721 for lumber and house building.   Perley, *Early Hist. of New Brunswick*, 20.   It is assumed that these figures were on a sterling basis.

Scotia. So far as possible, compensation was to be made in land grants. In June, 1783, General Haldimand asked Lord North about settlements for the loyalists. The Governor of Quebec received instructions about land grants July 23, 1783.[1] Surveys began immediately and were pushed forward with all possible speed.[2] Eight townships were surveyed in the neighborhood of Lake St. Francis, and five more at Cataraqui, or Kingston.[3] Other localities on the Sorel, along the St. Lawrence, and on the northern shores of Lake Ontario and Lake Erie were then plotted. There was no absolute uniformity in the size of the grants, although the general rule was to give every adult male and every widow 200 acres.[4] The provincial council in 1789 ordered the land boards to grant 200 acres each to all sons and daughters of loyalists " as they arrive to full age." [5] Loyalists on the Sorel received 60 acres each and a town lot.[6] Civil and military officials were given larger grants.[7] Stephen De-Lancey received 1,000 acres,[8] and Major Van Alstine, 1,200 acres.[9] These lands were granted free from all expense.[10] In upper Canada 3,200,000 acres were given loyalists who settled there before 1787. About 730,000 acres went to loyalist militiamen,[11] 450,000 to discharged soldiers and sailors, 225,000 to magistrates and barristers, 136,000 to

---

[1] *Can. Archs.* (1885), 285.

[2] *Ibid.* (1885), 375. " It swelled the expense." *Ibid.* (1886), 414, 417.

[3] *Ibid.* (1885), 310; Kingsford, *Hist. of Canada*, vii, 218.

[4] Caniff, *Hist. of Prov. of Ontario*, 165; *Can. Archs.* (1886), 428, 457, 585, 586.

[5] *Ibid.* (1890), 245, 250, Nov. 9, 1789; *The United Empire Loyalists' Centennial* (1884), 127-128.

[6] *Can. Archs.* (1887), 440, (1886), 426.

[7] *Ibid.* (1886), 427, 428, 457, 585.

[8] *Ibid.* (1886), 428, May 24, 1784.

[9] Caniff, *Hist. of Prov. of Ontario*, 107.   [10] *Ibid.*, 165.

[11] All loyalists not otherwise designated were classed under this head.

executive councillors, 50,000 to five legislative councillors, 37,000 to clergymen, 264,000 to surveyors and helpers, 500,000 for schools, 93,000 to officers of the army and navy, and smaller tracts to prominent persons.[1] Field officers received 5,000 acres, captains 3,000, subalterns 2,000, and privates 200. Loyalist civilians were ranked with the disbanded soldiers, according to their losses and to services rendered.[2] In 1798 the grants were limited to tracts varying from 200 to 1,200 acres each.[3] At first grants were made in lots of 200 acres each. They were numbered, the numbers put in a hat and drawn out by the petitioners.[4] The surveyor acted as land agent and wrote the names of owners upon the map of the surveys.[5] This democratic method was denounced by the officers.[6] In 1788 "many applications" from people in the "States" were made for lands, and it was estimated that 20,000 or 30,000 "who were attached to the king's government" could be secured by inducements in land grants.[7] Governor Simcoe, under this belief, issued a proclamation in 1792 inviting them to Canada, but he was removed and his action nullified.[8]

By 1789 about 17,000 loyalists were settled above Montreal.[9] As soon as possible after surveys were made, loyalists were to be sent to settle the lands.[10] The early arrivals and the late-comers were to be treated alike.[11] The only test was loyalty.[12] During the spring of 1784 the officers were

---

[1] Caniff, *Hist. of Prov. of Ontario*, 176.   [2] *Ibid.*, 179.   [3] *Ibid.*, 180.

[4] *Can. Archs.* (1885), 367, Nov. 18, 1783.

[5] Caniff, *Hist. of Prov. of Ontario*, 180. Many of these maps are preserved in the Crown Land Department.

[6] *Can. Archs.* (1886), 429, 431.   [7] *Ibid.*, (1890), 218, 219.

[8] Caniff, *Hist. of Prov. of Ontario*, 190.   [9] *Can. Archs.* (1890), 236.

[10] *Ibid.* (1886), 410, Jan. 22, 1784, 412, 413.

[11] *Ibid.* (1886), 409, Dec. 29, 1783, 409, 421, 422. The soldiers, if any, were to be shown preference,   April 15, 1784.

[12] *Ibid.* (1886), 422.

busy making out lists of those desiring lands.[1]   A
circular letter was sent to the loyalist leaders explaining the
condition of the lands and the character of the grants.[2]
Some petitioned to settle on Missisquoi Bay, but the request
was refused for the public good, because of fear of trouble
with the United States.[3] Loyalists were permitted to settle
on seigniories, though crown lands were recommended.[4]
The movement towards the new settlement began in March,
1784,[5] and on April 16, the order was sent forth " That the
whole of the loyalists must move at once to their settlements."[6]   In May removal was well under way from all
points toward the west,[7] and by July they were drawing lots
and locating on their lands.[8] Of the eight townships situ-
ated above Lake St. Francis, those numbered from one to
five were settled by 1,462 of the King's Royal Regiment of
New York, and those from six to eight by 495 of Jessup's
Corps. Of the five townships at Cataraqui Captain Grass'
party of 187 took the first, 434 of Jessup's Corps the second,
310 of the King's Royal Regiment of New York and Major
Rogers with 299 the third, Major Van Alstine with 258
and some of Roger's men the fourth, and 303 soldiers of
various regiments part of the fifth. This made a total of
about 3,800 single men and heads of families.[9] At Lachine,
Montreal, Chambly, St. Johns, the Bay of Chaleurs, on the
Sorel, and at other places, were located enough loyalist set-

---

[1] *Can. Archs.* (1886), 411, 412, 413.

[2] *Ibid.* (1886), 414, March 4, 1784.   [3] *Ibid.* (1886), 462, 463.

[4] *Ibid.* (1886), 411, 414, (1888), 710.

[5] *Ibid.* (1886), 416, 417.

[6] *Ibid.* (1886), 420, 421, (1888), 957, 958.

[7] *Ibid.* (1886), 424, 425, 426, 432, 462, (1887), 439, 440.

[8] *Ibid.* (1887), 164, 226.   The provincial troops were located in corps as much
as possible. *Ibid.* (1886), 422.

[9] *Ibid.* (1888), 753, July, 1784, (1891), 5.

tlers to raise the number, by October, 1784, to 5,628.[1]
Counting those who were at Niagara,[2] on Lake Erie, in the
cities, on seigniories,[3] in Lower Canada, and those who came
later, the total would reach at least 20,000 and probably
25,000.[4] Being forced to "actually sit down upon their lots,"[5]
huts were immediately built by the settlers, and in a few
years were replaced by comfortable houses.[6] The settlement of the loyalists was still in progress in 1790.[7]

The homeless and landless exiles, defeated and at the
mercy of Great Britain, were fed, clothed and housed until a
distribution of land could be made.[8] When the war closed
3,204 "unincorporated loyalists" were receiving rations,
beds and blankets.[9] Although the Canadian officials had no
instructions to continue these supplies after the war, still they
did so.[10] The English government approved of the action,
ordered rations to be furnished to the needy and sent over
articles of use and comfort to them.[11] For the sake of
economy and to prevent frauds, all orders for supplies in
upper and lower Canada were signed by the agents.[12] Allowances were made only to those who settled on crown lands.[13]
Although loyalists were welcomed from the "States" after

[1] *Can. Archs.* (1888), 753, 754, (1891), 17.

[2] *Ibid.* (1891), 1.   [3] *Ibid.* (1888), 845.

[4] Caniff, *Hist. of Prov. of Ontario*, 636.   July 20, 1784, 620 loyalists petitioned
for land at Niagara. *Can. Archs.* (1881), 2–5.

[5] *Can. Archs.* (1886), 418, April 15, 1784.

[6] *Ibid.* (1888), 718, 719, (1885), 352, 354, 367, 368.

[7] *Ibid.* (1890), 245; *ibid.* (1883), 71, Sept. 16, 1791.

[8] *Ibid.* (1892), 419, Jan. 21, 1783, (1886), 409.

[9] Kingsford, *Hist. of Canada*, vii, 218.

[10] *Can. Archs.* (1888), 731, (1887), no. 91.

[11] *Ibid.* (1885), 286, April 8, 1784, 354, (1886), 409, Jan. 5, 1784, 411, Jan. 19,
1784.

[12] *Ibid.* (1886), 409, Dec. 29, 1783, and Jan. 5, 1784.

[13] *Ibid.* (1886), 423.

1784, they were not entitled to provisions.¹ The king's instructions forbade the liberal "privileges granted to those in Nova Scotia," but the royal agent was resolved to "grant all indulgences possible" and to beg the ministry for more.² The practice was adopted of feeding the loyalists until they could support themselves.³ In June 1785, 6,000 were still victualed for a year,⁴ and in 1787 loyalists still petitioned for three months' provisions.⁵ Some of the distressed were aided as late as September, 1791, when it was proposed to set aside certain lands "for the permanent support of distressed loyalists" and for those whose claims for compensation were not allowed.⁶

In addition to food, clothing and blankets were given to the loyalists. Supplies of this character were granted in 1783 at various points,⁷ asked for on all sides the next year⁸ and generously given.⁹ As late as June, 1787, clothing was still asked for and granted.¹⁰ "Clothing" here includes coarse cloth for trousers, Indian blankets for coats, hats and shoes.¹¹

The first work before the loyalists was to build homes, clear the land and cultivate small plots. In these lines the government rendered valuable and generous assistance. Some planks, bricks and nails were given out for houses.¹²

---

¹ *Can. Archs.* (1886), 423, 429. The loyalists sent from England to Upper Canada were also "entitled to indulgences." *Ibid.* (1890), 321.

² *Ibid.* (1886), 350, 411, 426, May 14, 1784, (1892), 431, (1894), 403.

³ *Ibid.* (1886), 409, 422, 430, 431, 434, 437, 438, 442, 443, 456, 459, (1887), 164, (1888), 718, 719.

⁴ *Ibid.* (1890), 159.   ⁵ *Ibid.* (1890), 187.   ⁶ *Ibid.* (1890), 304.

⁷ *Ibid.* (1886), 467, (1888), 956.   ⁸ *Ibid.* (1888), 718, 719.

⁹ *Ibid.* (1886), 409, 423, 427, 429, 430, June 3, 1784, 439.

¹⁰ *Ibid.* (1890), 187.

¹¹ Caniff, *Hist. of Prov. of Ontario*, 190.

¹² *Can. Archs.* (1886), 463, 433.

The loyalists asked for tools, and the request was readily granted,[1] although pronounced extravagant.[2] By July 26, 1784, tools arrived and the loyalists went to work [3] and from that time on they were distributed until all were supplied.[4] " An axe, a hoe, a spade and a plow " were " allotted to every two families ; a whip and cross-cut saw to every fourth family." To every five families a set of carpenter's tools was given. Pick-axes and sickles were also supplied.[5] Bateaux were placed at their disposal,[6] and grindstones,[7] corn-mills,[8] grist-mills [9] and saw-mills [10] were furnished. At first arms were refused, but later some guns were distributed among the settlers "for the messes, for the pigeon and wild-fowl season." [11]

To complete their outfits they were given seeds in considerable variety for the garden and farm.[12] These were sent out for distribution as late as November, 1788.[13] It was not intended, at first, to give them live stock,[14] but the resolve was soon changed, and one cow was allotted to every two families.[15] But it was very difficult to secure an adequate

---

[1] *Can. Archs.* (1886), 391, 414, 416, 423, 433.

[2] *Ibid.* (1886), 417, no. 157.

[3] *Ibid.* (1886), 437, 439, 441, 446, (1887), 165.

[4] *Ibid.* (1885), 357, Aug. 6, 1784, (1886), 427, 428, 463.

[5] Caniff, *Hist. of Prov. of Ontario,* 190; *Can. Archs.* (1888), 958.

[6] *Ibid.* (1886), 427, 435.   [7] *Ibid.* (1886), 426.

[8] Caniff, *Hist. of Prov. of Ontario,* 190.

[9] *Can. Archs.* (1886), 447, (1887), 263, 265, 266.

[10] *Ibid.* (1886), 428, 433.   [11] *Ibid.* (1886), 419, 427, 463.

[12] *Ibid.* (1886), 391, 416, 423, 433, 437, 439, (1887), 164; *ibid.* (1886), 417, 420, 428, (1888), 957, 958; *ibid.* (1891), 1; *ibid.* (1890), 305; *ibid.* (1886), 429, 437, 441, 446, 462, 463, (1887), 165.

[13] *Ibid.* (1890), 222.

[14] *Ibid.* (1886), 391, 414, 416, 423, 433.

[15] *Ibid.* (1886), 462, 463; Caniff, *Hist. oj Prov. of Ontario,* 190.

number.[1]   Bulls were supplied for neighborhoods.[2]   Hay was
furnished for the cattle.[3]   In a few years, however, the farms
were well cleared, yielded good crops, and live stock became
plentiful.   At first there had been considerable discontent,[4]
and numerous and angry cries for relief were raised, but as
the early hardships wore away, the people became comfortable and prosperous, and even boastful of their early sacri-
fices for loyalty to king and empire.[5]   Before the Canadian
loyalists were established on a self-supporting basis perhaps
$4,000,000 had been expended in surveys, official salaries,
clothing, food, tools and stock.

Lord Dorchester, formerly Sir Guy Carleton, requested
the council of Quebec " to put a marke of honor upon the
families who adhered to the unity of the empire, and joined
the royal standard in America before the treaty of separation in the year 1783."[6]   Therefore all loyalists of that description and their descendants were " to be distinguished by
the letters U. E. affixed to their names, alluding to their
great principle, the unity of the empire."[7]   A registry of
these U. E. loyalists was ordered to be kept.[8]   For a period
of over twenty years names were added to the list,[9] and the

---

[1] *Can. Archs.* (1888), 720.   At Cataraqui and Oswagatia a population of over
1000 had but 6 horses, 8 oxen and 18 cows.

[2] *Ibid.* (1886), 434.   [3] *Ibid.* (1886), 427, 428, 463.

[4] *Ibid.* (1886), 391, 414, 423, 425, (1889), 63, 66, 67, 68, 69, 78, (1883), 204,
(1887), 164, 441.   Some even deserted and returned to the United States.   *Ibid.*
(1886), 411.

[5] The commissioners who went to Canada to examine loyalists' claims said the
people were flourishing and apparently satisfied.   This was in the report of Jan.
24, 1788.   MS. *Transcript* . . *Books and Papers of* . . *American Loyalists,* vol.
2, p. 333, etc.

[6] *The United Empire Loyalists' Centennial,* (1884), 127–128.

[7] *Can. Archs.* (1890), 245.

[8] *Ibid.* (1890), 250; *The United Empire Loyalists' Centennial,* (1884), 127–128.

[9] *Can. Archs.* (1892), 386, Min. of Oct. 28, 1807; *cf. ibid.* (1883), 206; *cf.*
Caniff, *Hist. of Prov. of Ontario,* 156.

descendants of these hardy pioneers have taken great pride in continuing the title.

The claims of the wealthy loyalists could not be satisfied by lands. They demanded compensation in money. In part their claims were offset by lucrative offices. Rev. Charles Inglis was made bishop of Nova Scotia.[1] Sir John Johnson was made superintendent-general of the settling of the loyalists.[2] Beverly Robinson, Jr., Christopher Billopp, Isaac Wilkins and Abraham de Peyster were appointed to civil offices in New Brunswick.[3] Abraham Cuyler wished to be inspector of lands for Cape Breton.[4] William Smith became chief justice of upper Canada.[5] Gabriel G. Ludlow was first councillor, mayor and judge of St. John.[6] Colonel Edward Fanning was made lieutenant governor of Nova Scotia.[7] Many of the loyalists were appointed justices of the peace.[8] Brook Watson secured a royal office for Christopher Sower in New Brunswick.[9] The loyalist military officers were put on half pay, and in 1806 one hundred and ten were still on the pay-roll.[10]

From the time Cooper and Chandler fled to England in 1775 to escape revolutionary mobs in New York until peace was concluded, loyalists had found refuge there. Many,

---

[1] *Can. Archs.* (1883), 52, (1894), 403, 405, 407, 443, 447, 452, 454, 456, 461, 465.

[2] *Ibid.* (1783), 57, 71, (1886), 426, 463, 482, (1887), 163.

[3] *Ibid.* (1895), 17, 19, (1894), 467.   [4] *Ibid.* (1895), 23.

[5] MS. *Transcript . . of Books and Papers . . of American Loyalists*, vol. 11, p. 78.

[6] Lawrence, *Footprints of New Brunswick*, 10–12.

[7] MS. *Transcript . . of Books and Papers . . of American Loyalists*, vol. 17, p. 95.

[8] Murdock, *Hist. of Nova Scotia*, iii, 30.

[9] *New Brunswick Mag.*, i, 97.

[10] *Can. Archs.* (1892), 375–377. List given. *Cf. ibid.* (1886), 431, 432; *Parliamentary Register*, vol. 35, p. 209.

with their wives and families, were sent to Great Britain in
1778.   There was a general exodus thither of civil officers,
of those too old or infirm to bear arms, of " great numbers"
of clergy who had become obnoxious, of those who wished to
be neutral, and of many of the wives and children of loyalists
who were serving in the army or navy.[1]   Subsequent to 1775,
allowances were granted these loyalists from time to time as
temporary support until the war should end, when it was expected that all would return to their country.   These sums
were paid by the treasury board, without uniformity as to
time or amount, at first quarterly and later annually.[2]   The
amounts thus granted increased yearly until by 1782 more
than $200,000 was paid to 315 recipients.   Besides these
allowances for temporary support, $90,000 had been paid
during each of the three years preceding 1782 as compensation for special losses or services.   Many of these pensioners came from New York and received annuities ranging
from £500, which was paid to Oliver De Lancey and his
family, to £20, which Thomas Moore obtained.   Some of
them, like Dr. Myles Cooper, had received help for seven
years.[3]   In 1782 twenty-six loyalists from New York were
receiving about $18,000 yearly.

[1] Wilmot, *Historical View of the Commissioners for Enquiring into the Losses
. . of . . Loyalists.* 8, 9.

[2] *Ibid.*, 15, 16, 22.   These sums and those which follow in this chapter are obtained by reckoning the pound as approximately $5.00 ($4.86).

[3] Chief among the pensioners from New York were Timothy Hurst, £200; Samuel Bayard, £200; John Tabor Kempe, £200; Rev. John Vardill, £200; Samuel
Hoke, £200; Isaac Wilkins, £200; William Bayard, £200; William Edmeston,
£150; Lambert Moore, £115; Col. Abraham Cuyler, £100; Rev. Harry Munroe,
£100; Lieut. Thomas Webb, £100; Robert Auchmuty, £100, Samuel Kemble,
£100; Peter Van Schaack, £100; Richard Vandeburg, £100; John Pickering,
£80; Francis Stephens, £80; John Blockler, £60; and Matthew Sentis, £50.
MS. *Transcript . . of Books and Papers . . of Americam Loyalists.* vol. 2, pp.
72, 74, 80, 82, 84, 86, 94, 96, 98, 100, 102, 106, 108, 110, 112, 114, 116, 120, 122,
126, 128, 132, 134, 136.

The increased emigration of loyalists to England in 1782, and consequently the large number of claims for assistance, led parliament to suspend all donations until a committee could investigate both the old and the new claims, and pass on their merits. The committee dropped 81 persons from the list, thus reducing the existing annual grant of $200,000 to $158,500, and considered 428 new claims, on which they allowed over $87,000, making the total grant for 1783 $245,725.[1] Of the 428 fresh claims 223, or more than half, came from New York alone. Only twenty-five applications were refused.[2] No new grant was made above £200, and from that amount grants fell off to £5. Loyalty, actual loss and need were made the reason for assistance. Over $5,000 were paid to finally settle many claims of loyalists from New York, and about $35,000 were allowed them in annuities. With but few exceptions, these claimants were all resident in England. Among them were representatives of all social classes, from emancipated negro slaves[3] to the aristocratic land-owners[4] and merchants,[5] of both sexes,[6] of all ages and

[1] Wilmot, *Historical View*, etc., 16–23; *Can. Archs.* (1886), 480, 482, 552.

[2] Refusal was on the ground of "no claim," or because the claimant was not in need of help. John Tabor Kempe took £14,000 with him to England, yet asked for aid, but was refused it.

[3] John Ashfield, Thomas Farmer, John Jackson, David King, John Thompson and Benjamin Whitecuff.

[4] John Cumming, James McCara, Archibald Kennedy, Claude Saubier, Christopher Billopp, William Knox, John Rapalje, etc.

[5] Thomas Hughes, Thomas Miller, William Bayard who lost £100,000, Col. Cruger, John Weatherhead, Alexander Wallace, V. P. Ashfield, William Axtill, Isaac Low, Benjamin Booth.

[6] Mrs. Auchmuty, wife of the Trinity rector, Mrs. and Miss Dawson, Mrs. Jessup, Mrs. McAlpin, Mrs. Norman, Mrs. Paschall, Mrs. Catherine Ridout, Mrs. Mary Swards, Nelly Malloy, the Misses Kemp, Mrs. Mary Smith, Mrs. Mary Airy, Miss Eliz. Floyd, Mrs. Henrietta Colden, Mrs. Mary Browne, Mrs. Price, Mrs. Col. Fred. Phillips, Elizabeth Brinley, Mrs. Mary Henley, Elizabeth Macdonald, Mrs. Elizabeth Lawrence, Elizabeth McAlpin and Miss Jane Sidney.

of all trades and professions—soldiers, sailors, teachers, wine-merchants, brewers, clergymen,[1] lawyers, physicians, crown officers,[2] flax dressers, silver-smiths, farmers and shop-keepers.

" Numberless persons" flocked to England after the treaty of peace, mostly from New York, to secure compensation.[3] Altogether 5,072 loyalists, representing perhaps 25,000 persons in all, either in person or through agents, submitted claims for losses.[4]   These loyalists had a general agent appointed for each state.   James DeLancey acted for New York, and also served as agent for the whole " committee."[5] The claims examined by the " commissioners" in England, by June 10, 1789, numbered 939, and by commissioners in Nova Scotia and Canada 1,272.[6]   Others were withdrawn, or not pressed for settlement, or dropped without consideration.

The king urged parliament to treat the loyalists with " a due and generous attention," and hence that body, in July, 1783, appointed a " commission " of five members to classify the " losses and services of those who had suffered in their rights, properties and professions on account of their loyalty."   The commissioners were empowered to examine persons under oath, send for papers, and use the testimony of loyalists in England and America to determine the valid-

[1] Rev. John Doty, rector at Schenectady, Rev. John Mackenna, a Roman Catholic priest, Rev. Agnew, Dr. Charles Inglis, Rev. John Milner and Rev. Samuel Seabury.

[2] Stephen DeLançey, Judge Thomas Jones who lost £44,600; Colonel James DeLancey, sheriff of Westchester; John Tabor Kempe, attorney general of New York, who lost £98,000; George D. Ludlow, judge of the Supreme Court, who lost £7000; David Matthew, mayor of New York city, who lost 26,774 acres; Arthur Kendall, tide surveyor of New York; Andrew Elliott, lieutenant-governor of New York; Philip Skene, lieutenant-governor of Crown Point, who lost £39,189.

[3] Wilmot, *Historical View*, etc., 25-28.

[4] Kingsford, *History of Canada*, vii, 217; Jones, *Hist. of N. Y.*, ii, 663.

[5] Jones, *Hist. of N. Y.*, ii, 257-258.   [6] *Ibid.*, 661.

ity of claims. Most of the loyalists were frank and honest in their statements, but some were not.[1]

The "commission" first laid down rules of procedure and then began their inquiry in October.[2] Loyalists were by them divided into six classes. 1. Those who had rendered services to Great Britain. 2. Those who had borne arms against the revolution. 3. Uniform loyalists. 4. Loyalists resident in Great Britain. 5. Those who took oaths of allegiance to the American states, but afterward joined the British. 6. Those who armed with the Americans and later joined the English army or navy. Claimants had to state specifically in writing the nature of their losses.[3] So strict were the rules and so rigid were the secret examinations that the "Enquiry" was denounced by the loyalists as the "inquisition."[4] All claims were to be in by March 25, 1784, but the time was later extended till 1790.[5] On the first date 2,063 claims were presented, representing a loss of about $35,231,000 in real and personal property, $11,770,000 in debts, and $443,000 in incomes, making a total of nearly $47,500,000.[6]

The examination of these claims was no easy task—especially such claims as those of the DeLanceys. The board refused to allow compensation for losses in East and West

---

[1] Wilmot, *Historical View*, etc., 42–47. The "Compensation Act" is *23 Geo. III.*, ch. 80. Given in Jones, *Hist. of N. Y.*, ii, 653; *Parliamentary Register*, vol. 35, p. 205.

[2] Notices had been sent to the governors of Canada and Nova Scotia, to the commander at New York, and printed in the newspapers.

[3] Caniff, *Hist. of Prov. of Ontario*, 61. *Case of Aspden*, p. 119, gives report to commissioners, May 30, 1788, and has 11 classes.

[4] Wilmot, *Historical View*, etc., 65.

[5] *Ibid.*, 89; *29 George III.*, ch. 62; Jones, *Hist. of N. Y.*, ii. 658–659; *25 George III.*, ch. 76; *26 George III.*, ch. 68; *27 George III.*, ch. 39; *28 George III.*, ch. 40.

[6] Wilmot, *Historical View*, etc., 50.

Florida, or in the form of uncultivated lands, estates bought after the war, rents, incomes of offices received during the rebellion, anticipated professional profits; losses in trade, labor, or by the British army; losses through depreciated paper money, captures at sea and debts. Claims were allowed for loss of property through loyalty, for offices held before the the war, and for the loss of actual professional incomes. By July, 1784, claims amounting to $2,675,000 were settled for the sum of $1,010,000.[1] Next the claims of 1068 persons needing immediate relief were considered, and by December 23, 128 of these claims, aggregating $3,446,000, were paid off for the sum of $755,000. In May and July, 1785, 122 claimants, asking for $4,500,000, were granted $1,283,000.[2] A fifth report, made in April, 1786, allowed $1,252,500 for 142 claims, aggregating $3,666,500.[3] By April 5, 1788, the commissioners had examined 1,680 claims on which they allowed $9,448,000.

It was soon evident that, to do justice to the loyalists, commissioners must be sent to America. Hence Colonels Dundee and Pemberton were sent to Nova Scotia, while John Anstey went to New York.[4] They were to inquire into the claims of loyalists, and thus relieve them of the necessity of going to England. They had the same powers as the board at home and proceeded in the same manner. Their work began November 17, 1785, and lasted till 1789. The various governors were apprised of this ·arrangement and General Haldimand, governor of Canada, was instructed

[1] Wilmot, *Historical View*, etc., 50.   [2] *Ibid.*, 54–55.

[3] *Ibid.*, 59. The commissioners met in London from Aug. 9, 1785, to March 25, 1790, and examined the claims of loyalists. The MS. *Transcript . . of Books and Papers . . of American Loyalists*, vol. 9, has the minutes of the proceedings of the commissioners. The minutes are bare and meagre, however.

[4] Wilmot, *Historical View*, etc., 58; *Can. Archs.* (1890), 169, Feb. 10, 1786; 25 *George III.*, ch. 76; MS. *Transcript . . of Books and Papers . . of American Loyalists*, vol. 2, 35.

to co-operate with them by sending in loyalists' petitions.[1] Governor Hope of Quebec issued a proclamation, January 21, 1785, to loyalists having claims for losses, and ordered their leaders to collect and forward them. He asked the commissioners for an extension of time in which to prove losses, and urged them to make a journey to Quebec.[2] Governor Patterson also demanded an extension of time for the loyalists of Prince Edward Island.[3] The commissioners intended to go from Nova Scotia to New Brunswick and Canada to expedite matters. They sat at Halifax, St. Johns and Montreal.

The examinations began at Halifax.[4] Claims under the act of parliament of 1783 were first considered.[5] Some loyalists from the United States appeared before the commissioners, hoping for compensation amounting to about $24,000, for losses which resulted from loyal service, but their claims were invariably rejected. On June 10, 1786, the commissioners reported that 642 claims had been presented from Nova Scotia, Cape Breton, the Island of St. John and the United States, of which 199 were approved. Also 402 new claims from New Brunswick and 716 from Canada had been sent in. The losses examined amounted to $335,000. A second report was made September 30, 1786, submitting a list of forty old claimants and sixty-four new ones, mostly from Nova Scotia. Before the third report was made, March

---

[1] *Can. Archs.* (1886), 480, Haldimand to Watts, Jan. 6, 1783, 555; Comsrs. to Haldimand, Sept. 4, 1784; *ibid.* (1890), 168; *ibid.* (1895), 43.

[2] *Ibid.* (1890), 168, Jan. 29, 1785.

[3] *Ibid.,* 43; MS. *Transcript . . of Books and Papers . . of American Loyalists,* vol. 2, 351.

[4] Expresses were sent to Canada, New Brunswick, Cape Breton, St. Johns Island, and to Governor Parr, of Nova Scotia, to say that the work had commenced.

[5] Some were passed on at once while others, for various reasons, were delayed from one day to one year.

26, 1787, the commissioners had gone by land from Halifax to St. John, where they heard 110 old claims and 239 new ones. Thence they went to Quebec and Montreal, where they examined the 716 claims sent to Halifax, 77 old claims and 300 new ones, and reported January 24, 1788. In June of that year, a report was made on 356 additional cases. The sixth and final report was made after they returned to England. It reviewed the whole work and showed that twenty-five inhabitants of the United States had sent in claims, that 432 claims under the act of 1783, calling for $3,375,000, and 1799 claims under the act of 1785, asking for $3,536,000, were filed; that altogether 1401 claims were heard and 834 were for various reasons not heard. The commissioners allowed $1,061,000 on the 432 old claims and $1,684,000 on 969 new claims, or a total of $2,745,000 for claims passed on in America.[1]

Of the 1401 claims examined by the two commissioners, 877, or nearly two-thirds, were those of New York loyalists.[2] About two-thirds of the $6,911,000 claimed for losses and of the $2,745,000 allowed by the commissioners were also in behalf of the loyalists from that state. A reference to a few of the petitioners will sufficiently illustrate the character of the whole. Stephen Tuttle was a justice of the peace of Albany county, and joined the British in Canada. He was proscribed, and his property, valued at £2,539, was confiscated. He did not bear arms himself, but his five sons went into the British service.[3] Thomas Barclay, of Ulster county,

---

[1] MS. *Transcript . . of Books and Papers . . of American Loyalists*, vol. 2, 333; *Case of Aspden*, 119, gives the report also. The 34 MS. vols. in the Cong. Lib. at Washington contain the *Proceedings of the two commissioners at St. John, Halifax and Montreal*, in 1786–1788.

[2] MS. *Transcript . . of Books and Papers . . of the American Loyalists*, vol. 10, p. 253–378.

[3] *Ibid.*, vol. 17, p. 1–18. Nearly every claimant reported a loss of both personal and real property.

left in 1776 to avoid taking up arms against his king, and for
six years held the rank of major of loyalist troops.   He reported that both his personal and real property was confiscated and sold in the fall of 1776 — the first confiscation in
New York.   He lost £2,745.[1]   Isaac Wilkins, a representative of Westchester in the general assembly, went to England
for a year, in 1775, after which he returned, and lived on
Long Island.   For six years he received an annual pension
of £200.   Although able to sell his property at Westchester
for £2,500, still he claimed a loss of £3,600.   Because of his
brother's influence, he was not attainted.[2]

The " determinations on claims " by the commissioners in
America began December 5, 1785, and closed December 19,
1788.   The commissioners in each case considered three
things—loyalty, service, extent of loss—and fixed the allowance accordingly.   Loyalists padded their claims with en-
tries of every kind of loss.[3]   The policy of the commissioners was to refuse to allow claims for lands bought or
improved during the war — a very long list — trading ships
lost through capture by Americans, horses and grain taken
by Americans, damage done by British or Hessian troops,

---

[1] MS. *Transcript . . of Books and Papers . . of the American Loyalists*, vol.
17, 24–31, 38.

[2] *Ibid.*, 38–56.   One of the remarkable things about these loyalist claims is the
fact that few came from southern New York, especially Queens county, the very
center of loyalism.   Out of 466 petitions 155 were from Albany co., 85 from
Westchester co., 80 from Tryon co., 50 from Dutchess co., 46 from Charlotte co.,
15 from New York city, 9 from Orange co., 11 from Ulster co., 7 from Queens
co., 3 from Cumberland co., 3 from Richmond co. and 3 from Suffolk co.   Kings
county had no claimants.   In other words, from the very stronghold of loyalism, southern New York, there were but 27 loyalist petitioners, as compared with
439 above New York city.   This astonishing difference was due to the fact that
the loyalists of southern New York lost comparatively little through their loyalty
because protected by the British until peace was signed, when most of them either
remained on their lands unmolested, or were able to dispose of their property before emigrating.   *Ibid.*, 17 to 22.

[3] *Ibid.*, vol. 29, p. 9.

forage and stock furnished the British army,[1] rent of lands, houses and goods used by the British,[2] crops on the ground, certain debts, the fall in value of provincial paper money, robbery of cash, runaway negroes,[3] cost of living in New York city during the war, fines paid for refusing to drill with the militia, houses built during the war,[4] expenses and sufferings in prison, property mortgaged to its full value, losses or suffering after the war, uncultivated lands, defective titles, and losses of persons who were not Americans before 1775. " Loyal " and " bore arms " made a strong case and invariably led to compensation for property, real and personal, which was lost by confiscation.[5] Claimants were obliged to prove clear titles and positive loss. In some instances improvements on tenant farms were allowed.[6] The loss of the incomes of physicians,[7] lawyers,[8] clergymen,[9] and from civil offices which were held before the revolution, was compensated. Every effort was made to be fair, and to do justice to all. When judgment was rendered the commissioners strongly urged immediate liquidation of claims. Many loyalists, like Hugh Wallace, William Bayard, Sir John Johnson, and Stephen DeLancey, who had large fortunes at stake, went directly to England to adjust their claims.[10] After the

---

[1] MS. *Transcript . . of Books and Papers . . of the American Loyalists*, vol. 29, p. 12.

[2] *Ibid.*, 13.   [3] *Ibid.*, 77, 157.   [4] *Ibid.*, 37.   [5] *Ibid.*, 47, 97.

[6] *Ibid.*, vol. 30, pp. 117, 245. Out of 126 petitioners to the crown for compensation for losses incurred through loyalty, 115 asserted their loyalty from first to last, while only 6 acknowledged themselves whigs at first, and but 5 confessed to having signed the association. Nearly every petitioner tried to prove first that he had served in the British army in one capacity or another, and next that he suffered personal injury for his loyalty. Out of 150 who saw military service, 62 were imprisoned for their beliefs, 9 were attainted and 1 had had his property burned. *Ibid.*, vols. 17-23.

[7] *Ibid.*, vol. 29, p. 29, 61.   [8] *Ibid.*, 63.   [9] *Ibid.*, 105.

[10] *Can. Archs.* (1886), 482, 554.

commissioners left America, petitions were still sent to England, asking for payment of losses.[1]

The "board of commissioners," now all in England, made the twelfth and last report on May 15, 1789.[2] Altogether 5,072 claims were presented, and for a total of $50,411,000, but only 4,118 claims were examined. Of this number 343 were not allowed, 553 were not prosecuted, and 38 were withdrawn; the claims included in these 934 cases amounting to $10,000,000. Of the $40,411,000 asked for by the 3,184 claimants who remained, over $19,000,000 was paid.[3] At first loyalist soldiers were allowed 40 per cent. of their claims, while civilians got but 30 per cent., though finally no difference was made.[4] From time to time partial payments were made on claims allowed, but Pitt's scheme was finally carried into effect by the 28th, George III, Ch. 40, and gave general satisfaction.[5] It provided that incomes below £400 should be paid off in pensions at 50 per cent., between £400 and £1,500 at 40 per cent., and above £1,500 at 30 per cent.[6] British subjects resident in England were to receive property losses in full up to £10,000, 80 per cent. of losses above that sum up to £50,000, 50 per cent. above the £10,000 on losses between £50,000 and £200,000 and 30 per cent. above the £10,000 on losses over £200,000. All other classes of loyalists were to be paid the full sum allowed by the commissioners up to £10,000, 90 per cent. of amounts above that sum up to £35,000, 85 per cent. above £10,000 on losses between £35,000 and £50,000 and 80 per cent. above £10,000 on losses exceeding £50,000.[7]

---

[1] *Can. Archs.* (1894), 462. At least as late as March 18, 1789.

[2] Wilmot, *Historical View*, etc., 59–89; *cf.* Caniff, *Hist. of Prov. of Ontario*, 61.

[3] *Cf.* Kingsford, *Hist. of Can.*, vii, 217, note; Wilmot, *Historical View*, etc., 64.

[4] *Ibid.*, 58.   [5] *Ibid.*, 69–78.

[6] *Ibid.; cf.* Jones, *Hist. of N. Y.*. ii, 659.

[7] *Case of Aspden*, 121, 122.

The loyalists of New York figured very prominently in the compensation. Their property losses, as set forth in their claims, approximated to $10,000,000, or about one-fourth of the whole amount. The petitions for imperial compensation ranged from $60, claimed by Agnes Bethune, to $777,000, which was the estimated value of the confiscated estate of Frederick Philipse, Jr. The sums allowed varied in amount from $50, granted to Agnes Bethune, to $221,000, the highest sum, paid to Sir John Johnson. The proportion of the compensation to the claim for loss differed very much and was conditioned upon the character of each case. Some were thrown out entirely because "fraudulent," or because there was "no proof of the loss," and none were allowed in full.[1] The claims for losses included both

---

[1] On one claim for $1545 the commissioners allowed $1540. The character of the reductions may be learned from the following table giving the principal claims and the amounts allowed:

Name.	Loss.	Allowed.
Frederick Philipse, Jr.	$777,000	$210,000
Sir John Johnson	516,000	221,000
Oliver DeLancey	390,000	125,000
William Bayard	326,000	97,000
John Tabor Kempe	325,000	28,000
Beverly Robinson	344,000	128,000
Roger Morris	310,000	91,000
James DeLancey	284,000	160,000
C. W. Apthorp	144,000	10,000
Thomas Lynch	111,000	1,250
John Rapalje	106,000	53,000
Philip Skene	188,000	109,000
John Weatherhead	152,000	19,000
Hugh Wallace	86,000	20,000
John Peters	54,000	10,000
David Colden	51,000	14,000
Alexander MacDonald	66,000	4,000
John Munro	50,000	9,000
Guy Johnson	111,000	34,000
Thomas Jones	63,000	28,000

personal and real estate. Since not more than a dozen loyalists from New York were allowed more than £10,000 by
the commissioners, practically all sums granted were paid in
full.

Of the $400,000 allowed by the commissioners for losses
in annual incomes from offices and professions loyalists from
this state were granted $56,000.[1] The crown paid about
$79,000 in yearly pensions on these losses and of that sum
loyalists from New York received in annual grants $40,000,
or more than one-half of the total amount.

The total outlay on the part of England, during the war
and after it closed, for the loyalists, in food and clothing, in
temporary relief and annuities, in establishing them in Nova
Scotia and Canada, and in money compensation, amounted
to not less than $30,000,000. At least one-third of this
sum, and possibly more, was paid to loyalists from New
York, or spent in their behalf. The slow, sifting process of

Isaac Low	75,000	26,000
James Jauncey	65,000	52,000
Ebenezer Jessup	110,000	18,000
Edward Jessup	54,000	20,000
George Folliott	66,000	21,000
Brant Children	92,000	34,000
Daniel Claus	88,000	32,000
John Butler	48,000	27,000
Christopher Billopp	26,000	2,000
Robert Bayard	55,000	1,550
William Axtell	85,000	47,000
Mary Auchmuty	25,000	8,000

Other claims were paid off in like ratio. MS. *Transcript . . of Books and
Papers . . of American Loyalists*, vol. 11, p. 78, etc.

[1] Chief among the claimants were Andrew Elliott, $6,500; Rev. Charles Inglis,
$2,295; John Tabor Kempe, $10,170; William Smith, $11,500: Philip Skene,
$2,500; Rev. John Vardill, $2,500; Major Thomas Barclay, $1,000; and G. D.
Ludlow, $1,000. MS. *Transcript . . of Books and Papers . . of American
Loyalists*, vol. 11, p. 78, etc. The total yearly loss of professional salaries was
£80,000, on which £25,785 was granted in pensions.

compensation, and the enormous reductions from the original claims, gave rise to widespread discontent.   Numerous
pamphlets appeared, and letters were printed in the journals
denouncing the methods of the " Enquiry," and the unap-
preciative, .close-fisted policy of the English government.
But as time passed the bitterness disappeared, and the loyalists were proud of the fact that loyalism meant a sacrifice
in material possessions, as well as fidelity to the king and
the empire.

APPENDIX

THESE lists of confiscated property are as complete as the known material warrants. No doubt additional matter will be found when all the available manuscript sources of the revolutionary history of the state are brought to light. The lists are complete for the city and county of New York and for Suffolk county in the southern district. No complete record of the sales in Queens, Kings and Richmond counties has been found. The arrangement followed here is not found in the manuscripts, but is used in order to secure uniformity and to condense the material.

215]

FORFEITED ESTATES SOLD IN NEW YORK CITY FROM 1784 TO 1789 [1]

Date of Sale.	Loyalist Owner.	Purchaser.	Price.	Description and Remarks.
June 16, 1784	John Watts, Sr., attainted.	Robert Watts and John Watts, Jr.	£100	$11\frac{9}{10}$ acres of salt meadow land in Out Ward, back of land of Peter Stuyvesant and James De Lancey, extending to East River. Surveyed Feb. 23, 1751.
" "	" "	" "	2,000	Farm in Out Ward.
" "	" "	" "	500	Residence of John Watts, Sr., in Great Dock Street, South Ward.
June 29, 1784	James Jauncey, Esq., attainted.	Wm. Malcom.	1,700	Water lot, house and store houses in Montgomery Ward, S. side of Water St., from S.E. side Water St. 200 ft. into E. River, 27 ft. fronting Water St., W. by Water St., N. by water lot of George Peterson, E. by E. River, S. by Pier or wharf 18 ft. wide. Rent of £2 6d current money of N.Y. State to be paid yearly on March 25 to Mayor and Aldermen of N.Y. City.
" "	James Jauncey, Esq., attainted.	John Carrow.	625	House and lot in North Ward, E. side of Fair St. W. North St., N. by Nicholas Fletcher, E. by Vineyard, S. by Jacob Bronta. Breadth 23 ft. Length 117 ft.
July 2, 1784	Josh, T. D. St. Croix, convicted.	Wm. Newton.	700	House and lot in Montgomery Ward, W. side of Queen St. E. by Queen St., S. by John Duryea, W. by same, N. by Peter Ryker. 100 ft. by 20 ft. 2 in. and 16 ft. 16 in.
June 24, 1784	James Jauncey, attainted.	John McKisson.	1,750	Messuage and Dwelling House and lot on S. side of Queens St., East Ward. W. by Francis Lewis and James Jauncey's confiscated estate, E. by Nicholas Covenhaven, Thomas Ellison and Wm. Everitt. 128 ft. 8 in. by 22 ft. 6 in. and 22 ft.

[1] Copied from MS. Ledger in Register's Office, New York City.

Date of Sale.	Loyalist Owner.	Purchaser.	Price.	Description and Remarks.
June 23, 1784	Waldron Blauw, convicted.	Eleanor Blauw.	£1,001	Messuage or Dwelling House and lot in S. Ward. Front by Dock St. wharf, rear by confiscated lot of Blauw, W. by Wm. Milliner, deceased, E. by devise of Wm. Holland, deceased. 28 ft. 6 in. by 73 ft. 2 in. and 73 ft. 7 in.
July 6, 1784	Frederick Philipse, attainted.	Henry Wyckoff.	1,225	House and lot in Dock Ward, North side of Great Dock St. to Duke St. S. by Great Dock St., W. by Isaac Stoutenburg and L. Pintard, N. by Duke St., E. by Widow Lawrence.
June 30, 1784	Thomas White, attainted merchant.	Anna White, his widow.	3,500	Lots, Garden and Vineyard in North Ward.
July 8, 1784	Alexan. Wallace, attainted merchant.	John Quackenbos.	25	Lot No. 825 in Out Ward, drawn in lottery by Nicholas Bayard, Esq.
"	James Leonard, convicted.	Anthony Post, carpenter.	225	Tenement and lot in West Ward on N. side of Little Queen St. S. by Little Queen St., W. by Samuel Ellis, N. by Christopher Stymus, E. by Joseph Nott.
"	Edward Ward, convicted.	Henry Tiebout.	1,150	Dwellings and lots (2) in West Ward on N. side of Dey St. S. by Dey St., W. John Gosmer, E. by Widow Earl, N. by —.
July 9, 1784	Roger Morris, convicted.	John Berrian and Isaac Ledyard.	2,250	Farm and buildings on Harlem Heights in Out Ward—115 acres.
July 28, 1784	James Jauncey, attainted.	John Maley.	1,600	Dwelling and lot in Montgomery Ward on N. Corner of Water St. and Beekman's Slip. E. by Water St., N. by Wm. Moore, W. by Widow Paine, S. by Beekman's Slip.
"	David Matthews and Thomas White, attainted.	John Quackenbos.	62	3 lots in Out Ward. Nos. 923 and 1077 drawn in Nicholas Bayard's Lottery by David Mathews. No. 492 drawn in said Lottery by Thomas White.
"	Robert Bayard, attainted.	Christopher Hutton.	630	Farm and Buildings in Out Ward at Bloomingdale. N. W. by Highway, S. W. by Tennis Lamarindike, S. E. by Charles Ward Apthorpe and confiscated land of Oliver De Lancey, N. E. by confiscated land of Oliver De Lancey.

Date of Sale.	Loyalist Owner.	Purchaser.	Price.	Description and Remarks.
July 28, 1784	Henry White, attainted.	John Quackenbos.	£225	Lot on N. side Beaver St. S. by Beaver St., E. and N. by estate of John Van Vorst, W. by estate of Edward Heayster.
" "	" "	" "	225	Lot on E. side of Broadway. W. by Broadway, N. by Thomas Shipbow, E. by confiscated property of Henry White, S. by confiscated property of Edward Heayster.
Aug. 6, 1784	William Bayard, attainted.	John R. Myer.	1,350	2 houses and a lot in the Dock Ward on S. side of Little Dock St. E. by lot No. 28 of Edmund Seaman, W. by lot No. 6 of Thomas Brown, deceased, N. by Little Dock St, S. by confiscated property of Wm. Bayard. 37½ ft. by 71 ft.
July 28, 1784	William Axtell, attainted.	John Quackenbos.	190	Lot No. 12 in West Ward on N. W. side of Broadway, adjoining lands of Anthony Rutgers. 174 ft. and 178 ft. by 30 ft. in rear.
" "	" "	Nicho. Quackenbos.	240	Lot No. 1 in North Ward on Broadway. 380 ft. and 362 ft. by 30 ft. by 40 ft. in rear of Broadway.
Aug. 5, 1784	Isaac Low, attainted.	Sebastian Banneau.	1,150	2 dwellings and lot. W. by Smith St., N. by Augustus Van Horn, E. by Peter Van Brugh Livingston, S. by Wm. Thorn.
July 8, 1784	John Harris Cruger, attainted.	Malachy Treat.	800	Dwelling and lot in North Ward on N. side of Little Queen St. S. by Little Queen St., E. by —— Johnson, N. by Peter Bogart, W. by Dr. Bard (occupied by him).
June 16, 1784	Joseph Gidney, of Westchester Co., convicted.	William Strachan.	550	2 lots No. 317 and 318 in West Ward on W. side of Greenwich St. Part of land given to the Governors of New York College by Trinity Church. E. by Greenwich St., N. by lot No. 316, W. by lot No. 319, S. by lot No. 319. Lease for 61 years from March 25. Property had been leased to Gidney by Kings College, March 25, 1782.
Aug. 27, 1784	Robert McGinnis, convicted.	John Brown.	475	House and lot in Montgomery Ward on corner of Gold and Ann Sts. E. by Gold St., N. by Ann St., W. by lot of Joseph Varrian, S. by Francis Bassett.

Date of Sale.	Loyalist Owner.	Purchaser.	Price.	Description and Remarks.
Sep. 4, 1784	Waldron Blauw, convicted.	Jacobus Bruyn.	£850	House and lot in Dock Ward on Dock St. wharf, between dwelling and Water Lot. N. by Dock St., E. by Water Lot granted to Henry Hal, S. as far as right of Mayor and Alderman extends, W. by William Milliner.
"	John Weatherhead, attainted.	Rachel Weatherhead.	498-5-6	One house and lot on N. side of Queen St. S. by said St., E. by Effingham Lawrence, W. by Samuel Socket (deceased) and his heirs. Lot on Broadway adjoining lots of Samuel Johnston and heirs of Thomas Warner, through to New St. Lot on N. W. corner of Beaver and Broad Sts., adjoining land of John Alsop and widow Ten Eyck.
"	James De Lancey, attainted.	Edward Laight.	750	Lot in Out Ward at Corlears Hook. S. by Crown Point St., W. by heirs of Evert Byvanck, N. by Grand St., E. by lot in possession of daughter of Henry Vandenham, "and other lots of land."
Sep. 21, 1784	Robert Bayard, attainted.	John Plantain, shopkeeper.	295	House and lot on Crown St. N. W. by land of the late Heybert Van Wagenen, N. E. by land forfeited by Robert Bayard and by Samuel Ellis, N. E. by forfeited land of Widow Egberts.
Sep. 24, 1784	James Jauncey, attainted.	George Campbell, gardener.	270	Messuage and lot in Out Ward adjoining Wm. Bayard's confiscated land. W. by high water mark of Hudson River, N. by Bayard's confiscated property, E. by the road, S. by heirs of late Sir Peter Warren. 1¾ acres more or less.
July 28, 1784	Waldron Blauw, convicted.	John Maley.	850	Messuage and lot in Dock Ward on N. side of Little Dock St. S. by said St., W. by William Milliner, N. by widow Cornelia Blauw, E. by estate of Henry Holland.
Sep. 4, 1784	" "	Nicholas Romayne, physician.	250	Messuage and lot in North Ward on S. E. side of King St. S. E. by Philip Minthorn, S. W. by Samuel Ver Planck, N. W. by estate of Blanch Beajean.

Date of Sale.	Loyalist Owner.	Purchaser.	Price.	Description and Remarks.
Sep. 25, 1784	James De Lancey, attainted.	Philip Vicker.	£80	Lots No. 255 and 256 in Out Ward on E. side of First St. W. by First St., N. by lot No. 257, E. by lots No. 275 and 276, S. by lot No. 254.
" "	" "	George Workhart, gardener.	130	Lots No. 465, 466, 467, 468, 487, 489, 490 and 491 in Out Ward. W. by Second St., N. by lots No. 469 and 486, E. by Third St., S. by lots No. 464 and 492.
Sep. 27, 1784	" "	Adam Smith, gardener.	41	Lot No. 108 in Out Ward. W. by Bowery Lane, N. by lot No. 109, E. by lot No. 115, S. by lot No. 107. On chart of Evert Bancker.
Oct. 4, 1784	" "	David Morris, pilot.	150	"Certain Lots" Nos. 105, 106 and half of 104 in Out Ward. W. by Bowery Lane, N. by lot No. 107, E. by lots No. 117, 118 and 119, S. by half of lot No. 104.
Sep. 27, 1784	" "	Abraham Brinckerhoff, merchant.	88	Lots No. 259, 260, 271 and 272 in Out Ward. W. by First St., S. by lots No. 258 and 273.
Oct. 6, 1784	" "	John Quackenbos.	160	Lots No. 110, 111, 112 and 113 in Out Ward on E. side of Bowery Lane. W. by said Lane, N. by Grand St., E. by First St., S. by lots No. 109–114.
Oct. 19, 1784	James Jauncy, attainted.	John Delafield.	1,500	House and lot in Montgomery Ward on N. side of Van Cleef's St. S. by said St., W. by John Vreedenburgh, N. by land of late John Brown, E. by heirs of Benjamin Tanner. 27 ft. by 114 ft. and 112 ft.
Oct. 20, 1784	James De Lancey, attainted.	John Fleming, baker.	444	Piece of land in Out Ward made up of lots No. 68, 69, 70, 89, 90 and 91. W. by Bowery Lane, N. by lots No. 72 and 83, E. by First St., S. by lots No. 67 and 92. 75 ft. by 210 ft.
Oct. 21, 1784	Frederick Philipse, attainted.	Adam Gilchrist, merchant.	350	Five-sided lot in South Ward on E. side of New St. W. by New St., N. by Samuel Bard, E. by Adam Gilchrist, S. by Isaac Marschalk.

Date of Sale.	Loyalist Owner.	Purchaser.	Price.	Description and Remarks.
Oct. 22, 1784	James De Lancey, attainted.	John Quackenbos.	£898	Lot of 500 by 200 ft. in Out Ward at Corlaers Hook. S. by Crown Point St., W. by Ferry St., N. by Garden St., E. by High Water Mark of East River. Lot of 500 by 200 ft. in same place. S. by Garden St., W. by Ferry St., N. by N. Middle St., E. by High Water Mark of East River.
Nov. 2, 1784	" " "	Henry Whitman. Christo. Feigenheim. Frederick Boediger. Christian Will. George Dietrich. Anthony Apple.	369	Lots in Out Ward on E. side of First St., No. 52, 53, 54, 55, 56, 57, 261, 262, 263, 266, 267, 268, 269, 270. E. by First St. and Second St., N. by Abraham Housewert and Pump St., W. by lots Nos. 38, 39, 40, 41, 42, 43, 261, 262, 263, 264 and 265, S. by lot No. 271 and Abraham Brinckerhoff.
Nov. 6, 1784	Robert Bayard, attainted.	Philip Kissick, merchant.	46-10	Lot No. 952 in Out Ward. E. by, Elizabeth St., W. by lot No. 964, N. by lot No. 953, S. by lot No. 951. 25 by 94 ft. Lot 1003 in Out Ward. W. by Catherine St., E. by lot No. 985, N. by lot No. 1002, S. by lot No. 1004. 25 by 100 ft. Lot 1086 in Out Ward. S. by Oliver St., N. by lot No. 1090, E. by lot No. 1087, W. by lot No. 1085. About 25 by 96 ft.
Nov. 12, 1784	James De Lancey, attainted.	John Quackenbos.	90	Lots No. 284, 285, 310 and 311 in Out Ward. W. by Front St., N. by lots No. 286 and 309, E. by Second St., S. by lots No. 283 and 312.
Nov. 13, 1784	" "	Benjamin Walker.	93	Lots No. 786, 787, 788, 789, 790 and 791 in Out Ward. N. by De Lancey St., S. by lot No. 785, W. by Third St., E. by lots No. 792, 793, 794 and 795.
Nov. 15, 1784	" "	Elizabeth Capelet.	102	Lots No. 294, 295, 300 and 301. W. by First St., N. by lots No. 296 and 299, E. by Second St., S. by lots No. 293 and 302.
Nov. 16, 1784	" "	Mary Klein.	1,071	Lots No. 34 and 35 in Out Ward. W. by Bowery Lane, N. by lot No. 36, E. by lots No. 61 and 62, S. by lot No. 33.

Date of Sale.	Loyalist Owner.	Purchaser.	Price.	Description and Remarks.
Nov. 16, 1784	James De Lancey, attainted.	William Laight.	£405	Lot at Corlaers Hook. S. by Crown Point St., W. by Edward Laight, N. by Garden St., E. by Ferry St. 150 by 200 ft.
Nov. 18, 1784	"	John Gassner.	46	Lots No. 317 and 342 in Out Ward. W. by First St., N. by lots No. 318 and 341, E. by Second St., S. by lots No. 316 and 343.
"	"	Isaac Moses, merchant.	95	Lots No. 792, 793, 794, 795, 796 in Out Ward. N. by De Lancey St., S. by lot No. 797, E. by Fourth St., W. by lots No. 787, 788, 789, 790 and 791.
"	"	Bartholomew Labson, merchant.	99	Lots No. 676, 677, 678, 679, 680 and 681 in Out Ward. W. by Third St., N. by Pump St., E. by Fourth St., S. by lots No. 675 and 682.
Nov. 19, 1784	"	John Lawrence, lawyer.	392	Piece of land on the Bowery. W. by Bowery Lane, N. by Henry Kipp, E. by First St., S. by Isaac Roosevelt. 1/3 of a square between Bullock and De Lancey Sts., middle part.
"	"	John Gassner.	196	Lots from 698 to 705 in the Out Ward. N. by Eagle St., W. by Third St., E. by Christian Shultz, S. by lot No. 697.
"	"	Christian Shultz.	196	Lots from 706 to 713 in Out Ward. N. by Eagle St., E. by Third St., W. by John Gassner, S. by lot No. 714.
Nov. 28, 1784	"	Leonard Fisher.	27	Lot No. 121 in Out Ward. N. by lot No. 120, W. by lot No. 102, E. by First st., S. by lot No. 122.
"	"	Henry Zimerman, gardener.	186	Lots 526, 527, 528, 555, 556 and 557 in Out Ward. W. by Second St., N. by lot No. 529 and 554, E. by Third St., S. by Eagle St.
Nov. 23, 1784	"	Francis Dominic.	355	Lots 244 to 249 in Out Ward. W. by First St, N. by Fisher St., E. by Second St., S. by Division St.
"	"	Jacob Blanck.	2,023	Lot No. 7 in Out Ward. W. by Bowery Lane, N. by lot No. 8, E. by lot No. 27, S. by lot No. 6.

Date of Sale.	Loyalist Owner.	Purchaser.	Price.	Description and Remarks.
Nov. 26, 1784	James De Lacney, attainted.	John Byvanck. Peter Byvanck. Evert Byvanck. Abraham Byvanck. Mary Abeel.	£500	Lot in Out Ward at Corlaers Hook. S. by Crown Point St., W. by John Blanchard, N. by Grand St., E. by Edward Laight.
Nov. 29, 1784	"	Catherine Chapple.	89	Lots No. 42 and 43 in Out Ward. W. by Bowery Lane, N. by lot No. 44. E. by lots No. 52 and 53, S. by lot No. 41.
"	"	Mary Morrel.	131	Lots No. 46 and 47 in Out Ward. N. by Pump St., W. by Bowery Lane, E. by lots No. 48 and 49, S. by lot No. 45.
"	"	Henry Roome, merchant.	245	Tract in Out Ward at Corlaers Hook. N. by Middle St., E. by Ferry St., S. by Garden St., W. by Edward Laight.
Nov. 30, 1784	"	Alexander Finch, butcher.	392	Lot No. 897 to 912 in Out Ward. N. by Eagle St., E. by Orchard St., S. by lots No. 896 and 913, W. by Fourth St.
Dec. 1, 1784	"	John Buchanon.	271	Lots No. 74, 75, 84 and 85 in Out Ward. W. by Bowery Lane, N. by lots No. 76 and 83, E. by First St., S. by lots No. 73 and 86.
Dec. 4, 1784	"	Philip Ebert.	144	Lots No. 1258 to 1265 in Out Ward. N. by Eagle St., W. by lots No. 1250 and 1257, S. by lot No. 1266, E. by Essex St.
Dec. 2, 1784	"	Moses Sherwood.	96	Lots No. 1081 to 1086 in Out Ward. N. by Pump St., S. by Division St., W. by Orchard St.
"	"	Moses Sherwood.	149	Lots No. 102, 103, and half of 104 in Out Ward. W. by Bowery Lane, N. by half of lot No. 104, E. by half of lot No. 119, 120 and 121, S. by lot No. 101.
Dec. 3, 1784	"	Philip Oswald.	137	Lots No. 291, 292, 294, 301, 303 and 304 in Out Ward. N. by lots No. 293, 295, 300 and 302, W. by First St., E. by Second St., S. by lots No. 290, 293, 302 and 305.
Dec. 4, 1784	"	Henry Zimmerman.	120	Lots No. 497 to 500 and 519 to 522 in Out Ward. N. by lots No. 501 and 518, E by Third St., W. by Second St., S. by lots No. 496 and 523.

Date of Sale.	Loyalist Owner.	Purchaser.	Price.	Description and Remarks.
Dec. 4, 1784	James De Lancey, attainted.	Margaret Lydig.	£370	Lots No. 36, 37, 58 and 59 in Out Ward. W. by Bowery Lane, N. by lots No. 38 and 57, E. by First St., S. by lots No. 35 and 60.
" "	"	John Hembrow.	152	Lots No. 690 to 697 in Out Ward. W. by Third St., N. by lot No. 698, E. by Albertus Vanderwater, S. by Pump St.
Dec. 7, 1784	"	Mathew Tier, blacksmith.	130	Lot No. 41 in Out Ward. W. by Bowery Lane, N. by lot No. 42, E. by lot No. 54, S. by lot No. 40.
" "	"	Margaret Jordan.	48	Lots No. 290 and 305 in Out Ward. W. by First St., E. by Second St., N. by lots No. 291 and 304, S. by lots No. 289 and 306.
" "	"	Henry Zimmerman.	126	Lots No. 288, 289, 306 and 307 in Out Ward. W. by First St., E. by Second St., N. by lots No. 290 and 305, S. by lots No. 289 and 308.
Dec. 9, 1784	"	Elizabeth Gantz.	41	Lots No. 282 and 283 in Out Ward. W. by First St., S. by Pump St., E. by lots No. 312 and 313, N. by lot No. 284.
Dec. 10, 1784	"	Peter Mesier, merchant.	359	Lots No. 19 to 24 in Out Ward. N. by lot No. 155, W. by lots No. 25 and 9, S. by Division St., E. by First St.
" "	"	John Dietz, inn holder.	100	Lots No. 78 and 79 in Out Ward. W. by Bowery Lane, N. by Eagle St., E. by lots No. 80 and 81, S. by lot No. 77.
Dec. 11, 1784	"	John Dover.	83	Lots No. 48 and 49 in Out Ward. N. by Pump St., E. by First St., S. by lot No. 50, W. by lots No. 46 and 47.
" "	"	Dorothy Tounelong.	65	Parcel of land in Out Ward. E. by Bowery Lane, S. by Peter Webber, W. by ——, N. by Edward Mooney.
Dec. 15, 1784	"	Charity Miller.	90	Lots No. 1266 to 1272 in Out Ward. N. by lot No. 1265, E. by Essex St., W. by Peter Ogilvie, S. by lot No. 1273.
" "	"	Jacob Whiteman.	164	Lots No. 15 and 16 in Out Ward. N. by Fisher St., W. by lots No. 13 and 14, E. by First St., S. by lot No. 17.
" "	"	William Snyder.	529	Lots No. 9 and 10 in Out Ward. W. by Bowery Lane, N. by lot No. 11, E. by lot No. 24, S. by John Van Vork and Gabriel Furman.

Date of Sale.	Loyalist Owner.	Purchaser.	Price.	Description and Remarks.
Dec. 15, 1784	James De Lancey, attainted.	William Snyder.	£213	Lots No. 100 to 103 in Out Ward. W. by Bowery Lane, N. by lots No. 102 and 121, E. by First St., S. by lots No. 99 and 124.
"	"	Richard Anderson.	62	Lots No. 320 and 321 in Out Ward. W. by First St., N. by lot No. 322, E. by lots No. 338 and 339, S. by lot No. 319.
Dec. 17, 1784	"	Luke C. Quick.	342	Lots No. 97 to 99 and 124 to 126 in Out Ward. W. by Bowery Lane, N. by lots No. 100, 123, E. by First St., S. by lots No. 96 and 127.
"	"	Nicholas Harry.	60	Lots No. 316 and 343 in Out Ward. W. by First St., N. by lots No. 317 and 324, E. by Second St., S. by lots No. 315 and 344.
"	"	John Huffman.	120	Lots No. 314, 315, 344 and 345 in Out Ward. W. by First St., N. by lots No. 316 and 343, E. by Second St., S. by Eagle St.
"	"	James Stringham.	34	Lot No. 109 in Out Ward. W. by Bowery Lane, N. by lot No. 110, E. by lot No. 114, S. by lot No. 108.
Dec. 21, 1784	Thomas Jones, attainted.	Morgan Lewis.	1,400	2 messuages and lots at Mount Pitt. W. by Arundel St., N. and E. by forfeited lands of James De Lancey, S. by Grand St. 500 by 200 ft.
Dec. 24, 1784	James De Lancey, attainted.	Albertus Vandewater, Queens Co., surgeon.	236	Lots No. 874 to 888 and half of Lots No. 714 to 721 in Out Ward. W. by lots No. 690 to 697 and John Hembrow, N. by lot No. 713, E. by the other half of lots No. 714 to 721.
"	"	" " "	400	Lots No. 921 to 928 and 945 to 952 in Out Ward. W. by Fourth St., N. by lots No. 929 and 944, E. by Orchard St., S. by Eagle St.
"	"	" " "	88	Lots No. 539, 553 and 554 in Out Ward. Lot No. 530 W. by Second St., N. by lot No. 531, E. by lot No. 553, S. by lot No. 529. Lots No. 553 and 554 W. by lots No. 529 and 539, N. by lot No. 552, E. by Third St., S. by lot No. 555.

Date of Sale.	Loyalist Owner.	Purchaser.	Price.	Description and Remarks.
Dec. 24, 1784	James De Lancey, attainted.	Albertus Vandewater, Queens Co., surgeon.	£276	Lots No.1297 to 1304 and 1273 to 1280 in Out Ward. W. by Sixth St., N. by lots No. 1281 to 1296, E. by Essex St., S. by Eagle St.
Dec. 31, 1784	"	John Finck.	330	Lots No. 33, 60, 61, 62 in Out Ward. Lot No. 33 W. by Bowery Lane, N. by lot No. 34, E. by lot No. 62, S. by lot No. 32. Lots No. 60 to 62 E. by First St., N. by lot No. 59, W. by lots No. 33, 34 and 35, S. by lot No. 63.
Dec. 30, 1784	"	Jacob Mordecai.	66	Lots No. 275 and 276 in Out Ward. E. by Second St., W. by lots No. 255 and 256, N. by lot No. 214, S. by lot No. 277.
"	"	Gabriel Furman.	441	Lots No. 3, 4, 25, 26 and 27 in Out Ward. Lots No. 3 and 4 W. by Bowery Lane, N. by lot No. 5, E. by lot No. 27, S. by lot No. 2. Lots No. 25 to 27 W. by lots from No. 1 to 8, N. by lot No. 9, E. by lot No. 24, S. by Division St.
"	"	William Smith.	102-10	Lots No. 1751 to 1755 in Out Ward. W. by Suffolk St., N. by lot No. 1756, E. by lots No. 1778 to 1782, S. by Eagle St.
"	"	Abraham Cannon.	82	Lots No. 1779 to 1782 in Out Ward. E. by Arundel St., W. by lots No. 1751 to 1754, N. by lot No. 1778, S. by Eagle St.
"	"	Dennis Hicks.	61-10	Lots No. 1756 to 1758 in Out Ward. E. by lots No. 1775 to 1777, W. by Suffolk St., N. by lot No. 1759, S. by lot No. 1755.
"	"	Peter Kittetas.	66	Lots No. 277 and 278 in Out Ward. E. by Second St., W. by lots No.253 and 254, N. by lot No. 276, S. by lot No. 279.
"	"	Abigail Spicer.	58	Lots No. 1588 and 1589 in Out Ward. E. by Suffolk St., W. by lot No. 1587, N. by Eagle St., S. by Division St.
"	"	Lemuel Bunce.	82	Lots No. 1775 to 1778 in Out Ward. E. by lots No. 1775 to 1778, W. by Arundel St., N. by lot No. 1774, S. by lot No. 1779.
Dec. 31, 1784	"	John Lawrence.	240	Lot No. 4 in Out Ward. E. by Columbus St., S. by Grand St., W. by 50 ft. St., N. by Bullock St.

Date of Sale.	Loyalist Owner.	Purchaser.	Price.	Description and Remarks.
July 12, 1784	Hugh and Alexander Wallace, attainted.	Henry Will.	£1,300	Lot No. 15 and 2 Store Houses in East Ward on N. side of Hunter's Quay along Water St. into East River to Wharf of H. Cruger and Robert Murray. N. by Water St., S. by East River, W. by lot No. 16. Leased for 14 years at £25 yearly to Archibald Kennedy.
Jan. 12, 1785	James De Lancey, attainted.	John Lawrence, lawyer.	768	Lot No. 23 in Out Ward. W. by Attorney St, N. by North St., E. by Ridge St., S. by Stanton St.
" "	" "	George Tilford.	207	Lots No. 250, 251, 252, 279, 280 and 281 in Out Ward. W. by First St., N. by lots No. 253 and 278, E. by Second St., S. by Fisher St.
" "	" "	Abraham Houswert.	116	Lots No. 44 and 51 in Out Ward. W. by Bowery Lane, N. by lots No. 45 and 50, E. by First St., S. by lots No. 43 and 52.
Jan. 7, 1785	" "	John Balthus Doat. Dederick Hoyer. Jacob Reslor, Alexander Finck. Henry Arcularius. John Gassner. Philip Oswald. Christian Shultz. George Schmelzel.	150	Lots No. 494, 495, 523, 524 and 525 in Out Ward. W. by Second St., E. by Third St., S. by Pump St., N. by lots No. 497 and 522. For a united Lutheran Church. Purchasers were the trustees.
Jan. 13, 1785	William Bayard, attainted.	Richard Varick.	545	Lot in South Ward. S. by Dock St., W. by late John Watts, N. by Wyncoop St., E. by William Boyd.
Jan. 21, 1785	James De Lancey, attainted.	Adam Finck.	108	Lots No. 286, 287, 308 and 309 in Out Ward. W. by First St., N. by lots No. 288 and 307, E. by Second St, S. by lots No. 285 and 310.
" "	" "	John Passenger.	461	Lots No. 32 and 63 in Out Ward. W. by Bowery Lane, N. by lots No. 33 and 62, E. by First St., S. by Fisher St.

Date of Sale.	Loyalist Owner.	Purchaser.	Price.	Description and Remarks.
Dec. 4, 1784	James De Lancey, attainted.	Hayman Levy, merchant.	£95	Lots No. 783 to 785 and 797 to 800 in Out Ward. W. by Third St., N. by lots No. 786 and 796, E. by Fourth St., S. by lots No. 782 and 801.
Feb. 22, 1785	" "	Marinus Willet.	96	Lots No. 1446 to 1451 in Out Ward. N. by Grand St., E. by Norfolk St., S. by lot No. 1452, W. by lots No. 1440 to 1445.
" "	" "	Isaac Moses.	256	Lots No. 1430 to 1437 and 1454 to 1461 in Out Ward. S. by Eagle St., E. by Norfolk St., W. by Essex St, N. by lots No. 1438 and 1445.
Feb. 23, 1785	" "	Cornelius Bradford.	62	Lots No. 320 and 340 in Out Ward. W. by First St., N. by lots No, 320 and 349, E. by Second St., S. by lots No. 318 and 342.
" "	William Bayard, attainted.	Peter Mesier, merchant.	890	Dwelling house and lot in Dock Ward. S. by Little Dock St., E. by late Garret Van Horne, N. by William Bayard's confiscated property, W. by late John Oathout.
Feb. 25, 1785	James De Lancey, attainted.	Jonathan Parsee.	128	Lots No. 1438 to 1445 in Out Ward. W. by Essex St., N. by Grand St., E. by Marinus Willet, S. by lot No. 1437.
Feb. 23, 1785	" "	Moses Gale.	32	Lots No. 1452 and 1453 in Out Ward. E. by Norfolk St., N. by lot No. 1451, W. by lots No. 1438 and 1439, S. by lot No. 1454.
Jan. 25, 1785	" "	William Denning.	1292	Lot No. 29 in Out Ward. N. by Bayard, Watts and Rutgers, E. by the Sound, S. by North St., W. by Columbia St.
Mar. 10, 1785	Henry White, attainted.	Henry White, Jr.	519-12-5	Messuage and lot in West Ward. S. by late James Van Cortlandt, W. by Henry White, N. by estate of Walter Heyer, E. by Broadway.
" "	" "	" " "	45	Lot in West Ward. E. by Broadway, S. by Edward Covenhaven, W. by lot No. 6, N. by George Schmelzel. Water lot in West Ward. S. by Water lot of James Van Cortlandt, N. by Walter Heyer, to low water mark.

Date of Sale.	Loyalist Owner.	Purchaser.	Price.	Description and Remarks.
Mar. 10, 1785	James De Lancey, attainted.	Marinus Willett.	£1,200	Messuage and lot in East Ward. S. by Water St., W. by John Lamb and John Delamater, N. by John McChime, E. by Jacobus Van Zandt.
Apr. 20, 1785	Robert Bayard, attainted.	Philip Kissick, merchant.	10sh.	Right of a road through a piece of land.
May 10, 1785	James De Lancey, attainted.	Mary Forbes, spinster.	225	Messuage and lot in West Ward. W. by Broadway, N. by Philander Forbes, E. by Mary Watkins, S. by heirs of Alexander Forbes.
" "	" "	Philander Forbes.	490	Messuage and lot in West Ward. W. by Broadway, N. by Little Queen St., E. by Mary Watkins, S. by Mary Forbes.
" "	" "	Mathew Ballam.	64	Lots No. 253 and 254 in Out Ward. W. by First St., N. by lot No. 255, E. by lots No. 277 and 278, S. by lot No. 252.
" "	" "	Edward Dunscomb.	99	Lots No. 782 and 801 to 805 in Out Ward. Lot No. 782, W. by Third St., N. by lot No. 783, E. by lot No. 801, S. by lot No. 781. Lots No. 801 to 805, E. by Fourth St., S. by Bullock St., W. by lots No. 778 to 782, N. by lots No. 783 to 800.
" "	" "	Bartholomew Labuzen, gardener.	96	Lots No. 879 to 884 in Out Ward. N. by Pump St., E. by Orchard St., S. by lots No. 878 to 888, W. by Fourth St.
May 26, 1785	" "	William Leonard, inn keeper.	200	Lots No. 66, 67, 92 and 93 in Out Ward. W. by Bowery Lane, N. by lots No. 68 and 90, E. by First St., S. by lots No. 65 and 94.
June 1, 1785	" "	Morgan Lewis.	874	Block of 28 lots in Out Ward. S. by Bullock St., W. by Attorney St., N. by De Lancey St., E. by Ridge St. Half of lot No. 17 in Out Ward, 16 lots. S. by Rivington St., W. by Arundel St., N. by half of No. 17, E. by Attorney St.
June 3, 1785	" "	Coenrad Errenfreed.	106	Lot in Out Ward. E. by Bowery Lane, S. by Pell St., N. by Nicholas Lockman, W. by Stephen N. Bayard.

Date of Sale.	Loyalist Owner.	Purchaser.	Price.	Description and Remarks.
June 6, 1785	James De Lancey, attainted.	Joshua Ketcham.	£259	Lots No. 1828 to 1834 in Out Ward. S. by Bullock St., W. by lots No. 1847 to 1813. N. by lot No. 1827, E. by Arundel St.
"	"	Michael Connolly.	288	Lots No. 1389 to 1396 in Out Ward. S. by Rivington St., W. by Sixth St., N. by Peter Stuyvesant, E. by lots No. 1397 to 1407.
"	"	John Sanders.	180	Lots No. 475 to 480 in Out Ward. W. by Second St., N. by Pump St., E. by Third St., S. by lots No. 474 to 481.
June 7, 1785	"	Henry Livingston of Albany County.	944	Block No. 9 with 28 lots in Out Ward. S. by Bullock St., W. by Ridge St., N. by De Lancey St., E. by Pell St. Half of lot No. 17 in Out Ward. W. by Arundel St., N. by Stanton St., E. by Attorney St., S. by half of No. 17.
"	"	Philip Peter Livingston.	1,048	Block No. 13 with 22 lots in Out Ward. S. by De Lancey St., W. by Attorney St., N. by Rivington St., E. by Ridge St. N. half of No. 12 in Out Ward. N. by Rivington St., E. by Attorney St., S. by half No. 12, W. by Arundel St.
June 8, 1785	Roger Morris, attainted.	John Lamb and John Delamater, merchantt.	760	Tract in South Ward. N. by Stone St., W. by Broadway or White Hall St., S. by Widow Moore, E. by Clarkson.
June 7, 1785	James De Lancey, attainted.	Nicholas Fish.	908	Block No. 14 with 32 lots in Out Ward. N. by Rivington St., E. by Pitt St., S. by De Lancey St., W. by Ridge St. S. half of No. 12 in Out Ward. S. by De Lancey St., W. by Arundel St., N. by half of No. 12, E. by Attorney St.
June 8, 1785	Waldron Blauw, convicted, and James Watts, attainted.	John MacKesson.	380	2 lots. W. and N. by heirs of Henry Carmer, E. by half of No. 12, S. by Bridge St. 2 lots. W. by half of Henry Carmer, N. by Peter Stoutenburg and William P. Smith, E. by late Gerardus Myer, S. by Bridge St.
June 13, 1785	James De Lancey, attainted.	Isaac Gouverneur.	1,424	Lots No. 1514 to 1545 in Out Ward. N. by Rivington St., E. by Norfolk St., S. by De Lancey St., W. by Essex St.

Date of Sale.	Loyalist Owner.	Purchaser.	Price.	Description and Remarks.
June 13, 1785	James De Lancey, attainted.	John Keating, merchant.	£50	Lots No. 1242 to 1249 in Out Ward. S. by Pump St., W. by Sixth St., N. by lot No. 1250, E. by Peter Ogilvie.
June 14, 1785	Beverly Robinson and Frederick Philipse, attainted.	Isaac Hubble.	?	Certain piece of land in South Ward. W. by Broadway, N. by Widow Hoogwort, E. by John Ryfels, S. by Stone St.
July 8, 1785	Robert Bayard, attainted.	Morgan Lewis, Esq.	1,200	Messuage and lot in North Ward. N. E. by Maiden Lane, N. W. by Morgan Lewis and Widow Egberts, S. W. by Luke Kiersted, S. E. by Joseph Dunckley.
June 18, 1785	James De Lancey, attainted.	Frederick William. Barron De Steuben. Christ. Feigenheim. Anthony Apple. William Leonard. Christian Will. Frederick Boetticker. William Snyder. Jacob Sperry and Henry Will.	102	Lots No. 264 and 265 in Out Ward. N. by Pump St., E. by lots No. 266 and 267, S. by lot No. 263, W. by First St. Bought by the trustees of the German Reformed Church of New York City.
July 26, 1785	William Bayard, attainted.	James Abeel, merchant.	710	Messuage and lot in Dock Ward. N. W. by Great Dock St., S. E. by Peter Mesier, N. E., by Garret van Horne, S. W. by Isaac Moses.
July 27, 1785	James De Lancey, attainted.	John Evans, merchant.	185	Lots No. 462, 463, 464, 492 and 493 in Out Ward. S. by Fisher St. and Division St., W. by Second St., N. by lots No. 465 and 491, E. by Third St.
"	"	John Somerndike of Bloomingdale, farmer.	2,500	Tract 68 by 250 rods N. of Great Hills and S. of Adrian Van Schaik along North River.
"	"			200 acres on Hudson River next to Jacobus Van Cortlandt, above Cornelius Williams, bounded by Commons on E.

Date of Sale.	Loyalist Owner.	Purchaser.	Price.	Description and Remarks.
July 28, 1785	William Bayard, attainted.	John Thompson.	£1,200	Dwelling and lot in East Ward. S. E. by Queen St., S. W. by John Reade, N. W. by Cornelius Tiebout, N. E. by Abraham Kettetas. S. W. half in fee simple, N. W. half only for life of William Bayard and wife.
"	"	Melancton Smith and Henry Wyckoff, merchants.	1,020	Messuage, store-house and lot in Dock Ward. S. E. by Dock St, N. E. by Edmund Seaman, N. W. by John R. Myer, S. W. by late Thomas Browne.
July 29, 1785	James De Lancey, attainted.	Peter Hill.	480	One-third of block of 120 lots in Out Ward. From crossing of Grand and Second Sts. N. to Bullock St, W. to Essex St., S. to Grand St. To include Third, Fourth, Orchard and Sixth Sts., 50 ft. wide.
"	"	Lewis Ogden, merchant.	480	One-third of above tract, 5 squares.
"	"	Nich. Gouverneur, Jr.	480	One-third of above tract, 5 squares,
"	"	Peter Hill.	392	One-third of 3 squares of 84 lots in Out Ward. S. by Bullock St., W. by Orchard St , N. by De Lancey St., E. by Sixth St., 350 by 175 ft.
"	"	Lewis Ogden.	392	One-third of above three squares. S. by Bullock St., W. by Essex St., N. by De Lancey St., E. by Norfolk St., 350 by 200 ft.
"	"	Nich. Gouverneur, Jr.	392	One third of 3 squares. S. by Bullock St., W. by Norfolk St., N. by De Lancey St., E. by Suffolk St.
July 25, 1785	"	Edward Money.	320	Messuage and lot in Out Ward fronting on Bowery Lane. To Pell St. W. to Jacob Hoffman, E. 50 ft., N. 44 ft., E. 101½ ft. to Bowery Lane.
Aug. 2, 1785	Thomas Jones, Esq., attainted.	Morgan Lewis.	970	Tract and buildings in Out Ward. S. E. by Arundel St. and Division St., N. to S. Bullock St., E. to Margaret St., S. to Grand St., W. to Division St.

Date of Sale.	Loyalist Owner.	Purchaser.	Price.	Description and Remarks.
Sep. 10, 1785	James De Lancey, attainted.	David Campbell.	£170	Lots No. 107 and 116 in Out Ward. W. by Bowery Lane, N. by lots No. 108 and 117, E. by First St., S. by lots No. 106 and 117.
" "	" "	Peter Byvanck, merchant.	360	Tract in Out Ward. N. by High St., N. E. by Grand St., E. by East River, S. by Middle St., W. by Ferry St.
" "	" "	Peter Van Zandt, Esq.	260	Lots No. 76, 77 and 80 to 83 in Out Ward. W. by Bowery Lane, N. by lot No. 78 and Eagle St, E. by First St., S. by lots No. 75 and 84.
Sep. 12, 1785	John Weatherhead, attainted.	John Stoutenburg.	520	Tract in West Ward. From North River St. East 76½ ft. to Benjamin Logier, then S. W. around to North River St. again.
Sep. 13, 1785	William Bayard, attainted.	Thomas McFarran.	850	Water lot and Dock in Dock Ward. N. by Conger's wharf, S. W. by Thomas Browne, S. E. by East River, N. E. by Edward Seaman.
" "	James De Lancey, attainted.	William Beekman.	81	Half lots No. 889 to 896 in Out Ward. W. by Fourth St., N. by lot No. 897, E. by other half of lots, S. by Pump St.
" "	" "	" "	734	Lots No. 1408 to 1429 in Out Ward. S. by Division St., W. by Essex St., N. by Eagle St., E. by Norfolk St.
" "				Lots No. 338 and 339 in Out Ward. E. by Second St., S. by Cornelius Bradford, W. by Richard Anderson, N. by Francis Dominick.
" "	" "	" "	822	Lots No. 531 to 552 in Out Ward. W. by Second St., N. by Grand St., E. by Third St., S. by lots No. 530 and 553.
" "				Lots No. 666 to 671 and 686 to 689 in Out Ward. S. by Division St., E. by Fourth St., N. by lots No. 672 and 685, W. by Third St.
Oct. 6, 1785	" "	Isaac Varian.	360	Lots No. 71, 72, 73, 86, 87 and 88 in Out Ward. W. by Bowery Lane, N. by lots No. 74 and 85, E. by First St., S. by lots No. 70 and 89.

Date of Sale.	Loyalist Owner.	Purchaser.	Price.	Description and Remarks.
Oct. 6, 1785	James De Lancey, attainted.	John Lawrence.	£44	Lots No. 114 and 115 in Out Ward. E. by First St., N. by lot No. 13, W. by lots No. 108 and 109, S. by lot No 116.
" "	"	Michael Varrian, butcher.	220	Lots No. 469 to 474 and 481 to 486 in Out Ward. W. by Second St., N. by lots No. 475 and 480, E. by Third St., S. by lots No. 468 and 467.
Oct. 7, 1785	"	Nicho. Gouverneur.	392	One-fourth of 2 pieces of land marked G and H in Out Ward. S. by Crown Point St., W. by Nicholas Romayne, N. by lot marked F, E. by James Blanchard.
" "	"	Lewis Ogden.	392-3-4	One-third land in Out Ward marked P, E and F. S. by lot G, W. by Nicholas Romayne, N. by Division St. and Grand St., E. by heirs of Evert Byvanck.
Oct. 15, 1785	"	Daniel Show.	336	Lots No. 854 to 861 in Out Ward. N. by Stanton St., E. by Fourth St., S. by lot No. 862, W. by lots No. 846 to 853.
Oct. 17, 1785	"	Peter Webbers, grocer.	90	Lots No. 257, 258, 273 and 274 in Out Ward. W. by First St., N. by lots No. 259 and 272, E. by Second St., S. by lots No. 256 and 275.
Oct. 24, 1785	"	Wm. Denning, Esq.	384	Lots No. 1005 to 1036 in Out Ward. N. by Rivington St., E. by Orchard St., S. by De Lancey St., W. by Fourth St.
Oct. 25, 1785	"	John Webbers.	200	Lot on W. side of Bowery, in Out Ward. E. by Bowery Lane, S. by Dorothy Toumelong, W. by Joshua Pell, N. by Edward Mooney.
Dec. 17, 1785	"	Jonathan Lawrence, merchant.	1286	Lots No. 1329 to 1356 in Out Ward. S. by Bullock St, W. by Sixth St., N. by De Lancey St., E. by Essex St.
Dec. 19, 1785	"	"	448	Lots No. 1814 to 1827 in Out Ward. N. by De Lancey St., E. by Arundel St., S. by lots No. 1813 and 1828, W. by Suffolk St.
Dec. 20, 1785	"	Leonard Fisher, barber.	90	Lots No. 296 to 299 in Out Ward. N. by Eagle St., E. by Second St., S. by lots No. 295 and 300, W. by First St.
Jan. 14, 1786	"	John Vaugh, lime burner.	165	Messuage and lot in Out Ward. S. by Bowery Lane, E. and N. by James De Lancey, W. by Abraham De Peyster.

Date of Sale.	Loyalist Owner.	Purchaser.	Price.	Description and Remarks.
Jan. 24, 1786	James De Lancey, attainted.	John Quackenbos.	£386	Tract No. 10, 84 lots, in Out Ward. S. by Bullock St., W. by Pitt St., N. by De Lancey St., E. by Columbia St
" "	"	"	1,872	Tract No. 20, 96 lots, in Out Ward. S. by Rivington St., W. by Pitt St., N. by Stanton St., E. by Columbia St.
Jan. 30, 1786	"	"	1,536	Tract No. 15, 96 lots, in Out Ward. N. by Rivington St., E. by Columbia St., S. by De Lancey St., W. by Pitt St.
Jan. 31, 1786	"	Garret Abeel.	174	Tract No. 3 in Out Ward. E. by Ferry St., S. by Middle St., W. by Edward Laight, N. by High St.
" "	"	"	110	Tract at Corlaers Hook in Out Ward. N. and E. by Grand St., S. by High St., W. by Ferry St.
" "	"	John Quackenbos.	159	Tract No. 4 in Out Ward. N. by Ruff St., E. by Ferry St., S. by High St., W. by Edward Laight.
Feb. 3, 1786	"	"	608	Lots No. 399 to 430 in Out Ward. W. by First St., N. by Rivington St., E. by Second St., S. by De Lancey St.
" "	"	Nicholas Fish.	1,600	Lots No. 180 to 211 in Out Ward. W. by Bowery Lane, N. by Rivington St., E. by First St., S. by De Lancey St.
Feb. 25, 1786	"	John Quackenbos.	81	Lots No. 118 to 120 in Out Ward. N. by lot No. 127, E. by First St., S. by lot No. 121, W. by lots No. 103 to 105.
Mar. 6, 1786	"	"	462	Tract No. 7 in Out Ward. S. by Bullock St., E. by Attorney St., W. by Arundel St., N. by De Lancey St.
Aug. 16, 1786	Oliver De Lancey, attainted.	Isaac Roosevelt.	2,660	Tract on Broadway in West Ward. S. by heirs of Pier De Peyster, W. by Hudson River, N. by hers of Isaac Van Hook, E. by Broadway.
Jan. 11, 1785	James De Lancey, attainted.	John Quackenbos.	2,300	Tract No. 28 in Out Ward. S. by North St., W. by Pitt St., E. by Columbia St., N. by Bayard, Watts and Rutgers.
Sep. 20, 1784	"	William Arnold, rope-maker.	58	Half lots No. 889 to 896 in Out Ward. S. by Pump St., W. by other half of lots, N. by lots No. 897 and 912, E. by lots No. 913 to 920.
May 30, 1785	"	George Fisher, baker.	588	Lots No. 1899 to 1921 in Out Ward. S. by Stanton St., W. by Suffolk St. N. by Peter Stuyvesant, E. by Arundel St.

Date of Sale.	Loyalist Owner.	Purchaser.	Price.	Description and Remarks.
May 18, 1786	Josh. T. D. St. Croix, of New Rochelle Twp., Westchester Co., convicted.	Comfort and Joshua Sands, merchants.	£800	Two houses and lots in Montgomery Ward. E. by James St., N. by Rutgers St., W. by Jacobus Roosevelt, S. by Christopher Bancker.
May 30, 1786	James De Lancey, attainted.	Sarah Smith, spinster.	336	Lots No. 846 to 853 in Out Ward. W. by Third St., N. by Stanton St., E. by lots No. 854 to 861, S. by lot No. 845.
"	"	Hon. John Sloss Hobert.	672	Lots No. 838 to 845 and 862 to 869 in Out Ward. S. by Rivington St., W. by Third St., N. by lots No. 486 and 461, E. by Fourth St.
"	"	Isaac Roosevelt.	1,240	Lots No. 371 to 398 in Out Ward. S. by Bullock St., W. by First St., N. by De Lancey St., E. by Second St. Lots No. 1462 to 1485 in Out Ward. S. by Grand St., W. by Essex St., N. by Bullock St., E. by Norfolk St. Lots No. 1622 to 1645 in Out Ward. S. by Grand St., W. by Norfolk St., N. by Bullock St., E. by Suffolk St. Lots No. 1783 to 1806 in Out Ward. S. by Grand St., W. by Suffolk St., N. by Bullock St., E. by Arundel St.
June 20, 1785	"	Cornelius Ray, merchant.	388	Lots No. 588 to 603 in Out Ward. N. by De Lancey St., E. by Third St., S. by lots No. 587 to 604, W. by Second St. Lots No. 610 to 613 and 638 to 641 in Out Ward. W. by Second St., N. by lots No. 614 and 637, E. by Third St., S. by De Lancey St.
June 22, 1786	"	Andrew Moody.	400	Lots No. 1131 to 1134 in Out Ward. N. by Grand St., W. by Orchard St., S. by lot No. 1130, E. by lots No. 1135 to 1138.
June 26, 1786	"	Thomas Lawrence.	888	Lots No. 1767 to 1774 in Out Ward. N. by Grand St., E. by Arundel St., S. by lot No. 1775, W. by lots No. 1759 to 1766.
June 20, 1786	"	Cornelius Bradford.	56	Lots No. 318 and 342 in Out Ward. W. by First St., N. by lots No. 319 and 341, E. by Second St., S. by lots No. 317 and 343.

Date of Sale.	Loyalist Owner.	Purchaser.	Price.	Description and Remarks.
June 20, 1786	James De Lancey, attainted.	Ebenezer Young.	£224	Lots No. 240 to 243 in Out Ward. S. by Rivington St., E. by First St., N. by lot No. 239, W. by lots No. 212 to 215. Lots No. 614 to 617 and 634 to 637 in Out Ward. W. by Second St., N. by lots No. 618 and 633, E. by Third St., S. by lots No. 613 and 638.
July 10, 1786	"	John R. Meyer.	113	Lots No. 641 to 648 in Out Ward. W. by Second St., N. by lots No. 649, E. by lots No. 657 to 665, S. by Rivington St.
" "	"	James Smith.	72	Lots No. 649 to 656 in Out Ward. W. by Second St., N. by lots No. 1922 and 1927, E. by Third St., S. by lots No. 648 and 657.
"	"	Henry Ten Brook, merchant.	116	Lots No. 431 to 462 in Out Ward. W. by First St., N. by lots No. 435 and 458, E. by Second St., S. by Rivington St.
June 22, 1786	"	George Taylor.	1,612	Lots No. 1135 to 1150 in Out Ward. N. by Grand St., E. by Sixth St., S. by Eagle St., W. by lots No. 1119 to 1134.
June 29, 1786	"	Joseph Stringham, merchant.	664	Lots No. 977 to 980 in Out Ward. S. by Bullock St., W. by Fourth St., N. by lot No. 981, E. by lots No. 1001 to 1004.
June 26, 1786	"	Henry Ten Brook.	852	Lots No. 1285 to 1288 in Out Ward. N. by Grand St., W. by Sixth St., S. by lot No. 1284, E. by lots No. 1289 to 1292. Lots No. 1203 to 1206 in Out Ward. S. by De Lancey St., W. by Orchard St., N. by lot No. 1207, E. by lots No. 1231 to 1234. Lots No. 1211 to 1214 in Out Ward. W. by Orchard St., N. by lot No. 1215, E. by lots No. 1223 to 1226, S. by lot No. 1210.
"	"	John Lawrence, Esq.	600	Lots No. 1590 to 1593 in Out Ward. S. by Eagle St., W. by Norfolk St., N. by lot No. 1594, E. by lots No. 1618 to 1621. Lots No. 1594 to 1601 in Out Ward. W. by Norfolk St., N. by lot No. 1602, E. by lots No. 1610 to 1617, S. by lot No. 1593.

Date of Sale.	Loyalist Owner.	Purchaser.	Price.	Description and Remarks.
June 26, 1785	James De Lancey, Sr., attainted.	Daniel Show.	£656	Lots No. 1602 to 1609 in Out Ward. N. by Grand St., E. by Suffolk St., S. by lots No. 1601 and 1610, W. by Norfolk St.
" "	" "	James Bingham.	892	Lots No. 1614 to 1621 in Out Ward. S. by Eagle St., E. by Suffolk St., N. by lot No. 1613, W. by lots No. 1590 to 1597.
" "	" "	George Douglas, merchant.	345	Tract in Out Ward. S. E. by Division St., W. by Suffolk St., N. by Eagle St.
June 19, 1785	Henry White, Sr., attainted.	Henry White, Jr.	21,500	Dwelling, lot, store-houses, stables, etc., in East Ward. N. W. by Queen St., N. E. by Wm. Ludlow, Thomas and James Arden, S. E. by Thomas and James Arden, Water St. and Daniel Phoenix, S. W. by Daniel Phoenix and James Desbrosses.
June 29, 1785	James De Lancey, attainted.	Ephraim Brasher.	444	Lots No. 1207 to 1210 and 1227 to 1229 in Out Ward. W. by Orchard St., N. by lots No. 1211 and 1226, E. by Sixth St., S. by lots No. 1206 and 1231.
July 10, 1786	" "	William A. Forbes, sadler.	300	Tract in West Ward. W. by Broadway, N. by Mary Forbes, E. by Mary Watkies, S. by Reformed Protestant Dutch church.
June 29, 1786	" "	John R. Meyer.	794	Lots No. 1001 to 1004 in Out Ward. S. by Bullock St., W. by lots No. 977 to 980, N. by lot No. 1000, E. by Orchard St.
" "	" "			Lots No. 1807 to 1813 in Out Ward. S. by Bullock St., W. by Suffolk St., N. by lot No. 1814, E. by lots No. 1828 to 1834.
" "	" "	James Gray, merchant.	300	Lots No. 1714 to 1716 and 1727 to 1729 in Out Ward. W. by Norfolk St., N. by lots No. 1717 and 1726, E. by Suffolk St., S. by lots No. 1713 and 1730.

Date of Sale.	Loyalist Owner.	Purchaser.	Price.	Description and Remarks.
June 22, 1786	James De Lancey, attainted.	Michael McLachlan.	£918	Lots No. 1119 to 1130 in Out Ward. S. by Eagle St., W. by Orchard St., N. by lot No. 1131, E. by lots No. 1139 to 1150.
July 8, 1786	"	Magdalen Falkenham.	261	Lots No. 38 and 39 in Out Ward. W. by Bowery Lane, N. by lot No. 40, E. by lots No. 56 and 57, S. by lot No. 37.
July 25, 1786	"	Elizabeth Leonard.	411	Lots No. 13 and 14 in Out Ward. W. by Bowery Lane, N. by Fisher St., E. by lots No. 15 and 16, S. by lot No. 12.
June 29, 1786	"	Thomas Ivers.	320	Lots No. 1231 to 1234 in Out Ward. S. by De Lancey St., W. by lots No. 1203 to 1206, N. by lot No. 1230, S. by Sixth St.
Sep. 30, 1784	"	Philip Livingston.	392	Lots No. 1674 to 1705, in Out Ward. S. by De Lancey St., W. by Norfolk St., N. by Rivington St., E. by Suffolk St.
June 21, 1786	"	Isaac Roosevelt.	560	Lots No. 722 to 753, in Out Ward. N. by Grand St., E. by Fourth St., S. by Eagle St., W. by Third St.
" "	"	James Blanchford.	465	Tract in Out Ward. S. by Crown Point St., W. by tracts E, F, G and H, N. by Ruff St., E. by heirs of Evert Byvanck.
June 26, 1786	"	Lewis Morris.	308	Lots No. 1610 to 1613 in Out Ward. E. by Suffolk St., S. by lot No. 1614, W. by lots No. 1598 to 1601, N. by lot No. 1609.
June 29, 1786	"	Abijah Hammond, merchant.	478	Lots No. 981 to 1000 in Out Ward. W. by Fourth St., N. by lots No. 985 to 996, E. by Orchad St., S. by lots No. 980 and 1001.
" "	"	William Barber.	280	Lots No. 1223 to 1226 in Out Ward. E. by Sixth St., S. by lot No. 1227, W. by lots No. 1211 to 1214, N. by lot No. 1222.
Nov. 17, 1784	"	Peter Ogilvie, attorney.	80	Half of lots No. 1242 to 1249 in Out Ward. S. by Pump St., W. by other half of lots, N. by lot No. 1250, E. by lots No. 1266 to 1269.

Date of Sale.	Loyalist Owner.	Purchaser.	Price.	Description and Remarks.
June 29, 1786	James De Lancey, attainted.	George Fisher, baker.	£1,766	Lots No. 1 and 2 in Out Ward. W. by Bowery Lane, N. by lot No. 3 and 4, E. by lot No. 27, S. by Division St. Lots No. 11 and 12 in Out Ward. W. by Bowery Lane, N. by lot No. 13, E. by lots No. 17 and 18, S. by lot No. 10. Lots No. 96 and 127 in Out Ward. W. by Bowery Lane, N. by lots No. 97 and 126, E. by First St., S. by Eagle St. Lots No. 128 to 139 in Out Ward. W. by Bowery Lane, N. by Bullock St., E. by lots No. 140 and 151, S. by Grand St. Lots No. 140 to 143 in Out Ward. N. by Bullock St., E. by First St., S. by lot No. 144, W. by lots No. 136 to 139.
"	" "	" "	528	Lots No. 212 to 219 in Out Ward. W. by Bowery Lane, N. by lot No. 220, E. by lots No. 236 to 243, S. by Rivington St. Lots No. 236 to 239 in Out Ward. E. by First St., S. by lot No. 240, W. by lots No. 216 to 219, N. by lot No. 235; Lots No. 347 to 354 and 363 to 370 in Out Ward. S. by Grand St., W. by First St., N. by lots No. 355 and 362, E. by First St.
July 10, 1784	John Grigg, of Kinderhook, Albany Co., convicted.	John Lake.	30	Lots No. 130 to 137 in Out Ward near Fresh Water. E. by Water St., W. by Fresh Water, N. by Fresh Water, S. by lot No. 138.
Dec. 7, 1784	James De Lancey, attainted.	Daniel Tier.	300	Lots No. 45 and 50 in Out Ward. W. by Bowery Lane, N. by lots No. 46 and 49, E. by First St., S. by lots No. 44 and 51. Lots No. 64, 65, 94 and 95 in Out Ward. W. by Bowery Lane, N. by lots No. 66 and 93, E. by First St., S. by Pump St.
May 31, 1785	" " "	William Boyd.	738	Lots No. 1235 to 1241 in Out Ward. S. by Rivington St., W. by Orchard St., N. by Peter Stuyvesant, E. by Sixth St. Lots No. 1397 to 1407 in Out Ward. S. by Rivington St., W. by lots No. 1389 to 1396, N. by Peter Stuyvesant, E. by Essex St.

Date of Sale.	Loyalist Owner.	Purchaser.	Price.	Description and Remarks.
May 31, 1785	James De Lancey, attainted.	Henry Tiebout.	£1,189	Lots No. 1546 to 1577 in Out Ward. S. by Rivington St., W. by Essex St., N. by Stanton St. and Peter Stuyvesant, E. by Norfolk St.
Aug. 16, 1784	"	Comfort Sands and Jas. Dunlap, merchants.	1,700	Tract and buildings in Out Ward. E. by Bowery Lane, N. by John Vaugh, W. by Moravian Cemetery, S. by Pell St. and Edward Mooney.
June 19, 1786	"	Anthony Post, corporal.	77	Lot No. 8 in Out Ward. W. by Bowery Lane, N. by lot No. 9, E. by lot No. 27, S. by lot No. 7.
Sep. 20, 1786	"	William Thurston, blacksmith.	80	Lots No. 913 to 920 in Out Ward. W. by John Lewis, N. by lot No. 912, E. by Orchard St., S. by Pump St.
" "	"	James Galloway, rigger.	80	West half of lots No. 1087 to 1094 in Out Ward. W. by Orchard St., N. by lot No. 1095, E. by John Crasson, S. by Pump St.
Oct. 7, 1786	"	Janet Montgomery.	1,032	One-sixth of Square No. 25 in Out Ward. E. by Columbia St., S. by Stanton St., W. by Pitt St., N. by the Square.
" "	"	"	540	Square No. 21 in Out Ward. S. by Rivington St., W. by Columbia St., N. by Stanton St., E. by High Water Mark.
" "	"	"	200	Half of square No. 24, 16 lots, in Out Ward.
" "	"	"	609	Square No. 22, 29 lots, in Out Ward. W. by Arundel St., N. by Peter Stuyvesant and North St., E. by Ridge St., S. by Stanton St.
June 29, 1786	"	Robert Lenox, merchant.	200	Lots No. 1215 to 1218 in Out Ward. W. by Orchard St, N. by Rivington St., E. by lots No. 1219 and 1222, S. by lot No. 1214.
" "	"	Samuel Kerr.	268	Lots No. 1219 to 1222 in Out Ward. W. by lots No. 1215 to 1218, N, by Rivington St., E. by Sixth St., S. by lot No. 1223.

Date of Sale.	Loyalist Owner.	Purchaser.	Price.	Description and Remarks.
June 26, 1786	James De Lancey, attainted.	John Mason, minister.	£720	Lots No. 1281 to 1284 in Out Ward. W. by Sixth St., N. by lot No. 1285, S. by lot No. 1280, E. by lots No. 1293 to 1296.
"	"	Daniel Neven.	404	Lots No. 1289 to 1292 in Out Ward. W. by lots No. 1285 to 1288, N. by Grand St., E. by Essex St., S. by lot No. 1293.
"	"	Hugh Walst.	368	Lots No. 1763 to 1766 in Out Ward. W. by Suffolk St., N. by Grand St., E. by lots No. 1767 to 1770, S. by lot No. 1762.
Jan. 10, 1786	"	Joseph Hallett.	480	Lots No. 1759 to 1762 in Out Ward. W. by Suffolk St., N. by lot No. 1763, E. by lots No. 1771 to 1774, S. by lot No. 1758.
Jan. 11, 1786	"	Joseph Hallett and Daniel Phoenix.	840	Tract No. 19, 32 lots, in Out Ward. W. by Ridge St., N. by Stanton St., E. by Pitt St., S. by Rivington St. Tract No. 16, 56 lots, in Out Ward. W. by Columbia St., N. by Rivington St., E. by East River, S. by De Lancey St.
June 20, 1786	"	Joseph Stringham.	180	Lots No. 582 to 587 and 604 to 609 in Out Ward. S. by Bullock St., W. by Second St., N. by lots No. 588 and 603, E. by Third St.
July 11, 1786	"	Abraham Cannon.	600	Tract in Out Ward. S. by Grand St., W. by Cannon St., N. by Bullock St., E. by East River.
Sep. 1, 1784	"	Mary Stiles.	95	Lot No. 40 in Out Ward. W. by Bowery Lane, N. by lot No. 41, E. by lot No. 55, S. by lot No. 39.
"	"	Francis Dominick.	150	Lots No. 17 and 18 in Out Ward. E. by First St., S. by lots No. 19 to 24, W. by lots No. 11 and 12, N. by lot No. 16.
Sep. 13, 1784	"	" "	288	Lots No. 322 to 338 in Out Ward. N. by Grand St., E. by Second St., S. by lots No. 321 and 339, W. by First St.
Mch. 1, 1785	James Jauncey, attainted.	John Lamb, Esq., and John Delamater, merchants.	675	Messuage and lot in East Ward. S. by Water St., W. by Christopher Smith, N. by Francis Lewis, E. by Marinus Willett, Esq.

Date of Sale.	Loyalist Owner.	Purchaser.	Price.	Description and Remarks.
Jan. 11, 1785	James De Lancey, attainted.	John Delamater and John Lamb, merchants.	£4,028	Tract No. 26, 36 lots, in Out Ward. S. by Stanton St., W. by Columbia St., N. by North St., E. by East River. N. E. corner of tract No. 24, 9 lots, in Out Ward. N. by North St., E. by Pitt St., S. and W. by No. 24. S. W. corner of No. 24 in Out Ward. S. by Stanton St., W. by Ridge St., N. and E. by No. 24. Tract No. 5, 24 lots, in Out Ward. S. by Grand St, W. by Columbia St., N. by Bullock St., E. by Cannon St. Tract No. 11, 62 lots, in Out Ward. S. by Bullock St., W. by Columbia St., N. by De Lancey St., E. by East River. N. half of tract No. 25, 48 lots, in Out Ward. N. by North St., E. by Columbia St., S. by rest of No. 25, W. by Pitt St.
Feb. 1, 1785	"	Francis Gantz.	50	Lots No. 312 and 313 in Out Ward. S. by Pump St., W. by lots No. 282 and 283, N. by lot No. 311, E. by Second St.
May 31, 1785	"	John Quackenbos, gentleman. "	752	Lots No. 1037 to 1068 in Out Ward. S. by Rivington St., W. by Fourth St., N. by Stanton St., E. by Orchard St.
June 29, 1786	"	"	1,294	Triangle tract No. 27, 22 lots, in Out Ward. N. by Peter Stuyvesant, E. by Pitt St., S. by North St.
June 21, 1786	"	John Gasner. Jacob Sperry. Christo. Fiegenheim.	152	Lots No. 1250 to 1257 in Out Ward. N. by Eagle St., E. by lots No. 1258 to 1265, S. by lot No. 1249, W. by Sixth St.
Sep. 30, 1784	"	John Egbert, carpenter.	150	Messuage and lots No. 1581, 1586 and part of 1580 in Out Ward. N. by Eagle St., E. by lot No. 1587, S. by Division St., W. by part of lot No.1580.
July 10, 1786	John Griggs, farmer, of Albany county, convicted.	John Murray, merchant.	10	House and lot in Out Ward near Fresh Water. E. by the late Hufnagle, S. by the late John Kingston, W. by lot No. 119, N. by Cross St.
Dec. 15, 1784	James De Lancey, attainted.	John Lamb.	96	E. half of square No. 3 in Out Ward. N. by Bullock St., E. by Sheriff St., S. by Grand St., W. by other half of No. 3.

Date of Sale.	Loyalist Owner.	Purchaser.	Price.	Description and Remarks.
Dec. 15, 1784	James De Lancey, attainted.	Marinus Willett.	£96	W. half of square No. 3 in Out Ward. N. by Bullock St., E. by other half of No. 3, S. by Grand St., W. by Margaret St.
Nov. 19, 1784	"	Henry Kipp, merchant.	392	One-third square between Bullock and De Lancey Sts. in Out Ward. W. by Bowery Lane, N. by De Lancey St., E. by First St., S. by John Lawrence, Esq.
" "	"	Isaac Roosevelt.	392	One-third of above square. W. by Bowery Lane, N. by John Lawrence, E. by First St., S. by Bullock St.
June 29, 1786	"	Abijah Hammond, merchant.	792	Lots No. 985 to 996 in Out Ward. N. by De Lancey St., E. by Orchard St., S. by lots No. 984 and 997, W. by Fourth St.
July 28, 1784	James Jauncey, attainted.	Isaac Stoutenburgh.	315	Lot and a half in West Ward. S. by Dey St., W. by lot No. 56, N. by late Janetje Ryerson, E. by lot No. 54.
Sep. 13, 1784	James De Lancey, attainted.	Alexander Finch, butler.	32	Lot No. 529 in Out Ward. W. by Second St., N. by lot No. 530, E. by lot No. 554, S. by lot No. 528.
Aug. 24, 1784	"	Mary Watkies.	200	Messuage and lot in North Ward. N. by Little Queen St., E. by Widow Winterlow, S. by Reformed Dutch church, W. by Philander Forbes.
Dec. 13, 1784	"	John McKesson, Esq.	180	Messuage and lot in Out Ward. W. by Bowery Lane, N. by lot No. 7, E. by lot No. 27, S. by lot No. 4.
Aug. 24, 1784	"	" "	80	Lots No. 778 to 781 in Out Ward. S. by Bullock St., W. by Third St., N. by lot No. 782, E. by lots No. 802 to 805.
Sep. 20, 1786	"	John Lewis, rigger.	40	Lots No. 913 to 920 in Out Ward. W. by William Arnold, N. by lot No. 911, E. by William Thurston, S. by Pump St.
July 10, 1786	"	Abigail Spicer, widow.	29	Lot No. 1587 in Out Ward. N. by Eagle St., E. by lot No. 1588, S. by Division St., W. by lot No. 1586.
Sep. 9, 1786	"	Wm. McGilbert, Esq.	480	Lots No. 1111 to 1118 in Out Ward and E. half of lots No. 1087 to 1094. W. by half of lots No. 1087 to 1094, N. by lots No. 1095 and 1110, E. by Sixth St., S. by Pump St.
" "	"	" "	640	Lots No. 1095 to 1110 in Out Ward. S. by lots No. 1094 and 1111, W. by Orchard St., N. by Eagle St., E. by Sixth St.

Date of Sale.	Loyalist Owner.	Purchaser.	Price.	Description and Remarks.
Sep. 9, 1786	James De Lancey, attainted.	Wm. McGilbert, Esq.	£720	Lots No. 501 to 578 in Out Ward. S. by lots No. 500 and 579, W. by Second St., N. by Eagle St., E. by Third St.
Jan. 11, 1785	" "	Morgan Lewis.	912	16 acres of Salt Meadow in Out Ward. S. and W. by Watts, Bayard and Rutgers, N. by Peter Stuyvesant, E. by Stuyvesant's Creek.
June 19, 1786	Oliver De Lancey, attainted.	Wm. Denning, Esq.	950	Land and water lot in West Ward. E. by High Water, S. by heirs of Peter Warren, N. by corporation of Trinity Church, W. by Hudson River.
May 30, 1785	" "	" "	1,750	Tract in West Ward. S. by Oyster Party Line, W. by Lombard St., N. by heirs of Sir Peter Warren, E. by late Lambert Moore.
				Tract in West Ward. E. by Lombard St., S. by estate of Richard Schuckburgh, W. by High Water on Hudson, N. by heirs of Sir Peter Warren.
				Water lot in West Ward. E. by above tract, S. by Richard Schuckburgh, N. by Water Lot of heirs of Sir Peter Warren, W. by high water mark to low water mark and 200 ft. into the river.
Sep. 27, 1786	William Bayard, attainted.	Charles McKnight, Physician.	1,050	Messuage and 2½ acres of land at Greenwich in Out Ward. E. by Greenwich St., S. by late George Campbell, W. by Hudson River, N. by heirs of Sir Peter Warren.
" "	Oliver De Lancey, attainted.	" "	350	Land in South Ward. E. by Nicholas Cruger, S. by Nicholas Cruger, Stephen De Lancey and Solomon Simpson, W. by John Ryfle.
July 5, 1787	James De Lancey, attainted.	" "	560	Lots No. 220 to 235 in Out Ward. S. by lots No. 219 and 236, W. by Bowery Lane, N. by Stanton St., E. by First St.
Aug. 16, 1787	" "	Philip Jacobs, merchant.	910	Messuage and land in Out Ward. W. by Bowery Lane, N. by Gabriel Furman, E. by lot No. 27, S. by Division St.

Date of Sale.	Loyalist Owner.	Purchaser.	Price.	Description and Remarks.
Aug. 16, 1787	James De Lancey, attainted.	John Delafield, merchant.	£810	Lots No. 11 and 12 in Out Ward. W. by Bowery Lane, N. by lots No. 13 and 14, E. by lots No. 17 and 18, S. by lots No. 9 and 10.
"	"	Cornelius C. Roosevelt, merchant.	1,120	Messuage and 2 lots in Out Ward. W. by Bowery Lane, N. by lots No. 97 and 126, E. by First St., S. by Eagle St.
"	"	William Beekman, gentleman.	570	Lots No. 673 to 675 and 682 to 684 in Out Ward. W. by Third St., N. by lots No. 676 and 681, E. by Fourth St., S. by lots No. 672 and 685.
"	"	Edward Dunscomb, Esq.	400	E. half of lots No. 714 to 721 in Out Ward. S. by Pump St., E. by Fourth St., N. by lot No. 713, W. by half lots No. 714 to 721.
"	"	Daniel Williams, of Westchester co., farmer.	190	Lot No. 878 in Out Ward. W. by Fourth St., N. by lots No. 879, E. by lot No. 885, S. by lots No. 874 to 877.
"	"	John Delafield.	560	Lots No. 1578 and 1579 in Out Ward. S. by Division St., W. by Norfolk St., N. by Eagle St., E. by John Egberts.
"	"	James Beekman.	2,760	Lots No. 132 to 135 in Out Ward. W. by Bowery Lane, N. by lot No. 136, E. by lots No. 144 to 147, S. by lot No. 131.
"	"	Jacob Reed.	2,000	Lots No. 140 to 157 in Out Ward. E. by First St., S. by Grand St., W. by lots No. 128 to 139, N. by Bullock St. Lots No. 128 to 131 in Out Ward. S. by Grand St, W. by Bowery Lane, N. by lot No. 132, E. by lots No. 136 to 139. Lots No. 136 to 139 in Out Ward. W. by Bowery Lane, N. by Bullock St., E. by lots from 140 to 143.
"	"	Ebenezer Young.	1,800	Lots No. 212 to 215 in Out Ward. S. by Rivington St., W. by Bowery Lane, N. by lot No. 216, E. by lots No. 240 to 243.
"	"	James Saidler.	480	Lots No. 236 to 239 in Out Ward. E. by First St., S. by lot No. 240, W. by lots No. 216 to 219, N. by lot No. 235.

Date of Sale.	Loyalist Owner.	Purchaser.	Price.	Description and Remarks.
Aug. 16, 1787	James De Lancey, attainted.	Jacob Reed.	£540	Lots No. 216 to 219 in Out Ward. W. by Bowery Lane, N. by lot No. 220, E. by lots No. 236 to 239, S. by lot No. 215.
"	"	Caleb Swan.	960	Triangular lot △ in Out Ward. S. by John McCane, W. by Bowery Lane, N. by Pierre Van Cortlandt. Tracts A, B and C in Out Ward. S. by Stanton St., E. by First St., N. by Pierre Van Cortlandt, W. by John McLane.
"	"	Bazeleel Howe.	420	Lots No. 347 to 349 in Out Ward. S. by Grand St., W. by First St., N. by lot No. 350, E. by lots No. 368 to 370.
"	"	Simon Van Antwerp.	315	Lots No. 350 to 352 in Out Ward. W. by First St., N. by lot No. 353, E. by lots No. 365 to 367, S. by lot No. 349.
"	"	John Stagg, Jr.	220	Lots No. 663 to 665 in Out Ward. S. by Rivington St., W. by lots No. 641 to 643, N. by lot No. 662, E. by Third St.
"	"	William W. Gilbert.	195	Lots No. 660 to 662 in Out Ward. E. by Third St., N. by lot No. 659, W. by lots No. 643 to 645, S. by lot No. 663.
"	"	Dennis McGuire.	220	Lots No. 657 to 659 in Out Ward. E. by Third St., S. by lot No. 660, W. by lots No. 646 to 648, N. by lot No. 656.
"	"	Dominick Lynch.	1,300	Tract in Out Ward. N. by Crown Point St., S. by High Water Mark, W. by Ferry St.
"	"	John Lawrence.	330	Lots No. 365 to 367 in Out Ward. E. by Second St., S. by lot No. 368, W. by lots No. 350 to 352, N. by lot No. 364.
"	"	John Siemon, of Westchester co.	220	Lots No. 353 and 354 in Out Ward. W. by First St., N. by lot No. 355, E. by lots No. 363 and 364, S. by lot No. 352.
"	"	Cornelius Ray.	500	Lots No. 355 to 358 in Out Ward. W. by First St., N. by Bullock St., E. by lots No. 359 to 362, S. by lot No. 354.
"	"	Edward Dunscomb.	530	Lots No. 362 to 364 in Out Ward. E. by Second St., S. by lot No. 365, W. by lots No. 353 to 355, N. by lot No. 361. Lots No. 806 to 809 in Out Ward. S. by De Lancey St., W. by Third St., N. by lot No. 816, E. by lots No. 834 to 837.

Date of Sale.	Loyalist Owner.	Purchaser.	Price.	Description and Remarks.
Aug. 16, 1787	James De Lancey, attainted.	Elsje Everson.	£240	Lots No. 818 to 821 in Out Ward. W. by Third St., N. by Rivington St., E. by lots No. 822 to 825, S. by lot No. 817.
"	"	Timothy Hutton.	330	Lots No. 359 to 361 in Out Ward. S. by lot No. 362, W. by lots No. 356 to 358, N. by Bullock St., E. by Second St.
"	"	John Delafield.	1,620	Lots No. 435 to 442 and 447 to 458 in Out Ward. S. by lots No. 434 and 459, W. by First St. and lots No. 443 to 446, N. by lot 443 and Stanton St., E. by Second St.
Aug. 17, 1787	"	John Quackenbos.	380	Lots No. 443 to 446 in Out Ward. S. by lot No. 442, W. by First St., N. by Stanton St., E. by lots No. 447 to 450.
"	"	John Delafield.	640	Lots No. 622 to 629 in Out Ward. S. by lots No. 621 and 630, W. by Second St., N. by Rivington St., E. by Third St.
"	"	"	375	Lots No. 1922 to 1927 in Out Ward. S. by lots No. 652 and 653, W. by Second St., N. by Stanton St. and Hon. Pierre Van Cortlandt, E. by Third St.
"	"	Isaac Norton.	240	Lots No. 834 to 837 in Out Ward. S. by De Lancey St., W. by lots No. 806 to 809, N. by lot No. 833, E. by Fourth St.
"	"	John Delafield.	820	Lots No. 810 to 817 in Out Ward. S by lots No. 809 and 834, W. by Third St., N. by lots No. 818 and 825, E. by Fourth St.
"	"	Aaron Stockholm.	220	Lots No. 822 to 825 in Out Ward. S. by lot No. 826, W. by lots No. 818 to 821, N. by Rivington St, E. by Fourth St.
"	"	Dominick Lynch.	1,760	Lots No. 1357 to 1388 in Out Ward. S. by De Lancey St., W. by Sixth St., N. by Rivington St., E. by Essex St.
"	"	James Walker.	125	Lots No. 871 to 873, in Out Ward. S. by Stanton St., N. and W. by Pierre Van Cortlandt, E. by Fourth St.
Aug. 18, 1787	"	Aaron Stockholm.	670	Lots No. 1068 to 1070 and 1079 to 1085 in Out Ward. S. by Stanton St., W. by Fourth St., N. by lots No. 1075 and 1078, E. by Orchard St.

Date of Sale.	Loyalist Owner.	Purchaser.	Price.	Description and Remarks.
Aug. 18, 1787	James De Lancey, attainted.	Abijah Hammond.	£350	Lots No. 1075 to 1078, F and G, in Out Ward. S. by lots No. 1074 and 1079, W. and N. W. by Fourth St. and Pierre Van Cortlandt, E. by Peter Stuyvesant.
"	"	Aaron Stockholm.	440	Lots No. 1734 to 1737 in Out Ward. S. by Rivington St., W. by Norfolk St., N. by lots No. 1710 and 1733, E. by Suffolk St.
"	"	Dominick Lynch.	200	Lots No. 1730 to 1733 in Out Ward. S. by lot No. 1734, W. by lots No. 1710 to 1713, N. by lot No. 1729, E. by Suffolk St.
"	"	John Delafield.	200	Lots No. 1710 to 1713 in Out Ward. ' S. by lot No. 1709, W. by Norfolk St., N. by lot No. 1714, E. by lots No. 1730 to 1733.
"	"	William Boyd.	250	Tract in West Ward. E. by New St., S. by Thomas Ellison, N. by Daniel Dunscomb.
"	"	Hon. Pierre Van Cortlandt, of Westchester co.	145	Triangle lot E in Out Ward. S. by Stanton St., W. by First St., N. by his own land.
Aug. 16, 1787	William Bayard, attainted.	William Boyd.	580	Tract of land in South Ward. W. by Robert Watts, N. by Wansort, E. by Wessel Wessels, S. by Bridge St.
"	James De Lancey, attainted.	Joseph Cheesman.	240	Lots No. 369 and 370 in Out Ward. E. by Second St., N. by lot No. 368, W. by lots No. 347 and 348, S. by Grand St.
"	"	Jotham Wright.	120	Lot No. 368 in Out Ward. E. by Second St., N. by lot No. 367, W. by lot No. 349, S. by lot No. 369.
"	"	Timothy Ketchem, of Dutchess co.	180	Lot No. 117 in Out Ward. S. by lot No. 118, W. by lot No. 106, N. by lot No. 116, E. by First St.
Aug. 17, 1787	"	Samuel Low.	260	Lots No. 618 to 621 in Out Ward. W. by Second St, N. by lot No. 622, E. by lots No. 630 to 633, S. by lot No. 617.
"	"	William Boyd.	260	Lots No. 630 to 633 in Out Ward. E. by Third St., S. by lot No. 634, W. by lots No. 618 to 621, N. by lot No. 629.

Date of Sale.	Loyalist Owner.	Purchaser.	Price.	Description and Remarks.
June 29, 1786	James De Lancey, attainted.	Abijah Hammond.	£128	Lots No. 1294 to 1296 in Out Ward. E. by Essex St., S., by lot No. 1297, W. by lots No. 1281 to 1284, N. by lot No. 1292.
Sep. 30, 1784	" "	Morgan Lewis.	576	Lots No. 1867 to 1898 in Out Ward. N. by Stanton St., E. by Arundel St., S. by Rivington St., W. by Suffolk St. Lots No. 1835 to 1842 and lots No. 1859 to 1866 in Out Ward. E. by Arundel St., S. by Rivington St., W. by Suffolk St., N. by N. half of the square.
" "	" "	Philip Livingston.	190	N. half of square in Out Ward. N. by Rivington St, E. by Arundel St., S. by S. half of square, W. by Suffolk St.
Jan. 11, 1785	" "	Morgan Lewis.	300	Square No. 18, 32 lots, in Out Ward. N. by Stanton St., W. by Attorney St., S. by Rivington St., E. by Ridge st.
May 31, 1785	" "	Garrit Van Horne.	300	Lots No. 1717 to 1726 in Out Ward. S. by lots No. 1716 and 1727, W. by Norfolk St., N. by Stanton St., E. by Suffolk St.
June 29, 1787	" "	John McLane.	289	10 lots in Out Ward. W. by Bowery Lane, E. by Stanton St.

"We, the subscribers, Commissioners of Forfeiture for the Southern District of the State of New York, do hereby certify that the foregoing, from page 1 to page 168, are true copies of abstracts of the sales of Forfeited Estates within the City and County of New York, being carefully compared with the original remaining in our office. * * * Containing in all copies of abstracts of three hundred and thirty-nine conveyances executed by us. Filed in the Clerk's Office of the City and County of New York, this twenty-fourth day of December, 1787."

ISAAC STOUTENBURG,

PHILIP VAN CORTLANDT.

" Abstract of certain lands, tenements, and hereditaments situate in the County of Suffolk, in the State of New York, Forfeited to the People of this State and sold by Isaac Stoutenburgh and Philip Van Cortlandt, Esquires, Commissioners of Forfeitures for the Southern District of the said State."[1]

Date of Sale.	Loyalist Owner.	Purchaser.	Price.	Description and Remarks.
July 28, 1784	Parker Wickham, attainted.	Nathaniel Norten.	£900	Farm and messuage of about 240 acres in Southold township cut by highway. Land N. of highway bounded on W. by Jonathan Jennings, Silas More and James Reeve, N. and E. by Timothy Wells and Nathan Goldsmith, S. by highway and Jonathan Jennings and Nathan Goldsmith. Land S. of highway bounded on E. by a lane, James Tuthill, a division of salt meadow lots and the creek, S. by the Bay, W. by Daniel Osburn and Thomas Wickham, N. by the highway and Thomas Wickham.
Aug. 5, 1784	" "	" "	1,030	Farm of about 800 acres and messuage at Riverhead. E. by Richard and Merrit Howell, S. by Peconic River and John Griffin, W. by said John Griffin and Jeremiah Wells, N. by the Sound. Tract of meadow, about 4 acres. S. by Peconic River, W. by Paul Reeves, N. by the Uplands, E. by Daniel Tuthill. Tract of meadow, about 4 acres. N. by Peconic River and adjoins land of Joseph Curen.
" "	Richard Floyd, attainted.	Benj. Talmage and Caleb Brewster.	730	The Middle of the Island Farm in Brookhaven township, 4½ lots, about 320 acres, "reserving to William Floyd, Esq, and to his heirs and assigns one lot and one-half lot of the above described lands claimed by him as his property." N. by William Clark, E. by William Smith, S. by John Homan, W. by Connecticut River.
" "	Parker Wickham, attainted.	Benj. Talmage and Caleb Brewster.	1,250	Tract in Southold township known as Robin's Island, about 350 acres. No definite boundary given.

[1] From the original in the Old Civil List Book in Clerk's Office, Suffolk county. Copy is in possession of O. B. Ackerly, No. 115 Broadway, N. Y., former County Clerk in Suffolk county.

Date of Sale.	Loyalist Owner.	Purchaser.	Price.	Description and Remarks.
Aug. 5, 1784	George Murison, attainted.	Joseph Brewster, of Brook Haven township.	£300	Tract of land called the "Long Lots," bounded on W. and E. by Benjamin Floyd, N. by Joseph Brewster, S. by the county road. Also the Benjamin Strog lot on Covam Road. Also the "John Joiner's Farm," Also a tract on Nassikig Road west of Joseph Brewster. Altogether about 2400 acres.
"	Richard Floyd, attainted.	Benjamin Floyd.	3,112	A "certain messuage and farm" of about 600 acres in Brook-haven township. W. and N. by William Smith, E. by Nathaniel Woodhull, deceased, S. by the Bay. Also half a tract of woodland in same township. N. by William Smith or the middle of the Island, W. by William Smith, S. by William Floyd and Nathaniel Woodhull, deceased, E. by sundry proprietors. Number of acres not known.
"	"	Benjamin Floyd and Caleb Brewster.	288	Four lots at Nocamack in Brookhaven township, No. 1, bounded on S. by Daniel Petty, W. by the River, N. E. and E. by William Smith. No. 2, S. by William Smith, W. by the River, N. by William Floyd, E. by William Smith, No. 3, W. and N. by the River, E. by William Smith, S. by William Floyd. No. 4, W. and N. W. by the River, E. by William Smith, S. by William Smith. These four lots contain about 32 acres.

APPENDIX

Date of Sale.	Loyalist Owner.	Purchaser.	Price.	Description and Remarks.
Aug. 3, 1784	George Murison, attainted.	Mills Philips, yeoman.	£914	Messuage and farm. E. by Creek, N. by Joseph Longbottom, W. by Public Road, S. by Richard Woodhull. Also tract W. of Public Road with a "barn and other outhouses." E. by Public Road, N. and W. by said Road, S. by John Bennett. Also a tract in the "Old Field." S. by Nathan Woodhull and land of ——, E. and N. by the Bank, W. by Jonathan Thompson. Also lots No. 3, 4, 18, 19, 20, 21, 25 and half of 33 and 34 in the West Meadow. Also two "parcels of land" between Nathaniel Ackerly and Jonathan Halback called "Amendments." In all about 150 acres.

AN ABSTRACT OF THE SALE OF FORFEITED ESTATES—SOUTHERN DISTRICT—FOR PUBLIC SECURITIES.

Date of Sale.	Loyalist Owner.	Purchaser.	Price.	Description and Remarks.
Dec. 6, 1785	Frederick Philipse.	Stephen Sherwood.	£149	Farm of 24½ acres.
" "	"	Jacob Post.	29	10 acres at £2-18 s.
" "	"	Peter Bout.	40	Farm of 40 acres.
" "	"	Catherine Von Tassel.	339–10	150 acres at £3.
" "	"	John Lawrence.	660	220 acres at £3.
" "	"	William Ruton.	136–16	171 acres at 16s.
Dec. 22, 1785	"	Marmaduke Foster.	340	160 acres at £2-2s-6p.
" "	"	James Pierce.	300	100 acres at 60s.
June 7, 1786	"	Abraham Brown.	1,531-17-6	204½ acres at £7-10s.
Aug. 3, 1786	"	Stephen Carpenter & Nathan Holmes.	18	Half lot at Tarrytown.
" "	"	Mordecai Hale.	30	Lot at Tarrytown.
Sep. 9, 1786	James De Lancey.	William W. Gilbert.	640	16 lots No. 1095 to 1110.
" "	"	"	160	8 lots No. 1111 to 1118.
" "	"	"	720	8 lots No. 1119 to 1127.
" "	"	"	320	8 lots No. 1128 to 1136.
Sep. 27, 1786	William Bayard,	Charles McKnight.	1,050	Dwelling at Greenwich.
" "	Oliver De Lancey.	"	350	3 lots in South Ward, N. Y.
June 29, 1786	James De Lancey.	John McLane.	289	Lot near Bowery.
July 5, 1786	"	Charles McKnight.	560	16 lots No. 220 to 235.
Aug. 1, 1787	Frederick Philipse.	Cornelius Ray.	2,981	284 acres at £10-10s.
" "	Lewis Palmer.	Benjamin Sands.	420	110 acres at Cortlandt Manor.
Aug. 3, 1787	Frederick Philipse.	Anthony Post.	302–10	121 acres at £2-10s.
Aug. 9, 1787	"	Nicholas Bailey.	372–10	149 acres at 50s.
Aug. 16, 1787	James De Lancey.	Isaac Norton.	180	Lot No. 117.

Date of Sale.	Loyalist Owner.	Purchaser.	Price.	Description and Remarks.
Aug. 16, 1787	James De Lancey.	William Beekman.	£570	6 lots.
" "	" "	Edward Dunscomb.	400	Lots No. 714 to 721.
" "	" "	Daniel Williams.	190	Lot No. 878.
" "	" "	Thomas McFarran.	560	Lots No. 1578 and 1579.
" "	" "	James Beekman.	640	4 lots.
" "	" "	" "	640	4 lots.
" "	" "	Caleb Swan.	540	Lot on Bowery Lane.
" "	" "	" "	420	
" "	" "	Joseph Chesman.	360	3 lots.
" "	" "	John Stagg, Jr.	225	3 lots.
" "	" "	William McGilbert.	195	3 lots.
" "	" "	Dennis McGuire.	270	3 lots.
" "	" "	Dominick Lynch.	1,300	Water lot.
Aug. 17, 1787	William Bayard.	William Boyd.	580	Lot on Bridge St.
" "	James De Lancey.	Edward Dunscomb.	110	1 lot.
" "	" "	Cornelius Ray.	500	4 lots.
" "	" "	Timothy Hutton.	330	3 lots.
" "	" "	John Delafield.	1,620	20 lots.
" "	" "	Edward Dunscomb.	240	4 lots.
" "	" "	John Quackenbos.	380	4 lots.
" "	" "	William Boyd.	260	4 lots.
" "	" "	Thomas McFarren.	640	8 lots.
" "	" "	John Delafield.	375	6 lots.
" "	" "	Isaac Norton.	240	4 lots.
" "	" "	Thomas McFarren.	820	16 lots.
" "	" "	Cornelius Ray.	240	4 lots.
" "	" "	Aaron Stockholm.	220	4 lots.

Date of Sale.	Loyalist Owner.	Purchaser.	Price.	Description and Remarks.
Aug. 17, 1787	James De Lancey.	Dominick Lynch.	£1,760	32 lots.
"	"	William Boyd.	260	4 lots.
"	"	James Walker.	125	Triangular lot.
"	"	Aaron Stockholm.	670	14 lots.
"	"	PierreVan Cortlandt.	145	Triangular lot.
"	"	Abijah Hammond.	350	4 lots.
"	"	Aaron Stockholm.	440	8 lots.
"	"	John Delafield.	200	4 lots.
"	"	Dominick Lynch.	200	4 lots.
"	"	William Boyd.	250	1 lot on West New St.
"	Oliver De Lancey.	Philip Jacobs.	910	2 lots on Bowery Lane.
Aug. 16, 1787	George Fisher.	Thomas McFarren.	810	2 lots on Bowery Lane.
"	"	Cornel. C. Roosevelt.	1,120	2 lots.
"	"	Jacob Reed.	1,000	4 lots.
"	"	James Beekman.	1,480	8 lots.
"	"	Jacob Reed.	1,000	4 lots.
"	"	Ebenezer Young.	1,080	4 lots.
"	"	Jacob Reed.	940	4 lots.
"	"	James Saidler.	480	4 lots.
"	"	Bezalel Howe.	420	3 lots.
"	"	Simon Van Antwerp.	315	3 lots.
"	"	John Lawrence.	330	3 lots.
"	"	John Simeon.	220	2 lots.
"	"	Edward Dunscomb.	180	2 lots.

LIST OF FORFEITED ESTATES SOLD IN SULLIVAN, ORANGE AND ULSTER COUNTIES, MIDDLE DISTRICT, OF MINISINK PATENT.

Date of Sale.	Loyalist Owner.	Purchaser.	Price.	Description and Remarks.
Aug. 9, 1808	James De Lancey, attainted.	Thomas Dunn.	$200.09	Parcel of 107 acres farming land, subdivision No. 4 of lot No. 1 of the seventh allotment of Minisink Patent, Orange Co. From E. bank of Delaware River at N. corner of subdivision No. 3, running S. 8° 40′, W. 5 chains, S. 24°, E. 2 chains and 59 links, S. 75° 30′, E. 8 chains 40 links, S. 15° 30′, E. 5 chains 35 links, S. 46°, E. 12 chains, S. 27°, E. 1 chain 70 links, S. 51°, E. 58 chains 50 links to stake on N. bank of Mill Creek in S. E. line of lot No. 1, then along same N. 42° 15′, E. 16 chains 20 links, N. 55°, W. 90 chains to the Delaware River, then along it to place of starting.
Aug. 8, 1808	" " "	Jeremiah Lilly, of Lumberland, Ulster co.	470.34	134 acres of farming land in Minisink Patent, Orange Co., subdivision No. 7 of lot No. 1 of the seventh allotment. From E. bank of Delaware River at N. corner of subdivision No. 6, S. 42°, W. 5 chains, S. 29°, E. 17 chains 82 links, S. 68°, E. 14 chains 20 links, N. 61°, 15′, E. 30 chains to Delaware River, then along it to place of starting.
Sep. 4, 1807	Oliver De Lancey, attainted.	Benjamin Dodge, of Deer Park, Orange co.	112.88	166 acres of farming land in Minisink Patent, Orange Co., lot No. 18 of second division. From N. E. corner of lot No. 17 N. 55°, E. 19 chains 60 links, N. 27°, E. 6 chains to marked flat stone, N. 48°, W. 83 chains 50 links to marked trees on top of mountain, S. to N. W. corner of lot No. 17, S. 48°, E. 80 chains to place of beginning. (32 acres of this plot in N. E. corner are sold to Moses Skinner.)
" " "	" " "	Moses Skinner, of Deer Park, Orange co.	32.00	32 acres out of lot No. 18. From E. corner of lot No. 18 N. 48°, W. 17 chains 55 links, S. 52°, W. 16 chains 15 links, S. 43°, E. to S. E. by lot No. 18, N. E. to place of starting.

Date of Sale.	Loyalist Owner.	Purchaser.	Price.	Description and Remarks.
Feb. 21, 1809	John Weatherhead, attainted.	George Clark, of City of Albany.	$1,125.00	2,213 acres in Minisink Patent, Sullivan co., lot No. 15 of seventh allotment. From S. E. corner of lot No. 14 down the Delaware S. 11°, W. 1 chain 50 links, S. 23°, W. 23 chains, S. 17°, W. 4 chains, S. 13°, W. 8 chains, S. 17°, W. 3 chains, S. 12°, W. 13 chains to marked red oak opposite Loghawach River, S. 6° 30', E. 4 chains, S. 4°, E. 6 chains 75 links to S. E. corner, N. 44° 15', E. 737 chains to Jersey claim, then 31 chains to N. W. corner, S. 34° 45', W. 685 chains to start.
Sep. 18, 1807	"	Isaac Vail and Solomon Finch.	260.00	224 acres in Minisink Patent, lot No. 4 of second division. From N. E. corner of lot No. 3 N. 40°, E. 17 chains 5 links to a marked white oak tree, N. 48°, E. 6 chains to N. E. corner to flat stone marked No. 2, N. 48°, W. 99 chains 40 links to N. W. corner, then S. 34°, W. 23 chains 35 links to S. W. corner, then along lot No. 3 to place of start.
Sep. 1, 1807	"	George L. Wickham, of Goshen, Orange co.	300.00	1710 acres in Minisink Patent, Ulster co., lot No. 35 of first general division. From S. W. corner of lot No. 34 S. 44° 45', W. 74 chains 25 links, S. 45° 15', E. 230 chains 38 links, N. 44° 45', E. 74 chains 25 links, N. 45° 15', W. 230 chains 38 links to place of start.
Feb. 22, 1810	"	"	2,180.00	2180 acres in Minisink Patent, Sullivan co., lot No. 4, of seventh allotment. Down Delaware River 50° 30', E. 15 chains 50 links, S. 81° 30', E. 18 chains 15 links, S. 23° 30', E. 25 chains to S. E. corner, N. 44° 45', E. 436 chains to N. line of Minisink Patent, along said line 61 chains to N. W. corner, S. 44° 45', W. 407 chains to start.

Date of Sale.	Loyalist Owner.	Purchaser.	Price.	Description and Remarks.
Aug. 9, 1808	James De Lancey, attainted.	Oliver Corkins.	$744.76	172 acres in Minisink Patent, lot No. 6 of lot No 1 of seventh division. From E. bank of Delaware River at N. corner of subdivision No. 5 S. 85° 30', E. 20 chains, S. 70° 30', E. 30 chains 78 links to marked white oak, N. 5° E. 16 chains 40 links to marked white oak, N. 68°, W. 14 chains 20 links to stone pile, N. 29°, W. 17 chains 82 links to marked hemlock, N. 42°, E. 5 chains to Delaware and down it to start.
"	"	George D. Wickham, of Goshen, Orange co.	750.00	250 acres in Minisink Patent, subdivision No. 5 of lot No. 1 of seventh allotment. From E. bank of Delaware River at N. W. corner of subdivision No. 4 S. 65°, E. 69 chains 70 links to a stake, N. 42° 15', E. 52 chains to stake, N. 75° 30', W. 55 chains to stone pile on flat rock, N. 85° 30', W. 20 chains to Delaware River and then to place of start.
"	"	William Dunn, of Lumberland, Ulster co.	670.00	134 acres in Minisink Patent, subdivision No. 2 of lot No 1 of seventh allotment. From E. bank of Delaware River at N. W. corner of subdivision No. 1, N. 42 15', E. 39 chains to stake and stones, S. 55°, W. 19 chains 20 links to rock oak tree, N. 31°, W. 30 chains to large rock, N. 45° 15', W. 16 chains to a white pine stump, N. 57° 40', W. 4 chains 40 links to pitch pine stump, S. 83° 50', W. 10 chains 70 links to a stake and stones, S. 51°, W. 8 chains 58 links to Delaware River, then down it to place of start.
Sep. 1, 1809	John Weatherhead.	Samuel Sherwood.	670.00	1702 acres in Minisink Patent, subdivision No, 40 of first division. From N. W. corner of lot No. 39 S. 45° 15', E. 186 chains to S. E. corner, N. 44° 30', E. 75 chains to George Moor's house, N. 41°, E. 17 chains N. E. corner, N. 45° 15', W. 184 chains, S. 44° 45', W. 92 chains to place of start.

Date of Sale.	Loyalist Owner.	Purchaser.	Price.	Description and Remarks.
Aug. 9, 1808	James De Lancey, attainted.	Thomas Dunn, Lumberland, Ulster co.	$702.18	249 acres in Minisink Patent, subdivision 3 of lot No. 1 of seventh division. From E. bank of the Delaware at N. E. corner of subdivision No. 2, N. 50° E. 8 chains 58 links, N. 83° 50', E. 10 chains 70 links, S. 57° 40', E. 4 chains 40 links, S. 45° 15', E. 16 chains to rock, S. 31°, E. 30 chains, S. 55°, E. 54 chains 70 links to S. E. lot No. 1, N. 42° 15', E. 21 chains to N. bank of Mill Creek, N. along Mill Creek 51°, W. 58 chains 50 links, N. 27°, W. 1 chain 70 links, N. 46°, W. 12 chains, N. 15° 30', W. 5 chains 35 links, N. 75° 30', W. 8 chains 40 links, N. 24°, W. 2 chains 59 links, N. 8° 40', E. 5 chains to the Delaware River, down it to place of starting.
Mar. 26, 1813	" "	William Dunn.	130.00	119 acres in Minisink Patent, subdivision No. 1 of lot No. 1 of the seventh allotment. From a stake on E. bank of the Delaware between lots No. 1 and 2 of seventh division N. along division line 42° 15', E. 34 chains 20 links to stake and stones in S. corner of subdivision No. 3 laid out for Thomas Dunn, N. 55°, W. 35 chains 50 links to N. E. corner of subdivision No. 2 laid out for Wm. Dunn, S. 42° 15', W. to Delaware River 29 chains, down it to starting point.
" "	Oliver De Lancey.	David Dill, of New Windsor, Orange co.	540.00	1720 acres in Minisink Patent, Sullivan Co., lot No. 6 of first division. From W. end of lot No. 5 S. 44° 45', W. 75 chains 50 links, S. 45° 15', E. 227 chains 84 links, N. 44° 45', E. 75 chains 50 links, N. 45°, 15', W. 277 links 84 chains to starting point.

Date of Sale.	Loyalist Owner.	Purchaser.	Price.	Description and Remarks.
Mar. 26, 1813	James De Lancey, attainted.	David Dill, of New Windsor, Orange co.	$400.00	942 acres in Minisink Patent, Sullivan Co., part of lot No. 1 of seventh division. From division line of lots No. 1 and 2 at N. E. corner of subdivision No. 4 of lot No. 1 N. 50°, W. 20 chains 30 links to subdivision No. 5, N. 42° 15', E. 52 chains, N. 75°, W. 24 chains 22 links to subdivision No. 6, N. 5°, E. 16 chains 40 links to subdivision No. 7, N. 61° 15', E. 30 chains, N. 30°, E. 32 chains, N. 61° 15', E. 30 chains, N. 30°, E. 32 chains, N. 61°, W. 32 chains to the Delaware, up it to sub-division No. 8, S. 80° 15', E. 30 chains, N. 32° 15', W. 24 chains 15 links to N. boundary of Minisink Patent, S. 86° 15', E. to division line between lots No. 1 and 2, S. 42° 15', W. to place of start.
(No date given in MS.)	" "	Jonathan Dexter.	239.00	92 acres in Minisink Patent, subdivision No. 8 of lot No. 1, in seventh division. From E. bank of Delaware river where N. boundary of the Minisink Patent strikes it down S. 16°, E. 27 chains to stake and stones, S. 80° 15', E. 30 chains to stake and stones, N. 23° 15', E. 24 chains 50 links to N. boundary of said patent, along same N. 80° 15', W. 48 chains to place of starting.
June 10, 1819	John Weatherhead.	John G. Wheat, of Manakatine, Sullivan co.	62.70	91.2 acres of Minisink Patent at Manakatin, Sullivan Co., part of lot No. 34 of second division. From N. W. corner of lot No. 33 S. 49° 12', E. 47 chains to W. line of White and Crawford Patent, N. 41°, E. 19 chains 20 links to S. line of lot No. 35, N. 49° 12', W. 48 chains to line of marked trees E. of lot No. 3, S. 38°, W. 19 chains 20 links to place of start.
		Total	$9,508.95	Total acres sold, 12,231.2.

Forfeited Estates Sold in the Middle District.

Money received by the State Treasurer, G. Banker, "For Lands sold by the Commissioner of the Middle District."

Date of Sale.	Loyalist Owner.	Purchaser.	Price.	Description and Remarks.
June 15, 1780	George Falliot,	Moses Bulkly.	£18,150	217 acres in North East precinct, Dutchess co.
Sep. 23, 1780	Beverly Robinson.	Alexander Kidd.	3,000	111 acres in Fredericksburg precinct.
Sep. 30, 1780	"	John Newbury.	2,000	125 " "
"	"	William Duer.	19,750	150 acres.
"	"	Cornelius Cooper.	10,450	196 acres.
"	"	Robert Morris.	21,650	300 acres.
Oct. 9, 1780	Charles Inglis.	Dick Wynkoop.	120	Right in a lot near Kingston, called Vroman's Wey.
Oct. 25, 1780	Beverly Robinson.	Oke Ludam.	920	Lot near Kingston called Crooks Orchard.
"	"	James Hays.	4,560	252 acres in Fredericksburg precinct.
"	"	David Close.	500	159 " "
"	"		150	30 " "
"	"		600	59 " "
"	"	Joseph Chandler.	2,500	200 " "
"	"	Timothy Hatch.	3,350	100 " "
Nov. 17, 1780	Charles Inglis.	Jedediah Mills.	33,700	490 " "
Nov. 23, 1780	Beverly Robinson.	Burnet Miller.	17,400	426 " "
"	"	Comfort Sands.	9,800	189 " "
"	"	" "	17,050	300 " " Amenia
Nov. 28, 1780	George Falliot.	Lewis Delavergne.	8,900	Farm in Amenia precinct.
Dec. 3, 1780	Charles Inglis.	Paul Johnson.	26,900	250 acres in Charlotte precinct.
"	"	Rufus Herrick.	7,750	360 " " "
"	George Falliot,	Josiah Gale.	6,210	70 acres in Amenia precinct,
Dec. 6, 1780	"	Samuel Herrick.	53,000	300 acres.
Dec. 18, 1780	Charles Inglis.	Elihu Bardslee.	12,350	100 acres in Charlotte precinct.
		Josiah Gale.		

Date of Sale.	Loyalist Owner.	Purchaser.	Price.	Description and Remarks.
Jan. 4, 1781	Beverly Robinson.	Nehemiah Stibbins.	£17,750	250 acres.
Jan. 16, 1781	Charles Inglis.	Abraham Frees.	2,350	Lot near Kingston called Crooks Height.
April 10, 1781	Beverly Robinson.	William B. Alger.	36,135	250 acres.
		Total	£336,995	

These payments were in full and procured deeds.

The following partial payments were made for forfeited lands bought.

Date of Sale.	Loyalist Owner.	Purchaser.	Price.	Description and Remarks.
Sep. 30, 1780	(No names given.)	William Forman.	£5,188	(No description given.)
Oct. 25, 1780		Robert Watts.	1,000	
Jan. 3, 1781		Thomas Reed.	150	
Jan. 28, 1781		John Williams.	3,003	
Nov. 14, 1781		David Heacock.		
" "		John Burch.	10,378	
" "		Roswell Wilcox.		
" "		Joseph Philipse.		
" "		Ephraim Warner.		
			£19,719	

"PUTNAM COUNTY LANDS CLAIMED BY JOHN JACOB ASTOR."

Date of Sale.	Loyalist Owner.	Purchaser.	Price.	Description and Remarks.
Apr. 20, 1781	Roger Morris.	Jesse Hunt.	£455	193 acres in lot No. 9, in Putnam county.
Mch. 1, 1781	"	William Smith.	110	3¼ acres.
Apr. 20, 1781	"	Ebenezer Philips.	218-14	162 acres.
Jan. 4, 1782	"	Ezra Gregory.	106	106 acres.
Jan. 17, 1781	"	Jonathan Brown.	723	351 acres.
May 2, 1781	"	Jonathan Crane.	265-16	123 acres.
Dec. 24, 1781	"	Edmond Mead.	139-14	218 acres.
June 1, 1781	"	Charles Graham.	790	316 acres.
" "	"	John Drake.	262	262 acres.
" "	"	Abram Hyatt.	135	70 acres.
" "	"	Joseph Gregory.	83	279 acres.
" "	"	John Crane.	82	164 acres.
" "	"	John Berry.	12-13-9	50¾ acres.
Aug. 20, 1781	"	Philip Leek.	232- 4	129 acres.
Oct. 1, 1781	"	Moody Howe.	192	259 acres.
" "	"	James Sacket.	207	138 acres.
" "	"	Isaac Townsend.	149-12	156 acres.
" "	"	Seth Paddock.	264	293 acres.
" "	"	Nathan Green.	124-10	269 acres.
" "	"	Thomas Lowrie.	90	119 acres.
" "	"	Silas Paddock.	144	174 acres.
" "	"	John Gove.	547-11	106 acres.
" "	"	Timothy Delavan.	95- 8	237 acres.
Nov. 10, 1781	"	Benjamin Crosby. / Enoch Crosby.	843	276 acres.
" "	"	Benjamin Crosby. / Enoch Crosby.	144	103 acres.
" "	"	Stephen Field.	428	405 acres.
" "	"	Joshua Horton.	200	262 acres.

Date of Sale.	Loyalist Owner.	Purchaser.	Price.	Description and Remarks.
Nov. 10, 1781	Roger Morris.	Jehrel Boutor.	£91–12–6	198 acres.
" "	"	Maurice Smith.	180	206 acres.
" "	"	"	70	142 acres.
" "	"	Nathaniel Delavan.	330–12	228 acres.
Dec. 27, 1781	"	Ezra Richards.	168– 6	187 acres.
Dec. 28, 1781	"	Jacob Ellis.	146	146 acres.
" "	"	Peleg Bailey.	67–18–6	123 acres.
" "	"	Frederick Pinckney.	22	29 acres.
" "	"	William Lovelace.	43	107½ acres.
Jan. 3, 1782	"	Moses Richard.	155–14	177 acres.
" "	"	Mary Haines.	270–18	301 acres.
Jan. 4, 1782	"	Isaac Pearce.	113	126 acres.
" "	"	John Platt.	88– 4	100 acres.
" "	"	Edward Rice.	215	284 acres.
Jan. 5, 1782	"	David Paddock.	197	304 acres.
" "	"	Hannah Nickerson.	173	229 acres.
Jan. 7, 1782	"	Nehemiah Wood.	102–18	147 acres.
Jan. 8, 1782	"	John Field.	283– 4	354 acres.
" "	"	Uriah Wallace.	75–18	69 acres.
" "	"	Jeremiah Mead.	81–15	111 acres.
Jan. 9, 1782	"	David Cowen.	110– 8	92 acres,
" "	"	John Townsend.	50	100 acres.
" "	"	John Dau.	87– 9–9	99¼ acres.
" "	"	Isaac Paddock.	172–16	153 acres.
" "	"	Moses Gage.	84	97½ acres.
" "	"	John Dickinson and Daniel Bull.	30– 4	17 acres.
" "	"	John Dickinson.	157–10	210 acres,
" "	"	James Cock.	3	6 acres in lot No. 5.
" "	"	Herman King.	284	284 acres in lot No. 9.

Date of Sale.	Loyalist Owner.	Purchaser.	Price.	Description and Remarks.
Mch. 29, 1782	Roger Morris.	Michael Stutt.	£108-11	167 acres in lot No. 9.
Mch. 30, 1782	"	John Avary.	55- 6	159 acres.
" "	"	Josiah Falkner.	18	43 acres.
Apr. 19, 1782	"	Peter Bedeau.	151-18	217 acres.
" "	"	Jabes Berry.	75- 4	188 acres.
" "	"	Peter Mabee.	63	105 acres.
" "	"	"	30-12	68 acres.
" "	"	Peleg Wixsorn and Shubal Wixsorn.	67-11	193 acres.
" "	"	Israel Pinckney.	131- 7-9	114¼ acres.
" "	"	Comfort Chadwick.	14-10-8	68⅓ acres.
Apr. 20, 1782	"	William Smith.	215	172 acres.
" "	"	John Haight.	218-12	256 acres.
" "	"	William Wright.	56- 5	125 acres.
" "	"	Abner Daly.	45	90 acres.
" "	"	James Cock.	26- 4	131 acres.
" "	"	William Hitchcock.	53-11	178 acres.
" "	"	Peter Banker.	44-14	149 acres.
" "	"	John Jean.	48-10	194 acres.
" "	"	Solomon Field.	267	267 acres.
Apr. 22, 1782	"	Caleb Palmer.	75	75 acres.
" "	"	John Crane & others.	198	360 acres.
" "	"	Charles Surrine.	99 - 8	198¾ acres.
" "	"	Joseph Gregory.	52	130 acres.
" "	"	John Merrit.	47- 5	94½ acres.
" "	"	William Yeomans.	60	122 acres.
" "	"	James Surrine.	42-18	143 acres.
May 30, 1782	"	William Smith.	43	71 acres.
May 31, 1782	"	"	94- 4	314 acres.
" "	"	James Surrine.	67- 4	111 acres.

Date of Sale.	Loyalist Owner.	Purchaser.	Price.	Description and Remarks.
May 31, 1782	Roger Morris.	John Le Clare.	£26-14	89 acres in lot No. 9.
June 1, 1782	"	Charles F. Wiserfell.	109-12	137 acres.
" "	"	John Berry and John McLeon.	113- 4	141½ acres.
" "	"	John Oakley.	133-16	111 acres.
" "	"	Joseph Cole and Daniel Cole.	126-10	230 acres.
June 3, 1782	"	John Gearman.	108	72 acres.
" "	"	David Smith.	95- 8	318 acres.
" "	"	Nathaniel Nott.	53-18	98 acres.
" "	"	Joseph Haskins.	104- 8	174 acres.
June 4, 1782	"	Ebenezer Cole.	12-15	36½ acres.
" "	"	Isaac Russequa.	58-10	130 acres.
" "	"	John Gunang.	71- 4	178 acres.
June 6, 1782	"	Gilbert Haight.	14- 8	48 acres.
June 7, 1782	"	Isaac Lounsbury.	141-15	202 acres.
" "	"	William Field.	80	100 acres.
" "	"	Billy Trowbridge.	656	287 acres.
" "	"	Jonathon Stokon.	48-16	97 acres.
June 11, 1782	"	Charles Agas.	57-14	94 acres.
" "	"	Thomas Bryant.	32- 8-9	129¾ acres.
" "	"	Isaac Roads.	99- 9	221 acres.
" "	"	Hannah Brewer.	98-10	98¼ acres.
" "	"	Elisha Cole.	64-12-6	117½ acres.
" "	"	" "	234- 9	396¾ acres.
June 13, 1782	"	Isaac Barrett.	42- 7	121 acres.
June 15, 1782	"	Samuel Delavan.	78- 8	112¼ acres.
Oct. 20, 1782	"	Isaac Austin.	50-12	92 acres.
Nov. 4, 1782	Robert Morris and Beverly Robinson.	Nathan Lane.	119- 0-3	278¾ acres.

Date of Sale.	Loyalist Owner.	Purchaser.	Price.	Description and Remarks.
Nov. 4, 1782	Beverly Robinson.	John Smith.	£68– 5	165 acres in lot No. 4.
Nov. 12, 1782	Roger Morris.	Thomas Kirkham.	134– 8	336 acres in lot No. 9.
" "	"	Charles Herag.	67– 4	112 acres,
Nov. 13, 1782	"	John Adams.	36– 6	90¼ acres,
" "	"	Abel Van Scog.	21	120 acres.
" "	"	Robert Hugson.	217–16	363 acres.
" "	"	James Dunn.	3	30¾ acres.
" "	"	Daniel Knap.	97–10	162⅔ acres.
Nov. 14, 1782	"	Robert Russell.	21–15	62¼ acres.
" "	"	John Secor.	49–18	124¾ acres.
" "	"	Isaac Secor.	55–16	124 acres.
Nov. 15, 1782	"	John Davis.	17– 8	116 acres.
" "	"	Moses Knap.	115	230 acres,
Nov. 16, 1782	"	Timothy Carver.	71	355 acres.
Nov. 13, 1782	"	Jacob Van Scog.	13– 4	88 acres.
Nov. 16, 1782	"	Abigal Clerk.	79– 4	132 acres.
Nov. 18, 1782	"	Ebenezer Lockwood.	57–12	144 acres.
" "	"	Isaac Bodeau.	92–10	94½ acres.
" "	"	John Begua.	66	132 acres,
Nov. 19, 1782	Beverly Robinson.	Philip Button.	17– 4	43 acres in lot No. 4.
" "	Roger Morris.	Sylvanus Covert.	14–14	49 acres in lot No. 9.
" "	"	Gilbert Haight.	15–13	60¾ acres,
" "	"	Mahar Nielson.	66– 5	132½ acres,
" "	"	William Higby.	64	128 acres,
" "	"	Sporiah Hopkins.	16–12	83 acres.
Nov. 21, 1782	"	Henry Charlick.	95–15	383 acres,
" "	"	Jonathan Miller.	28	106½ acres,
Apr. 20, 1782	"	Cornelius Adriance.	6– 6	74 acres,
June 13, 1783	"	Ichobad Morvin.	84–16	460¾ acres.
June 16, 1783	"	Benjamin Bloomer.	138– 4–6	270½ acres.

Date of Sale.	Loyalist Owner.	Purchaser.	Price.	Description and Remarks.
June 16, 1783	Roger Morris.	Thomas Adams.	£67–12–6	298¾ acres in lot No. 9.
" "	"	Gilbert Bloomer.	44–16–4	315 acres.
" "	"	Jeremiah Hugsrow.	141–15	166 acres.
June 17, 1783	"	Thomas Russell.	24–16	296 acres.
" "	"	Joseph Hustis.	174	108¼ acres.
" "	"	John Barton.	27– 1–3	
" "	"	Wid. Charity Hastis.	109–10	219 acres.
Jan. 29, 1783	"	Peter Dubois.	253– 3–8	293 acres.
Apr. 4, 1783	"	Israel Knap.	21	120 acres.
Apr. 8, 1783	"	Joseph Farringtone.	248	310 acres.
Apr. 10, 1783	"	Solomon Hopkins.	136– 4	341 acres.
Apr. 14, 1783	"	Benjamin Knap.	19– 2–6	127½ acres.
" "	"	William Hitchcock.	2–12	26 acres.
" "	"	John Van Amber.	51–18	346¼ acres.
" "	"	Christo. Townsend.	61	122 acres.
June 2, 1783	"	Solomon Hopkins.	42–12	82 acres.
July 7, 1786	"	Martin Willsie.	55– 6–6	109½ acres.
June 7, 1786	"	Samuel Hawkins.	8– 2	54 acres.
June 14, 1786	"	William Boyd.	16– 8–1	93¼ acres.
June 16, 1786	"	Isaac Drew.	37	187 acres.
June 17, 1786	"	Comfort Chadwick.	29– 7	117½ acres.
" "	"	John Obrien.	115–10	210 acres.
June 18, 1786	"	Ebenezer Boyd.	22– 4–9	177½ acres.
June 20, 1786	"	"	23–12–6	157½ acres.
" "	"	David Frost.	33–12	168 acres.
" "	"	Judith Cromwell.	37–10	153 acres.
Oct. 15, 1786	"	Gilbert Weeks.	114	285 acres.
Oct. 22, 1786	"	Israel Knapp.	48– 6	168 acres.
Oct. 23, 1786	"	Richard Williams.	6–16–3	109 acres.
" "	"	Joseph Randle.	33– 4–6	221½ acres.

Date of Sale.	Loyalist Owner.	Purchaser.	Price.	Description and Remarks.
Oct. 23, 1786	Roger Morris.	John Booth.	£ 11-16	118 acres in lot No. 9.
Oct. 25, 1786	"	Samuel Carle.	111	370 acres.
" "	"	Lewis Crankite.	12-12- 6	101 acres.
Nov. 18, 1786	"	Thomas Horton.	24	160 acres.
" "	"	David Hanion.	21- 9- 8	200 acres.
" "	"	Paul Sparling.	4-10	54 acres.
Nov. 22, 1786	"	Abram Maybee.	65- 9	187 acres.
Nov. 23, 1786	"	Joseph Farington.	56- 8	141 acres.
" "	"	Consider Cushman.	27	180 acres.
" "	"	Samuel Hawkins.	10-16	27 acres.
" "	"	Richard Ayers.	30	200 acres.
" "	"	Justice Berrit.	18-18	130 acres.
Nov. 24, 1786	"	Robert Show.	38	190 acres.
" "	"	Lemuel Morger.	36-18-16	211 acres.
" "	"	Joseph Ogden.	3- 8	34 acres.
" "	"	John Russel.	2-18- 6	39 acres.
Nov. 25, 1786	"	Samuel Hunt.	23-10	117½ acres.
" "	"	Peter Bell.	41-13- 4	136½ acres.
Nov. 30, 1786	"	Abel Van Scog.	5-14	76 acres.
" "	"	Samuel Jones.	63- 1	294 acres.
Nov. 18, 1786	"	James Townsend.	52-16	352 acres.
" "	"	William Headon.	62- 6- 6	138½ acres.
Nov. 25, 1786	"	Jeremiah Sprage.	7- 7	98 acres.
Mar. 24, 1784	"	David Porter.	28-10	190 acres.
" "	"	Amy Haight.	7-12	76 acres.
" "	"	William Goodfellow.	12	66 acres.
	"	Ebenezer Boyd.	17- 5- 9	461 acres.
	"	"	13-16- 3	110½ acres.
	"	"	8- 5	220 acres.
	"	"	18-15	500 acres.

Date of Sale.	Loyalist Owner.	Purchaser.	Price.	Description and Remarks.
Apr. 26, 1784	Roger Morris.	Jacob Kniffen.	£53– 1– 8	260 acres in lot No. 9.
" "	"	Gilbert Bloomer.	39– 4	187 acres.
" "	"	Zacheus Newcomb.	8– 5	165 acres.
Nov. 20, 1784	"	Martin Wiltsie.	9	360 acres.
May 26, 1784	"	Isaac Rhodes.	2– 8	32¼ acres.
May 31, 1784	"	James Smalley.	11–12	232½ acres.
July 2, 1784	"	Henry Charlick.	25–13	171 acres.
Oct. 20, 1784	"	Moses Mead.	19– 4	266 acres.
" "	"	Justus Nelson.	1–12	8 acres.
" "	"	Mathew Swanck.	3– 4	16½ acres.
" "	"	Martin Wiltsey.	7–12	19 acres.
Feb. 10, 1785	"	Joseph Farington.	24	160 acres.
" "	"	Samuel Hawkins.	7–10	100 acres.
" "	"	Robert Fuller.	38–14	96 acres.
" "	"	Nathaniel Anderson.	53– 4	266 acres.
" "	"	Solomon Cornell.	2– 8	8 acres.
" "	"	Charity Heustes.	1– 4	4 acres.
" "	"	Daniel Dant.	15– 9	103 acres.
June 30, 1785	"	John Post.	4– 1–9	81¾ acres.
Feb. 10, 1785	"	Daniel Ter Boss.	100	500 acres.
" "	"	"	88	500 acres.
June 30, 1785	"	Benjamin Bloomer.	30–17	497 acres.
" "	"	Timothy Van Scoy.	86	430 acres.
" "	"	Johnson Deakins.	38	190 acres.
" "	"	James Nelson and	46	230 acres.
May 3, 1786	"	John Haight.	18– 0–5	341 acres in lot No. 3.
May 3, 1784	"	Israel Knapp.	Price not	354 acres.
" "	"	Cornelius Adriance.	given.	27 acres.
" "	"	Squire Baker.		30 acres.

Date of Sale.	Loyalist Owner.	Purchaser.	Price.	Description and Remarks.
May 3, 1786	Roger Morris.	John Haight.		30 acres.
"	"	Andrew Hill.		385 acres in lot No. 3.
"	"	Maurice Smith.		142 acres.
"	"	John Haight.		256 acres.
"	"	William Wright.		125 acres.
"	"	Cornelius Adriance.		21¾ acres.
"	"	Benjamin Bloomer.		460 4/10 acres.
"	"	Gilbert Bloomer.		290½ acres.
"	"	Joseph Huestis.		296 acres.
"	"	John Barton.		108 acres.
"	"	Charity Huestis.		219 acres.
"	"	Peter Dubois.		293⅛ acres.
"	"	Jno. Van Amburgh.		340¼ acres.
"	"	Martin Wiltsie.		528½ acres.
"	"	Judith Cromwell.		153 acres.
"	"	Gilbert Weeks.		285 acres.
"	"	Israel Knapp.		168 acres.
"	"	David Hamion.		200 acres.
"	"	Paul Sparling.		54 acres.
"	"	Gilbert Bloomer.		187 acres.
"	"	Nathaniel Anderson.		266 acres.
"	"	Daniel Ter Boss.		1497 acres.
"	"	Benjamin Bloomer.		430 acres.

Total acreage in lots No. 3, 5 and 9 50,849
Land under water.............. 1,357
Highways 420
Land sold by Roger Morris.......... 600
Land sold by the Commissioners...... 39,100

Total acres disposed of 41,477
Acres still unsold........ 9,372

Not till 1819 did Henry Livingston declare that all the land was sold.

Note.—The returns of the sales for the rest of the state are incomplete and are therefore withheld for future publication.

BIBLIOGRAPHICAL NOTE

This dissertation is the product, almost entirely, of a study of original sources. The field was unworked, and consequently it was no inconsiderable task to find the available material, which was scattered over a wide area, part of it being at Washington, D. C., part in England, part in Nova Scotia, New Brunswick and Canada, but most of it in the state of New York. So far as known, everything available that could throw any light upon the loyalists of New York was examined and used. Most of the matter relating to events before July 4, 1776, was taken from printed sources, while that of the later period was found in manuscript sources. Wherever secondary material has been used, due credit will be found in the foot-notes of the text.

The purpose of this bibliographical note is not to give an exhaustive list of sources consulted, but to indicate the unprinted material and the most important printed authorities for this subject.

I. Original Sources

1. Unprinted.

Assembly papers, vols. 25–28, *Forfeited estates.*

These papers were arranged by the secretary of state in 1831 from documents on file in the assembly. They are a miscellaneous collection of petitions, reports of committees, minutes of revolutionary boards, accounts of the state treasurer, and lists of forfeited estates, and throw light upon every phase of loyalism. These volumes are in the state library at Albany, N. Y.

Proceedings of the Albany committee of correspondence, 1775–1778. 2 vols.

This is the only complete record of the acts of a county inquisitorial board in New York which is available. It affords an excellent picture of the methods used to dispose of obnoxious loyalists. It furnishes an example of what was done in the other counties. These volumes are in the state library at Albany, N. Y., and were bought from the descendants of Matthew Visscher in 1848.

Minutes of the commissioners for detecting conspiracies, 1778–1781. 2 vols.

These volumes show the attitude of the new state toward the loyalists, their numbers and activity, and how they were treated in the later stages of the war. These papers belonged to Leonard Gansevoort, Jr., secretary of the commissioners, and in 1850 were given to the New York state library by his grandson, Dr. Thomas Hun, of Albany.

Sir William Johnson papers, 1738–1790.   26 vols.

Vols. 1–22 were bought by Lieut.-gov. Taylor at the sale of confiscated property during the revolution. The MSS. in the other four volumes were purchased by the state in 1863. There is an excellent index. These papers shed much light on the colonial period after 1738 and show the feeling of this powerful family toward the movement for independence.

George Clinton papers.   52 vols.

These papers were bought by the state of New York in 1853 and 1883. They contain material for a military history of the revolution and show how the loyalists were treated by the military power. Some of these papers have been printed by the state historian.

New York assembly journals, 1693–1775.

From these papers the development of early political groups may be traced.

Henry Stevens papers.

These papers were added to the New York state library in 1875. They contain some material about loyalism in Cumberland and Gloucester counties.

Papers laid before the Provincial Congress, 1775–1778.   16 vols.

Vol. 24 contains the credentials of delegates for 1775; vol. 30 relates to the associations in 1775; vols. 31–33 contain petitions presented during the years 1775 to 1777; and vols. 34–39 are made up of miscellaneous papers. Some of these papers appear in the Calendar of historical manuscripts relating to the war of the Revolution.

Beverly Robinson estate, 1777–1780.

This is a detailed account of the sales of personal property belonging to Beverly Robinson and other loyalists by the commissioners of sequestration. It is the only report of this kind preserved for the use of students of the revolution. It shows what was done in all the counties north of New York city.

Papers relating to the Vermont controversy, 1777–1799.

These documents reflect the loyalist sentiment in the counties which became Vermont.

Council minutes.   28 vols.

These journals give the executive, legislative and judicial proceedings of that body and help to reveal the rise of parties in the colony. The minutes of the council as a legislative body have been printed.

Minutes of the Provincial Congress, Provincial Convention, Committee of safety and Council of safety, 1775–1778.   10 vols.

These bodies governed New York from 1775 to 1778 and their minutes reflect the attitude of the revolutionary governmental bodies toward the loyalists. These 10 vols. are transcripts from 6 vols. of original minutes and were printed at Albany in 1842.

Revolutionary papers, 1775–1777. 12 vols.

These papers supplement the minutes of the extra-legal bodies. They also were printed in 1842.

General John Lacey papers, 1773–1782.

These afford some information concerning the loyalists.

Proceedings against the disaffected persons of Queens and Richmond counties, 1776.

These minutes record the acts of a committee appointed by the Provincial Congress to suppress obnoxious loyalists. The forms of summons, the details of the trials, and the disposition of the cases are given. With the occupation of southern New York by the British the work of the committee ceased.

New York treasurer's journal, 1775–1784. 2 vols.

This journal has a complete record of the moneys paid to the committees having charge of the loyalists, and of the sums received from the sales of confiscated and forfeited property. It is in the state library at Albany, N. Y.

Accounts of the New York treasurer, 1775–1784.

The amounts turned over to the state at various times by the commissioners of sequestration of personal property are here given for each county. The sums realized from forfeited real estate are also stated. This record is in the state comptroller's office at Albany, N. Y.

Forfeited estates sold in New York city, 1784–1787.

This is the most complete and detailed list of the loyalists whose property was forfeited, and also of the purchasers of it, that is known to exist for any section of the state. Each piece of property sold is fully described and the price is stated. This volume is in the register's office, New York city.

Abstract of forfeited estates in Suffolk county.

This describes the sale of the few forfeited estates in Suffolk county with the owners, purchasers, price and character of the property. It is in the Old Civil List Book, in the Suffolk county clerk's office.

Report of sales by the commissioner of forfeitures of the eastern district, 1784–1789.

This report gives the names of the owners and the purchasers of forfeited estates, the date of sale, the location of the property, and a description of it. This is in the office of the state surveyor and engineer, Albany, N. Y.

Forfeited lands—Timothy Thomson.

This is a bundle of papers in the state surveyor and engineer's office at Albany, N. Y. The letters and deeds show that the confiscated lands belonged to John Thompson and Mr. Fox and wife.

Forfeited estates—Minisink Patent.

This is a bundle of deeds which were given by the surveyor general to purchasers of eighteen lots owned by James De Lancey, Oliver De Lancey and John Weatherhead. This also is in the office of the state engineer.

Commissioners of forfeitures' memorandum of sales for the 16th and 17th of September, 1787.

This gives copies of the deeds granted by the commissioners for the western district. In same place as preceding.

P. Sternberg's application for forfeited lands.

This relates to the patent of Jersey field, which was divided, and the portion falling to loyalists forfeited and sold—about 95 lots. This led to trouble as late as 1808. In same place as preceding.

Application for forfeited lands.

This contains applications for forfeited lands after 1808. In same place as preceding.

Commissioners of forfeitures—" 77."

This bundle contains certificates of the loyalty of applicants, and other facts about them. In same place as the preceding.

Forfeited lands sold by the surveyor general—" 76."

This gives accounts of the various patents, divers applications, affidavits of appraisers, etc. In same place as preceding.

Commissioners of forfeitures.

This has various claims and cases, certificates of loyalty, etc. In same place as preceding.

Commissioners of forfeitures from 1 to 50.

This contains claims of the discovery of forfeited lands under the act of 1803 giving the finder 25 per cent. In same place as preceding.

Copies of deeds for forfeited estates—Glens Falls.

The surveys and descriptions are given. In same place as preceding.

Forfeited lands—Dutchess and Westchester counties—" 73."

This bundle coutains the reports of the appraisers of lands sold by the surveyor general, and the deeds. In same place as preceding.

Forfeited lands at Kayaderasseras.

This gives the deeds of lands sold by the surveyor general from 1804 to 1808. In same place as preceding.

Forfeited lands in Dutchess county.

This contains reports of the appraisements and of the surveys of the lands belonging to Robert Morris and wife, and B. Robinson and wife. In same place as preceding.

Copies of deeds for forfeited lands—Lott and Magin's patent—" 50."

These lands were sold by the surveyor general Simeon De Witt from 1803 to 1805. In same place as preceding.

Stevens, B. F.   Fac similes of Manuscripts in European Archives relating to America, 1773–1783.

This collection contains many important references to the loyalists of New York. In Columbia University library, and in the state library at Albany, N. Y.

Transcript of the manuscript Books and Papers of the Commission of Enquiry into the Losses and Services of the American Loyalists held under Acts of Parliament of 23, 25, 26, 28 and 29 of George III., preserved amongst the Audit Office Records in the Public Record Office of England, 1783–1790.

This is the most valuable and most complete collection of material concerning the loyalists now open to students.   These papers include applications, memorials and petitions of the loyalists to the British government for aid and compensation.   They show the loyalty, the services and the losses in real and personal estate of the loyalists.   They give the examinations and decisions on claims for temporary relief.   They contain the minutes of the commissioners on loyalists' claims in England and in America, and also the determinations of the commissioners.   These papers give the first public view of authentic and official information regarding the loyalists.   Until this transcript was made, the British government held these documents to be strictly private.   The collection is very rich in biographical material likewise.   Volumes 1–13, 17–24, and 29–31, 33, 34, 41–46, deal with New York loyalists.   This valuable material is in the Lenox Library in New York city.

Proceedings before the commissioners, Pemberton and Dundas, between 1786 and 1788, at St. John's, Halifax and Montreal. 34 vols.

These are evidently the rough minutes of the commissioners, which were afterwards transcribed, and the transcripts deposited in the Public Record Office in England. These volumes are in the Congressional Library at Washington, D. C.

2. PRINTED.

The printed original sources consulted are known, for the most part, and need not be discussed at great length. Only the most important will be given.

I. PAMPHLETS.

Chandler, *A Friendly Address to all Reasonable Americans.*

Chandler, *What Think Ye of Congress Now?*

Cooper, *The American Querist; or Some Questions Proposed Relative to the Present Disputes between Great Britain and her American Colonies,* 1774.

Cooper, *A Friendly Address to all Reasonable Americans on the Subject of our Political Confusions,* 1774.

Cooper, *A sermon preached before the University of Oxford,* Dec. 13, 1776.

Inglis, *Plain Truth, Addressed to the Inhabitants of America.*

Inglis, *Additions to Plain Truth.*

Inglis, *The True Interest of America Impartially Stated in Certain Strictures on a Pamphlet entitled Common Sense,* 1776.

Inglis, *Letters of Papinian in which the Conduct, Present State and Prospects of the American Congress are examined.*

Observations on the fifth article of the Treaty with America and on the necessity of appointing a Judicial Enquiry into the Merits and Losses of the American Loyalists. Printed by order of their Agents, 1783.

This pamphlet states the case of the loyalists in 1783. It is in the Lenox Library, New York city.

Case and claim of the American loyalists impartially stated and considered, 1783.

This is in the Lenox Library, New York city.

The case of the Right Rev. Charles Inglis against the U. S., 1799.

This is in the Lenox Library, New York city.

———— *The Loyal or Revolutionary Tory: being some Reflections on the Principles and Conduct of the Tories.* London, 1783.

Seabury, *Free Thoughts on the Proceedings of the Continental Congress, held at Philadelphia, Sept. 4, 1774.*

Seabury, *The Congress Canvassed; or, An Examination into the Conduct of the Delegates, at their Grand Convention held in Philadelphia, Sept., 1774.*

Seabury, *A View of the Controversy between Great Britain and her Colonies.*

Seabury, *An Alarm to the Legislature of the Province of New York, occasioned by the present Political Disturbances in North America.* New York, 1775.

Wilkins, *My Services and Losses in Aid of the King's Cause during the American Revolution.* Ed. by Paul L. Ford, Brooklyn, N. Y., 1890.

These pamphlets set forth the attitude of the extreme loyalists, and are essential to a right comprehension of their position. They show the heart and brain of the genuine tory in the early part of the contest. The fourteen pamphlets of Joseph Galloway, of Pennsylvania, and those of other loyalists, a description of which may be found in Tyler, *Lit. His. of Am. Rev.*, supplement these of the loyalists of New York.

2. NEWSPAPERS.

Bradford's *New York Gazette*, 1725–1740.

This paper was inclined to champion the " court party."

Zenger's *New York Weekly Journal*, 1733–1744.

This journal was founded to oppose the administration of Governor Cosby and consequently reflects the opinions of the popular party.

Gaine's *New York Mercury, or New York Gazette and Weekly Mercury* (1763), 1752–1783.

This paper was on the patriot side when the revolution began, but it changed to a loyalist sheet upon the arrival of the British in 1776, and was devoted to the crown throughout the war. It is a good reflection of the loyalists' views and acts.

Holt's *New York Journal, or General Advertiser*, 1766–1785.

Holt edited the first Whig newspaper in New York city, and it was consistent throughout the whole struggle. In 1776 it removed to Kingston, and in 1777 to Poughkeepsie. It gives an account of the loyalists from a whig standpoint.

Rivington's *New York Gazette, or the Connecticut, New Jersey, Hudson's River and Quebec Weekly Advertiser, or New York Loyal Gazette* (1776), *or New York Royal Gazette*, 1733–1787.

From the first this journal took the royal side. Its extreme toryism led to its destruction by a whig mob in 1775. Rivington went to England to secure a new press, and when the British were in possession of New York city he returned and served as the royal printer throughout the revolution. His paper was the official organ of loyalism, and set forth its extreme views.

Other papers were printed in New York city during the revolution, but they throw little additional light on the loyalist party. Gaine, Holt and Rivington give three different pictures of loyalism, and are very valuable to a proper understanding of the movement. These papers are in the Lenox Library and the New York Historical Society Library in New York city.

3. MEMOIRS, DIARIES, ETC.

Curwen, *Journal and Letters*. Edited by Ward in 1842.

This is the journal of a loyalist who lived in England from 1775 to 1784, and which, consequently, depicts loyalism from that point of view.

Hutchinson, *Diary and Letters*.

He was the loyalist governor of Massachusetts, and discussed loyalism from the standpoint of a royal officer true to the crown.

Jay, *Correspondence and Public Papers*. Edited by Henry P. Johnson. 4 vols.

This collection gives the attitude of a moderate whig toward the loyalists.

Jones, *History of New York during the Revolution.*   2 vols.

⌐This is the work of a partisan, who gives an excellent picture of the revolution from the standpoint of a stern loyalist, but who is unreliable in many of his facts.   The appendix by Edward F. De Lancey is particularly valuable.

Moore, *Diary of the American Revolution.*   2 vols.

This is a collection of material from the newspapers of the revolution, and has much good material pertaining to the loyalists.

Morris, *Diary and Letters of Gouverneur Morris.*

This gives the attitude of a conservative whig towards the loyalists.

Simcoe, *A Journal of the Operations of the Queen's Rangers from the ena of the year 1777 to the conclusion of the American war.*

Smith, *History of New York.*

This work covers the colonial period from the bias of the Presbyterian party.

Wilmot, *Historical View of the Commission for Enquiring into the Losses, Services, and Claims of the American Loyalists.*   London, 1815.

This is the best discussion of the method England took to compensate the loyalists for their losses.

4. ARCHIVES AND COLLECTIONS.

Brymner, *Canadian Archives,* 1883–1889.   8 vols.

These archives are especially rich in material on the migration, settlement and compensation of loyalists.

Calander of historical manuscripts relating to the war of the Revolution.   2 vols.

This contains credentials of delegates, election returns, military returns, petitions, association papers and other valuable material arranged in chronologic order.

Calendar of New York historical manuscripts.   vol. 2.

This gives a digest of much useful matter between 1664 and 1776.

Collections of the New York Historical Society.

This collection contains much material pertaining to the loyalists.   The Colden papers are especially valuable.

De Peyster and Stone, *Orderly Book of Sir John Johnson.*

This is an excellent defence of Sir John Johnson and the Mohawk loyalists.

Documentary History of the State of New York, by O'Callaghan.   4 vols.

There are some documents of value relating to loyalism in this work.

Documents relating to the Colonial History of the State of New York.   15 vols.

This work is full of material revealing the tendencies toward loyalism in colonial New York and also contains considerable matter on the revolutionary period.

Force, *American Archives.*

This work is very valuable for the history of the loyalists from 1774 to 1777.

Journals of the American Congress, 1774–1788.

Journal of the New York Provincial Convention and Congress.

Journal of the New York Assembly.

Memoirs of the Long Island Historical Society.

New York City during the Revolution.

Onerdonk, *Queens County Incidents.*

Onerdonk, *Revolutionary Incidents in Queens, Suffolk and Kings counties.*

II. SECONDARY SOURCES.

Every secondary source, which would throw light upon the New York loyalists, was examined so far as known. The general histories of New York, Nova Scotia, New Brunswick and Canada were examined, but proved to be of little use. The local histories of these regions, on the contrary, often furnished valuable information. Conspicuous among these numerous works is Dawson, *Westchester County.* Some biographies like Van Schaack, *Life of Peter Van Schaack* and Leake, *Life of John Lamb,* have proved helpful. Sabine, *Biographical Sketches of Loyalists of the American Revolution,* has been particularly valuable. Ryerson, *Loyalists of America,* has also rendered some assistance. So numerous were the secondary sources consulted, and so comparatively small was their contribution to the subject, that there would be little propriety in appending a list of them here.